Gay Ideas

Gay Ideas

Outing
and
Other
Controversies

Richard D. Mohr   4·2·93

BEACON PRESS / BOSTON

BEACON PRESS
25 Beacon Street
Boston, Massachusetts 02108

Beacon Press books are published under the auspices of
the Unitarian Universalist Association of Congregations.

99 98 97 96 95 94 93 92   8 7 6 5 4 3 2 1

Text design by David Bullen

The frontispiece is of an ACT UP demonstration in San
Francisco, June 21, 1990, during the Sixth International AIDS
Conference and is used by permission of AP/Wide World.

Drawings by Rex are provided by Drawings by Rex under
international copyright law, P.O. Box 347, San Francisco, CA
94101.

Drawings by Tom of Finland are provided by the Tom of Finland
Foundation under international copyright law, P.O. Box 26658,
Los Angeles, CA 90026, (213) 250-1685.

The endpiece is Edward Weston's *Neil*, 1922. Courtesy of the
Krannert Art Museum and Kinkead Pavilion, University of
Illinois, Urbana.

Library of Congress Cataloging-in-Publication Data

Mohr, Richard D.
  Gay ideas: outing and other controversies / Richard D. Mohr.
    p. cm.
  Includes bibliographical references and index.
  ISBN 0-8070-7920-0
    1. Gay liberation movement—United States. 2. Gays—Civil
rights—United States. 3. Homosexuality—Moral and ethical
aspects.
  I. Title.
HQ76.8.U5M64 1992
305.9'0664—dc20   92-4686
                                                          CIP

for Robert W. Switzer

Life is good—he makes it so.

At any rate, from the start, we have helped form our own code of conduct by listening to stories.

Andrew Holleran, "Sex Quiz" (1991)

A Klee painting named "Angelus Novus" shows an angel looking as though he is about to move away from something he is fixedly contemplating. His eyes are staring, his mouth is open, his wings are spread. This is how one pictures the angel of history. His face is turned toward the past. Where we perceive a chain of events, he sees one single catastrophe which keeps piling wreckage upon wreckage and hurls it in front of his feet. The angel would like to stay, awaken the dead, and make whole what has been smashed. But a storm is blowing from Paradise; it has caught in his wings with such violence that the angel can no longer close them. This storm irresistibly propels him into the future to which his back is turned, while the pile of debris before him grows skyward. This storm is what we call progress.

Walter Benjamin, Thesis IX from "Theses on the Philosophy of History" (1940)

CONTENTS

ILLUSTRATIONS

Gay Ideas

A Gathering of Eyes

1950: If God made them equal, I hate God! I hate God! I hate God!
*Southern matriarch while being carried upstairs after collapsing on
hearing the news that her grandson would be the only white attending
Howard University Law School.*[1]

1990: There is no God if homosexuals are allowed into heaven.
*A fundamentalist minister disrupting in Hoboken the Episcopal
ordination of a noncelibate openly gay priest.*[2]

And how did these stories end? Well, the grandson got his law degree
from Howard, also one from Yale, taught law at Notre Dame Law
School, became President Kennedy's special assistant for civil rights,
and in that capacity was responsible for bringing Kennedy together
with Martin Luther King, Jr. He helped found the Peace Corps, became the first male president of Bryn Mawr College, and eventually
became, first by appointment, then by election, a U.S. senator from
Pennsylvania.[3]

What of the gay priest? Just a month after his ordination, he was
tossed out of his ministry—not through successful fundamentalist protest but by his own gay congregation, which had been the main political
force behind his ordination. His perceived priestly failing was that he
espoused two beliefs that he might well have gleaned from gay male
experience. One was that sex is a good that improves people's lives and
could do so even for celibates. The other was that monogamy is not an

essential component of marriage—or, differently put, the sacrifices that people make in order to value their relations as sacred, as beyond calculations of utility, need not be sexual sacrifices. These gay ideas were too much for his lesbian and gay male parishioners, who seemed to be looking to non-gay Hoboken for their values and sense of worth. He was condemned too by his now rueful ordaining bishop, who had gone against church teachings by ordaining a sexually active, openly gay person in the first place, but thereby made the *New York Times*. Eventually the bishop would make the *Times* again—for "outing" the New Testament's Saint Paul as a self-loathing homosexual. The priest was not defrocked: ecclesiastical hearings for heresy would have been just too messy. But parishless and under the press of survival's necessities, he retired to do what everyone does whose fifteen minutes of fame have expired. He began to write a book.[4]

Gays are so fearsome, it seems, that they can, like blacks of the recent past, be perceived to make God cease to be God, cease even to exist. This fearsomeness too seems to make gays skittish in relation to each other and so produces grotesqueries of soul and action of the sort that we see in the priest's tale and that cannot be entirely or even satisfactorily relieved by comedy staged in the face of such dissolution.

This book addresses, in diverse ways, how I think gays ought to represent and position themselves in the wider world and suggests how they ought to act in relation to each other, given that this does not appear to be the messianic era, but at best is the time of the prophets. Still, as the German-Jewish thinker, mystic, pessimist, harbinger of the postmodern, and suicide Walter Benjamin put it: "Like every generation that preceded us, we have been endowed with a *weak* Messianic power. . . . [Each era] is shot through with chips of Messianic time."[5]

This book is intended to provide indicators of, gestures toward, and recognitions of the existence for gays of such chips of messianic time in the present, pervaded though it be with both screaming and silent horrors—the basher's bat swung, the respirator useless, torturing, unplugged. As a witness to some of the horror, I had thought of placing an asterisk by the name of each man mentioned, discussed, or quoted in the book who has died of AIDS. But the idea was only seconds in the thinking—the names mounting up—before my mind shut down from depression, anxiety, embarrassment, shame, and exhaustion. In any case, a storm was blowing from paradise.

Justice, I believe (and will argue along the way), is not to be found right around the corner, over the next hillock. Nor is even the path to justice known nor its occurrence predictable and assured. The chapters of this book would like to be, and can at most be, muffled whispers from justice echoing off current gay, sometimes specifically gay male, experience, bearing messages not so much of hope but of righteousness. They, like gospel music, can herald only good news, not good times, and, even at that, only news of limited word and vision.

The book addresses sudden topics, like outing and ACT UP, concerns that flash up in moments of danger, but it is intended for the long haul. It suggests courses of action and styles of ideas appropriate even when the usual machinery of social reform, particularly participatory democracy, benefits gays but little. It explores three forms of social institutions in which gays represent themselves to the wider world and through which they intervene in each others' lives, political, cultural, and educational institutions that gays might profitably and nobly develop now even when justice is remote.

In an earlier book, *Gays/Justice*, I addressed what might be called "civic relations"—relations between citizen and government.[6] There, I argued that for lesbians and gay men the ideals of classical liberalism—values like dignity, privacy, equality, and presence—are the right ideals around which to configure the relation of the individual to the state. Here, my focus widens and shifts, moving from narrowly civic to more general social relations, specifically those between a community and the society of which it is a part, those between a community and its members, and those between members of a community. I will suggest that the same set of values that animates liberal democracy and that ought to govern civic relations ought also to govern these more broadly gaged and diversified relations. The book argues that the values that should be realized in education, messianic politics, and cultural rites are

3

the social ideals of liberty as privacy, equality as nondegradation, the precedence of dignity over happiness, and the primacy of individual presence over group power.

I admit that in many ways liberal values have failed to be realized for gays in civic life and are unlikely to be realized there any time soon. But this defeat, for now and the foreseeable future, does not mean that they are the wrong ideals: there are some storms that will not allow the passage of any ship however well built. The defeat, or at least current abeyance, of liberal social reform notwithstanding, liberal values can still serve as proper guides for action among gays themselves during the time of the prophets. The practical failure of liberal humanism in gay politics does not mean that gays should seek their values in the range of communal, communistic, or communitarian ideals, ideals that in many forms are still in rigid force domestically even as they are collapsing by the day elsewhere in the world. Instead, liberal values offer untapped potential to illuminate and liberate an understanding of why gay lives and gay life—lesbian and gay male social forms—are worth cherishing and fighting for and why gay men and lesbians ought not to submit either to crushing oppression from current political forces or to dissipating indeterminacy from the contemporary intellectual forces of deconstructionism, historicism, and relativism. If all norms are socially relative, as most gay academics now hold, there can be no concept of oppression, only more or less pervasive regimes of knowledge, discourse, and power.

Liberalism stamps itself on the intellectual style of this book as well as on its content. The book's eight chapters are highly interdisciplinary, crossing—both moving between and blending—analytic philosophy, social philosophy, gay studies, cultural studies, literary studies, legal studies, and American studies, with bits of history, sociology, and opera studies thrown in. Sometimes the chapters are postdisciplinary—epigrammatical, smarmy, arch, strolling, strutting, reveling, hectoring, yarn spinning. The book presses the themes and ideals of classical liberalism not only into (for them) unusual social areas but also into academic and intellectual areas where such ideals have usually been thought to be least at home, least effective, least insightful—areas

4

either thought recalcitrant to liberal analyses (like cultural studies and gender studies) or simply abandoned to the academic Left (like the standing and nature of gay studies as an academic discipline). The book tries to show that liberal principles are richer, more subtle, and of greater consequence than current academic thinking allows. They can even be poetic, even be a charm, or a lure, tethered and tossed, awaiting its falcon's strike.

Politics

Gays in America have fewer rights than do barnyard animals in Sweden. Part I explains why this arrangement probably will not undergo substantial change any time soon, but it also suggests ways in which to live morally even when it looks as though the goals of gay justice are very far off, if discernible at all.

The first chapter addresses that form of intracommunity intervention that has come to be called "outing" and that has electrified lesbian and gay politics as nothing else in its history. Is it morally permissible for someone to make public another person's homosexuality without regard to whether that person desires it to be known? I argue yes— outing is even morally expected behavior. I hope that even if, under criticism, every one of the chapter's substantive claims proves false, the various distinctions drawn in the chapter will advance the debate by clarifying the issues and stakes involved in outing. The second chapter—"On Some Words from ACT UP"—briefly argues that gays should be wary in politics of quick Leftward-leaning ideological fixes. The third chapter—"Black Law and Gay Law"—examines in detail one way in which society's treatment of gay men and lesbians has affected for the decidedly worse the whole of American life. The part's final chapter—"Social Lenses, Social Progress"—programmatically analyzes the central roles that the concept "homosexuality" serves in society's defining itself to itself and suggests in consequence that, in politics, the era's weak messianic force for gay men and lesbians consists of enacting those strategies that tend to establish individual dignity standing in the face of social adversity, rather than those strategies that, at the individual's expense, try to modulate, circumvent, overturn, or accommodate it.

Culture

The book's central chapters explore gay males' appropriation for themselves and representation to others of men's worlds and death's dominion. One chapter queers a canonical text—Wagner's final opera, *Parsifal.* The other normalizes a queer text—The NAMES Project's quilt memorial to those felled by AIDS. The cultural task for gays now is the restoration of institutional sites for awe. Traditionally, religion has provided the home for awe. Here, I offer two other, gay homes for it.

The part's first chapter—"Text(ile)"—is an elegy with seduction on its mind. Politically, the chapter tries to entice and then appropriate for the cause of liberalism the high emotional charges that radiate from and circulate around the mourning of mass death in the AIDS crisis. Textually, the chapter tries to rehabilitate elegy from its current academic status as the falsest genre within the falsest of literary movements: Romanticism. The part's second chapter—"'Knights, Young Men, Boys'"—reads together the virtually all-male world of *Parsifal* with contemporary gay draftsmen's and photographers' renderings of the gay male psyche in order to examine the morality of explicitly masculinist cultures. The chapter attempts to show that gay men have more to offer democracy than democracy has had to offer gay men.

Together the two chapters of this part might be taken to suggest that, just as gay men now have generations without generation, so too gay men can have religion without gods.

Identity

This part asks how lesbians and gay men ought to position themselves socially as subjects who have themselves as objects of inquiry. Its first chapter gives a negative account, the second a positive account, of what gay studies should be, by examining how homosexual identity should be understood. The latter constructive chapter—"Gay Studies as Moral Vision"—argues that gay studies should be viewed chiefly as a normative project. The part's critical chapter—"The Thing of It Is"—attempts to trim the excesses of the currently leading model of lesbian and gay studies, the view that homosexuality is to be viewed exclusively as a social or cultural artifact or construction, so that lesbian and gay studies more or less reduces to the study of social history—and a short one at that—while nature and science are debunked respectively as *poseur* and self-deception. Academic lore has it that, when asked what he did as a philosopher, Sidney Morgenbesser answered: "Well, I draw a few distinctions. I clarify a few concepts. It's a living." This chapter falls in that tradition.

Still, stiff analysis to the side, one of the broad themes running as a leitmotif through the book is that the time has come for gay intellectuals to stop being afraid of nature—both the concept and the thing. It is past the time when "denaturalizing" this or that or nature itself is further productive of truth or interest. Natural law doctrine—the view that obligations can be found embedded in nature—can be killed only so many times before it is dead. And the paranoia-driven tendency among academics now to see everything as socially confected, such that the bad old charges of sexual or genderal unnaturalness are avoided, simply ends up tossing out the good with the bad. It is time for gays to assume roles in the environmental and animal rights movements from which they have been absent in large part because of the ideology of social construction, by whose lights nothing in nature or nature itself could matter except as someone has an arbitrary interest in it. Although nature sends us viruses, it is also the source, causally or by inspiration, of bodies, sensations, pleasure, beauty, and wonderment. In providing the discreteness of our bodies and the critical capacities of our minds, nature lays the nurturing ground for the values of liberal individualism. America could do worse than looking to nature and gays for an understanding of the basic, if only half acknowledged, values of its better self.

The book was completed during a term when I was freed from teaching by the University of Illinois's Center for the Study of Cultural Values and Ethics. The costs of publication prints and reproduction rights for the book's graphics have been defrayed through the generous patronage of Seth Joseph Weine and by grants from the Playboy Foundation and the University of Illinois's Research Board. I thank the following people for having substantially advanced the book, variously by offering comments, raising questions, assisting research, securing funding, improving grammar, and sustaining spirit: Claudia Card, John Littlewood, Jane Williams, Ed Stein, Kevin Hill, Timothy F. Murphy, Jerry McCarthy, James Rachels, Lee C. Rice, Mark Chekola, Greg Pence, John Boswell, Martha Nussbaum, Rhonda R. Rivera, James Miller (Boston), James Miller (London, Ontario), Deborah Merritt, Kal Alston, Robert Michael Doyle, Ann Miller, Allen Ellenzweig, John Clum, David F. Greenberg, Noretta Koertge, George Greenia, Wayne Koestenbaum, Judith Butler, James Saslow, Andrew Koppelman, Eugene F. Rice, Jr., Alycee J. Lane, Barbara Andic, Arthur S. Leonard, and Paul Siegel. Particular thanks go to Simon D. Stern, in correspondence with whom many of the book's ideas had their first sounding and response, to my husband and lover, Robert W. Switzer, for his stewardship and loving, and to my editor, Deborah Chasman, and the director of Beacon Press, Wendy J. Strothman, for much, but especially for their courage and honor when courage and honor were necessary.

New Year's Day 1992
Urbana, Illinois

Politics

*All at once they started yelling "faggot" and
"fucking faggot." . . . One of them missed me with
a beer can. . . . College and my literary education
agreed that I should see myself as a random
conjunction of life's possibilities, certainly an
enviable, luxurious point of view. But it's hard to
draw on that as a model when four men are chasing
you down the street. What life will that model
sustain, and when aren't we being chased?*

Robert Glück, *Elements of a Coffee Service*
(1982)

CHAPTER I

The Outing Controversy: Privacy and Dignity in Gay Ethics

Mr. Naimy was helping pull the casket from the hearse, when his friend's father begged him to tell a relative that he had died of anything but AIDS. And please, emphasize that he was not gay.

"I told him I couldn't lie any more."[1]

I. Definition and Theses

"Outing" is making publicly acknowledged the sexual orientation of a homosexual without regard to whether the person is willing to have this information publicly acknowledged. It is making publicly acknowledged what most lesbians and gay men wish to be kept secret—their identity, what they are, possibly who they are. Usually outing will simply make a person's sexual orientation publicly known, but where a person's gayness is already publicly known but not publicly acknowledged—as in the case of the "open secret"—outing will disrupt the codes of silence that block public acknowledgment of gay lives.

With few exceptions, outing has been opposed in the gay press, and (to my knowledge) it has been universally opposed within the national gay litigative and political communities, including the National Gay and Lesbian Task Force. Others too have weighed in against outing: Fran Lebowitz, Mike Royko, Miss Manners, Randy Shilts, Barbara Bush, Eric Bentley, Joan Rivers, Jane Rule, Madonna, the National Organization of Women, and congressional anti-gay ringleader Representative William Dannemeyer.[2] And emotions run high. Fran Lebowitz, whose buddy Malcom Forbes was outed posthumously, calls outing "despicable" and "beneath contempt."[3]

Like abortion and affirmative action, outing raises a welter of norms that are difficult to disentangle from each other and whose recommendations seem to collide with each other. Just for starters, the issue invokes considerations of privacy, secrecy, freedom, coercion, truth, lies, knowledge, the first amendment, sex, sexuality, dignity, and happiness. I will first argue that all the arguments against outing are variously conceptually confused or factually unfounded, especially the argument that outing damnably violates privacy rights (secs. II–VII). I will then go on to argue that if proper weight is given to the dignity of the openly gay person who outs others—tellingly the least-discussed figure in the debate—outing is justified in almost all cases as a matter of course (sec. VIII to the end). Outing is both a permissible and an expected consequence of living morally. Outing is to the gay person who lives morally what a ship's wake is to the ship that causes it as the ship cuts its course to its destination.

II. Privacy versus Secrecy

The most common argument deployed against outing is that outing violates the outed person's right to privacy. But, at heart, this argument, not much more than a slogan, confuses privacy and secrecy. Privacy, taken in a moral sense and put broadly, is control over the access that others have to one. Secrecy, broadly, is the intentional concealment of something, usually information. Control of access is the core of privacy; hiding is the core of secrecy.[4]

Further, when privacy is held to apply to something in a normative sense, the application in turn invokes certain norms. Indeed, any act, possession, or relation that is private *in a normative sense* invokes a right to it, a right barring unwanted access to it by others. Thus, not surprisingly, the term "privacy" occurs most frequently in the phrase "right to privacy." So when I say, for instance, that some occurrence of a sexual act is private (and mean thereby more than the simple description that it was performed out of sight), the act is covered by a right to privacy. No one, especially the state, can claim a right to spy on it or to prohibit its occurrence.[5]

I emphasize normative, not purely descriptive, uses of privacy, for there are some merely descriptive senses of privacy that in fact do not automatically invoke the protection of a right. One such case is the sense of private in "private property." When I say to a wayward hunter, "Son, this is private property," I mean simply that it is mine rather than his, or someone else's, or the state's, or nobody's. What rights I have over my property flow from the concepts of property and ownership rather than from this descriptive sense of the private—what is mine.

Now, another merely descriptive definition of the private, one that standardly occurs in dictionaries, is indeed secrecy: "removed from public view or knowledge; not within the cognizance of people generally" *(OED)*. The two definitional variations here simply answer, "Removed," "Not within," to the descriptive question, "Where is it?" Importantly, this descriptive sense of privacy—the secret—does not invoke the protection of a right. Just think of common linguistic convention. One never hears the expression "the right to secrecy." Even those who would love to invoke such a right for themselves as a cover for their doings—for example, government, police, and military conspirators—invoke a different justificatory cant for their secrecy, appealing to "national security" or "public safety." The reason why we never hear of a "right to secrecy"—why that phrase rings false—is that things variously secret fall across the entire moral spectrum and many of them could never plausibly claim the protection of a right.

At one end of the spectrum, the good end, one can note, for example, that secrecy in one's thoughts and the inner dialogue such secrecy safeguards from harsh judgments of others are necessary to the development of the privacy of one's thoughts, to their truly being one's own.

Even if the harsh judgments are not accompanied with actual invasions, say, with drugs and electrodes, and so do not violate bodily integrity, still the judgments must be blocked if personal thought is to be free. Thus, secrecy in our ideas is a precondition of one's very status as an autonomous moral agent—a person, that is, with ends of her own and the ability to revise those ends. Such secrecy is morally protected as a right not because of the nature of secrecy but because of the nature of privacy and personhood.

But note too that my private ideas—the ones I truly believe—may well be quite public, may even be published; they need not be maintained as secret at all still to be private. Privacy and secrecy overlap, but they are not coextensive. As Sissela Bok nicely puts it: "Privacy need not hide and secrecy hides far more than what is private." For our purposes, she gives an especially illustrative example of nonhidden privacy: "A private life is rarely a secret life."[6] Just think of marriage, for example: who one marries is a private matter, but it is virtually never a secret matter. The person who would be continuously closeted, continuously secreted, about his private life, then, is not invoking a moral norm, a moral rule. He is morally abnormal. He is invoking an exception that to be warranted requires appeal to a compelling higher-order reason to justify it. But that higher-order principle—if there is one— cannot be privacy since normally one's private life, one's own affairs, are not a secret. They cannot be intruded on, but they are usually known and acknowledged.

At the other end of secrecy's moral spectrum, one may note that every evil that succeeds in a world that is potentially just does so because of secrecy. And the more massive the evil, the greater the need for secrecy in order for it to succeed. For police brutality to succeed requires a uniform code of silence at the precinct house. Or, if the police do do their job, a code of silence in the white community can effectively prevent them from prosecuting the murderers of blacks, as it did in Bensonhurst.[7] The Holocaust was facilitated by secrets: its administrators and bureaucrats were officially designated and known to each other as "The Keepers and Bearers of Secrets," and indeed the closing gambits of the Holocaust were failed attempts to disguise and hide by elimination the concentration camps, to keep it all a secret from historical cognizance. So it is a good thing that to act in secret is not automatically to act by right. The true assertion that something is secret is the start of moral inquiry, rather than, as in the case of a true assertion of privacy, the inquiry's end.

III. Gay Secrecy and Gay Privacy: The Content of the Alleged Right against Outing

Although normative privacy and secrecy overlap, there simply is no normative privacy, no content to the right to privacy, that covers the secret that is the closet. I will argue that no legitimate gay privacy interest is violated by making public the secret of someone's sexual orientation.

When I tell someone that someone else who does not want to be known as a homosexual is a homosexual, I convey a secret. That which is hidden is revealed. Metaphorically, I open the person's closet door to another, who sees the person inside as homosexual. It is the person's sexual orientation that I am revealing. I am saying that the person is someone whose erotic energies and sexual desires are directed toward members of the same biological sex as the person.

But the door that I open is not the door to the person's bedroom or to a cubicle at the baths. I am not revealing, making unhidden, the secrecy of the person's sexual *behavior.* I am not reporting, for instance, what could only have been gotten through spying, stealth, or coercion. I may simply have seen the person as a regular at a gay bar, or participating in a gay pageant or gay pride parade, or hanging out in gay areas of town, or working in a campaign for an openly gay candidate, or I may have read his name in gay newspapers. This catalog of "maybes" is not random. They are public events in which one Oliver Sipple participated prior to his thwarting a 1975 assassination attempt on President Gerald Ford. They are public events that a California appellate court cited as more than sufficient to dismiss summarily an invasion of privacy suit that Sipple lodged against the *San Francisco Chronicle*, whose columnist Herb Caen had undeniably implied that the ex-marine hero was gay.[8]

There are many ways of inferring from public signs that someone is gay.[9] But I might also know that a male is gay because, say, he has wolfed down my cock with gusto. But there is a world of difference between my reporting to the press that he is gay and my detailing to the press his sexual activities. The success of sex in our unedited lives presupposes the creation of sanctuary, a presumption that what one is doing is not being watched and subjected to judgment—even or especially through the indirect agency of one's partner himself.[10] Therefore, prospective secrecy—a presumption that what we are doing in our sexual fumblings will be kept just between us—is necessary for the privacy of sex, just as a right to secrecy in my ideas is necessary for their privacy. A right to secrecy covering one's sexual actions derives from a right to privacy in sexual behavior. Here, again, the right that attaches to secrecy is not freestanding, flowing from the nature of secrecy itself, but is pendant from some other, freestanding right. People who would out someone by giving detailed accounts of her sexual gymnastics would indeed be violating a privacy right. But to report on someone's sexual orientation is not to report on her sexual behavior.

Vito Russo puts the distinction between sexual action and sexual identity nicely: "When I say my brother and his wife are heterosexual, that doesn't mean I'm talking about their sex lives. Likewise, when we say someone is gay, we're talking about *sexual orientation*, not their sexual activity. It's not our fault that every time someone says 'gay,' people think 'sex.' That's *their* twisted problem."[11] Moreover, when I say that Sally and Steve are married and that *those* are their children—claims that no one would think were invasions of privacy—I have actually conveyed more information and grounds for inferences about their actual sexual behavior than if I report that someone is gay. For the marriage commits the couple to having had intercourse, the consummation of marriage—that without which marriages are not marriages in Western civilization. And their children's existence presumptively implicates them as having left themselves open to HIV

16

transmission in their sexual behavior. But the marriage and the children are completely compatible with Steve being entirely gay: his sex acts may have been possible only because he was fantasizing about having sex with a guy—although too, of course, he may never actually have done that.

It is sexual acts, and derivatively talk of them, not sexual orientations, that are protected by privacy. The reporting of sexual orientation does not violate any of the senses of privacy that are legitimately invoked in sexual matters. As we have seen, it does not violate privacy in its most central dimension as what is not to be spied on.[12] Nor obviously does it, like rape, violate rights to bodily integrity, which constitute another central part of our conception of normative privacy. Nor does such reportage prevent one from fulfilling the crucial role that sexual behavior plays in central, personally affecting values: as the chief portal to ecstasy, as recurrent natural need, and as the near occasion of, undergirding for, and necessary prompt to marital love. Such central, personally affecting values are values that make up the private in the sense of the personal.[13] Nor does the reporting of sexual orientation violate privacy viewed as necessary sanctuary and repose in sexual behavior. Open gays have as much sanctuary and repose in their nonintruded on, nonreported on sex acts as closet cases do. All the senses of sexual privacy that are relevant to gays—the status of not being spied on, the integrity of the body, the importance of personally affecting values, and the need for sanctuary—all these were in fact violated by the Supreme Court's decision in *Bowers v. Hardwick*, which upheld against constitutional privacy challenge ten-year prison sentences for consensual "homosexual sodomy" performed in one's own bedroom.[14] But none of them is violated by outing.

––––––––

The founder of ACT UP, Larry Kramer, has called for the "outing" of the HIV status of politicians.[15] Does the absence of a right to secrecy covering the status of one's sexual orientation analogously entail that no right to secrecy covers one's HIV status? No. It has already been shown how in various ways a right to secrecy—call it "confidentiality"—can arise when secrecy is closely tethered to privacy. The same holds here. One of the basic forms of privacy is privacy in the relation of doctor and patient. The doctor-patient relation is private because one's doctor maintains the integrity of the very substrate of one's existence—one's body.[16] Medical records are both instrumental to and constitutive of the doctor-patient relation in the way that an actor's role is both instrumental to and constitutive of a play. Secrecy in medical records is necessary for the records to be private, and so a right to secrecy in one's HIV status is pendant from the privacy that inheres in the doctor-patient relation.

IV. The Form of the Alleged Right against Outing

In addition to the failure of the alleged right against outing to be covered in its content by normative privacy, the right in question also has difficulties of form. Note that this putative right is not simply a garden-variety immunity right against others, that is, a right *not to be coerced by others* to do or not do something. In particular, the alleged right is not an unobjectionable immunity right against self-incrimination. For the outer is not forcing the outee to say anything about himself that he does not want to say. The outee is free to tell the truth, tell a lie, or remain silent. Indeed, all three options have been exercised by those outed. Rather, the alleged "no outing" right, unlike any common immunity right, is asserted as a positive demand-claim, that is, a right *to coerce others* to do or not do something. Specifically, the alleged right is a demand-claim that a specific person keep from repeating what he in fact knows about the closet case's identity—a right, that is, morally to place a gag order on someone. That the right asserted has both the general structure of a positive demand-claim and the specific form of a gag order should make it highly suspect.

A gag order squelches speech and so makes the purported right suspect as a direct violation of freedom of speech. There are, of course, culturally and constitutionally standard exceptions to rights of free speech: obscenity, slander (saying damaging falsehoods about a person), libel (printing damaging falsehoods about a person), and fighting words (those words that automatically, precognitively incite the hearer to strike out at the speaker present to hand). But none of these exceptions applies to outing.

Some state laws and state court interpretations of common law do, however, recognize a possibility of invading privacy by means of words and hold it as a legally admitted exception to free speech rights.[17] In these cases, the purported invasion of privacy by words (where this is not simply the first reporting of information acquired illegitimately) resembles an obscenity truly said of an individual, like calling someone who fucks his mother a "motherfucker." It is reporting something disgusting but true about an individual. The legal standard in California is that "the matter made public must be one which would be offensive and objectionable to a reasonable person of ordinary sensibilities . . . a morbid and sensational prying [revealing information] . . . so offensive as to shock the community's notions of decency."[18] However, a "reasonable person" or a "community standards" exception to a right controverts what a right is if the exception ultimately is analyzed in terms of majoritarian values. For rights are areas where the individual's rather than the group's values are permitted to prevail. So, on the one hand, if allegedly privacy-generating disgust is measured simply by popular opinion, then the exception to free speech cannot stand, for rights at law are immunities against majority rule.[19] On the other hand, if an objective, culturally neutral standard of disgust, offense, indecency, and morbidity is employed to generate a privacy that can be violated by speech, the person outed can claim such a violated right *only* if he views himself as properly, in the nature of things, disgusting for being gay—views his very existence as being like the experience of accidentally but permanently stepping into a rotting, exposed corpse. That this sense of privacy is committed to a vision of gay being as sempiternal horror may well explain why ultraconservatives, like Congressman Dannemeyer, oppose outing. I hope it is not the reason why the National Gay and Lesbian Task Force opposes outing.

That the "no outing" gag order is a demand-claim, which coerces what other people must do, makes it doubly objectionable. Those who oppose outing claim that, as a matter of moral right, one person—the potential outee—can place on another specifiable person—the potential outer—*without that person's consent* a duty to do something for him, to restrict her independence for his sake. The alleged duty is to keep the closet case's secret secret. On the part of the person with the alleged duty, such keeping entails a complex web of actions and omissions, including lies, deceptions, and morally coerced silences. Now I may have nonvoluntary moral positive duties to others, like the duty to be charitable, but these are not duties to specifiable individuals. Having a moral obligation to be charitable does not give any particular individual—*this* mendicant—a right claim on my wallet. At common law, there is only one such involuntary duty between specifiable individuals, and it is telling. The duty is the duty of a parent to his own child. If I return home to find my house aflame with my child in it, I have a duty to call the fire department. I have affirmative obligations for the welfare of my child. Even without my consent, my child can place a duty on me, a demand-claim to do something for him that restricts my independence. But he is the only person who may do so. Third parties—parties with whom I have no contractual agreements—have no right to demand things of me. They cannot demand that I limit my independence—in the case of outing, my speaking and printing—for their sake even to the point of saving their lives. To claim that they can is to invert the totality of moral opinion of the West and to constitutionalize the Marxist view that my abilities exist simply as instruments to fulfill the needs of other people, whoever they may be.

The rule that there are no involuntarily assumed third-party obligations, however, also cuts against one argument frequently given *for* outing. The argument runs to the effect that the closet case enjoys various benefits from the lesbian and gay community—enhanced access to socializing, to sexual partners, to gay professional services, and the like—benefits that she would not have if the community did not exist. From this indisputable fact, the argument tries to conclude that, since the closet case is benefited by the community, she in turn owes it to the community to do her part for the community by coming out and shouldering her share of the work required to produce the benefits she enjoys. If the person does not voluntarily fulfill her obligation to come out, the community has a right (so it goes) to do it for her—by outing her, that is, naming her as responsible to the group to which she belongs and by which she is benefited.[20] The argument, however, arrives stillborn. Suppose a nice French restaurant has just opened in my town, a town otherwise bereft of good restaurants. I eat there a lot. I'm a regular. My life is benefited by its existence and its nouvelle cuisine. Time passes. Times get bad. The restaurant is failing. Its owner, needing capital, comes to me and says: "You have benefited from my restaurant's existence, so you have an obligation to do your part to help the restaurant survive." Now, if I do not give the owner five thousand dollars—the amount he needs—is it all right for him to steal it from me to enforce this alleged obligation? Obviously not. There is no such non-agreed-to obligation. But then obviously too, I have no non-agreed-to duty to the gay community even if, in its need, I do not come to its aid, however nice a thing, decent a thing, expected a thing that would be for me to do. We ought to stick to the vision of the Declaration of Independence and believe that communities exist to guarantee rights of individuals, and we should be very wary when the concept of community is used to generate obligations. For the tyranny of the majority will almost always be found there working in finely sinuous, deeply insidious ways.

V. The Rhetoric of Privacy

Some Leftward-leaning gays have supported outing but thought that to do so entails abandoning privacy as a moral engine for reform—an engine that they want to see abandoned in any case as being too geared toward benefiting the individual at the expense of the collective.[21] Some have thought too that even the rhetoric of privacy should be abandoned as ineffective. One activist litigator holds that "focusing our political rhetoric on the realm of privacy not only mischaracterizes our goals but also reinforces the negative stereotypes that we are hidden, dangerous, and easily blackmailed and that we really care only about sex."[22] But this catalog of dangers is conceptually confused along lines already mapped. It mistakes privacy for enforced secrecy.

Privacy, a dimension of freedom, continues to provide a strong political rhetoric for gays, even stronger than the rhetoric of equality: for everyone, gay or not-gay, has many occasions to feel his or her privacy threatened or invaded. So everyone is a natural constituent, a natural audience for appeals to privacy. In contrast, the vast majority of people do not feel oppressed, do not feel that they are treated unequally, treated as socially degraded because of some (minority) group membership. So there is no natural sympathy "out there" for rhetorical strategies based on equality; at least they are more difficult to mount. And this difficulty, I suspect, explains why, although its aim was racial equality, the civil rights movement cast its slogans in terms of *freedom* rather than in rhetorically deadening terms of *equality*. Thus, certain motorcoach trips were called "Freedom Rides," not "Equality Rides." If you want an example of deflationary rhetoric, just substitute "equal" for "free" in the following line: "Free at last! Free at last! Thank God Almighty, we are free at last."

VI. Are Privacy Rights Waived by Hypocrisy?

The majority of gays who have taken a published stand opposing outing as a matter of general rule nevertheless have thought that there is a legitimate exception to the rule: they hold that it is morally permissible, indeed commendable, to out closet cases who have viciously attacked the gay community. These critics claim that the exception is justified by the closet case's hypocrisy, in virtue of which (so they claim) the closet case waives any right to privacy.[23] In trying to justify his threat to out gay, yet gay-baiting, Republican House members, openly gay U.S. Representative Barney Frank has thundered that, while there is a right to privacy, there is no right to hypocrisy.[24] I think that this is a bad argument.

First, the exception's rationale basically claims that one is justified in holding a person to his own standards: if he thinks gays should be punished, and he *is* gay, then (so it goes) he should be punished by his own lights.[25] At least, that person, it seems, cannot complain when he is punished. For he is being treated as he himself claims a person should be treated. But surely we want to hold a person not to his own standard but to the standard of justice, and if it is wrong to out people by the standard of justice, then it is wrong to do so even if they by their own standards think that they should be outed.

Second, one would hate to see something as strong as a fundamental right be forfeited as the result of something as weak as hypocrisy. If hypocrisy is enough to cause a right to be waived, then there will not be many rights around, for everyone has many occasions to be hypocritical. Indeed, hypocrisy is an expected consequence of living in relatively liberal times, the consequence, that is, of not being assigned a specific role that is the whole of one's life, but of having many diverse roles with no clear ranking between them. Torn between roles, a person "sells out" one role for another and so appears hypocritical. Indeed, it has been suggested that one of the core values and functions of privacy is just exactly to insulate from moral critique the conflicting values associated with our differing roles—so that we do not become entirely unhinged or explode as moral agents:

> Some writers have equated nondisclosure of self to others as tantamount to fraud, hypocrisy, deceit. [But] keeping people ignorant about what one is like in spheres they are not part of, or have no reasonable claim to knowledge about, is in no way morally tainted behavior. Generally, so long as a person does not misrepresent himself to those who, within the relevant domain, reasonably rely on his projected image, that person is not acting deceptively.[26]

In light of this understanding, consider closeted politicians who aggressively support anti-gay legislation, the sort of people with whom "hypocrisy" outers are most concerned. Within the domain of policy-oriented political rhetoric on gay issues—the writing of statutes, speeches on the House floor, that sort of thing—it is not in fact relevant what the speaker's sexual orientation is. What *is* relevant is how good the arguments are for or against the legislation and possibly what a politician's constituents think about the legislation, if she is viewed as representing them. So the politician is not being deceptive or punishably hypocritical if in this context she says one thing while being quite another. Ironically on this role-insulating view of privacy, contra Barney Frank, far from creating an exception to privacy, hypocrisy is something protected by it.

The political philosopher Judith Shklar has pointed out that charges of hypocrisy—charges that a person says one thing but does another or for convenience says conflicting things to different audiences—are politics on the cheap. For such charges simply punt on what the substantively correct political stand should be. Indeed, Shklar points out that in liberal democracies, where those who rule do so by the consent of the governed, politicians with their competing constituencies will be particularly subject to this process of selling out, of habitually failing to live up to promises and of professing beliefs they do not hold. Hypocrisy is part and parcel of public political life.[27] Hypocrisy is chiefly a sin of the intellect, a sin against reason, not a moral sin. Academics, not politicians, should worry about it.

Finally, even if all this is not persuasive, two examples should make it clear that, if privacy is a fundamental right, then hypocrisy does not waive it. First, imagine that I am very wealthy but that I say that I am poor, or at least act poor—I wear, for instance, Pat Nixon's cloth coat. But I support lower tax rates for the wealthy, say, because I honestly (if benightedly) believe that through the mechanisms of trickle-down theory everyone will be benefited by tax cuts for the wealthy. Have I waived my right to confidentiality in my tax statements at the IRS? Is it all right for some Leftist computer hacker who has gotten wind of my filthy riches to break into the IRS's records and reveal to the world my tax returns? The answer is obviously not, hypocrite though I be.

Or again—to use a real-life example—take televangelist and twelve-time convicted felon Jim Bakker. He regularly derided gays and anyone else not living the narrowest of sexual life-styles. Yet, as he fell from television greatness, both men and women among his staff came forward to vouch that he imposed on them for nonconjugal sexual favors. He was hypocrite supreme on matters sexual.[28] Yet do we suppose that in light of this hypocrisy it would be morally permissible for you or the government to go ahead and record with hidden video cameras his and Tammy Faye's marital sex acts? Again, obviously not, hypocrite though he be. So even if outing does indeed violate privacy rights (and I have argued that it does not), hypocrisy will not justify the selective outing of those gays who are viciously anti-gay.

One need not erase the value—the right—of privacy one jot or tittle in order to be able to support outing. Privacy need not be diminished as a political ideal or drilled with exceptions in order to be made consistent with the practice of outing. If a right to privacy were violated by outing, outing really would be, as some have claimed,[29] an act of terrorism, just as Operation Rescue's blocking of women's access to reproductive privacy is terrorism. But outing violates no right of privacy, and talk of outing as gay terrorism and gay fascism is rhetoric as vapid as it is overheated.

VII. A Right to the Closet?

If outing does not violate privacy rights, still perhaps there could be, independently of privacy, a right to the closet. I will approach this issue in two ways. First, I will suggest that there is something defeatingly odd about a right to the closet. Then I will argue that, once considerations of privacy are dropped, there is no alternative way to generate secrecy rights for the closet.

The dynamics of the closet do not comport with what a right is. At a minimum, a right means a permission to act in accordance with one's own desires, to live by one's own lights rather than by the dictates of others, whether the others are majorities or a tyrant or anyone else who might coerce one. "I have a right" means "I have permission to act as I want." But notice that this permission does not obtain for the closet case. The closet is coerced. For it makes a demand on the individual—to hide—that no one in the majority and no one in power would ever choose for himself. Like Sophie's "choice" of picking which of her two children is to be killed by the Nazis, the closet presents only an unreasonable "option."

25

The coercion compelling the closet is of two sorts. One is material or economic coercion. Lesbian novelist Sarah Schulman puts it bluntly: "Most gay people stay in the closet—i.e., dishonor their relationships—because to do so is a prerequisite for employment. Having to hide the way you live because of fear of punishment isn't a 'right,' nor is it 'privacy.' Being in the closet is not an objective, neutral, or value-free condition. It is maintained by force, not choice."[30] But even—or especially—gay people for whom considerations of employment are irrelevant, thanks to wealth, are closeted, for example, the "A" gays in Armisted Maupin's *Tales of the City* series. Vito Russo summarizes the situation of such people: "What all this boils down to is that people aren't afraid to come out because of career considerations, economic reasons, or even a desire for privacy. They don't want to come out because they've been taught on the most basic level that it's disgusting and dirty to be gay, and they believe it."[31]

It is the regard of others that does most of the coercing of gay people—a spiritual coercion, if you will. To be viewed by others as scum is not something people in power or the majority would choose for themselves even for a second. The avoidance of being so viewed therefore can hardly be considered a moral choice of a free agent. These two types of coercion cover most closet cases.[32] But if this is so, then the closet cannot be considered to be occupied as a matter of "right," for in occupying it one is simply following other people's dictates, not one's own lights.

VIII. Secrets by Agreement and the Code of Silence

Even if privacy does not generate rights to secrecy surrounding the closet, perhaps there is another way that rights to secrecy can come into being. The way that secrecy becomes a right without appeal to privacy is through consent. You tell me, "Now you've got to keep this secret; this is just between you and me." I nod agreement, say, "Cross my heart and hope to die," and then you tell me you're gay. If, in these circumstances, I then go to the media and let the elephant out of the bag, you have a legitimate complaint against me that I have violated your right to secrecy. The violation has the form of a promise broken, a contract breached. But outing is hardly ever such a violation.

Secrecy about the closet is virtually never the result of an agreement between two people. Rather, secrecy about the closet is a code within the gay community as a whole. There is an unspoken presumption, an unwritten rule, that one does not publicly report what one knows of another's sexual orientation. Some people would like to view the code as having been built up from, and so as having its moral force derived from, individual acts of consent. Thus, one objector to outing claims, "We [gays] have long *agreed* to allow each of us the dignity of deciding on our own moment to speak."[33] But no one signs on to this code; rather, one is born into it, just as black Americans for the better part of a century were born into a constitutional scheme with provisions for their slavery. Therefore, any justness that the code might have cannot be said to flow from the consent of the governed.

The gay community cannot be thought of as an artifice like, say, a stamp collectors' club or Alcoholics Anonymous. In such social groupings, as a condition of membership, one agrees to abide by the club's bylaws, and if one doesn't like the club's rules, one can set up one's own competing club. Rather, the gay community is a natural community in the way that English is a natural language but the computer languages Fortran and Cobol are not. If one is born in England of English parents, it is not an option to decide not to speak English as one's mother tongue but to set up linguistic shop instead in some artificial language, in the way one can, if one does not like some computer language, simply make up one's own. Gays simply find themselves immersed in the presumption of protecting each other's closets. Individual consent has nothing to do with it. And this presumption is firmly entrenched in gay social custom. Not maintaining The Secret is not easy. I have found that, even if one has consciously decided to abandon the custom, one still finds oneself unwittingly acting in accordance with it. Abandoning the custom, like speaking in nonsexist English, requires unlearning automatic responses.

Now, this code of silence and presumption of the closet is not just a rule. It is an industrial strength rule, one so strong as to be different in kind from usual rules: it is a rule that one breaks only if one wants to destroy the rule itself. We call this species of rules "conventions." Take jaywalking: the legal ban on jaywalking is a rule but not a convention. People jaywalk for self-interested reasons—to save seconds and steps. But people who jaywalk—virtually all Americans—are not attempting to destroy the rule against jaywalking when they do jaywalk. Indeed, they do not think that the ban is a bad one and do not demonstrate and vote to get rid of it. For even if the rule is never enforced, it is useful in adjudicating responsibility when accidents occur. By way of contrast, consider the rule breaking that is involved in desegregating lunch counters in the segregated South. If I am black and sit at the "whites only" section of a lunch counter, I am not breaking the rule for some self-interested end, to get some advantage just for me, thinking the while that others really should obey the ban. No, when I sit down, what I am trying to do is to destroy the "whites only" rule, and the only people who do consciously break the rule are those who want to destroy it. This rule—"whites only"—is a convention, not a mere rule.

A society's central values, those by which it defines itself to itself, are cast as conventions and not mere rules. Many of these conventional rules run so deep both in a society's conception of itself and in the behavior of its members that no one ever thinks to write the conventions into law. Thus, until the rule was challenged during the 1991 liberation of Kuwait, the Saudi government did not bother casting as law the convention that Saudi women are not permitted to drive cars. Similarly, although there is a near universal social practice barring gays from adopting children, it is illegal in only two states—New Hampshire and Florida. Or again, a bar to gay marriages is universal even though many states have marriage laws that make no reference whatever to the biology of spouses.

To break such a community-defining convention is to appear to be a traitor to the community. But what appears as treason to some can actually be social reform, as exemplified by civil disobedience, in which, when one breaks a current convention, one hopes thereby to establish a morally improved community. Breaking conventions—as in civil disobedience—is a way of finding out whether society's specific rules, however intensely held, in fact reflect society's overarching general values. Thus, in the late 1980s, although some American flag burnings inflamed more than cloth, they also revealed the nation's commitment to free speech when in 1989 and again in 1990 the Supreme Court ruled that burning the nation's flag was constitutionally protected expression and when a constitutional amendment to reverse the decisions failed in Congress.[34] So too, blacks sitting at the front of conventionally segregated buses helped reveal the nation's commitment to equality.

The gay community itself has both garden-variety rules and community-defining conventions. An example of a mere rule is the rule that, when in a gay bar a friend is having a conversation with someone whom he is cruising, one does not add oneself to the conversation. When a gay man breaks this rule, he does so usually for selfish reasons—envy, misplaced lust—or from stupidity. He is not trying to destroy the rule; indeed, he wants others to abide by the rule when he himself is cruising. In a society with few opportunities for gay men to connect with other gay men conversationally in ways that might lead to a relationship, say, at a company picnic, this rule has excellent social utility. But the gay community has conventions too. One such convention is that, in the conversations one conducts while picking someone up in a gay bar, one is expected to present oneself at the lowest common intellectual denominator and not to press to discover the other person's occupation. Another is the convention, sometimes posted, that there is to be no talking in orgy rooms at bathhouses. In both cases, the convention works to keep something that is potentially political and politically charged from becoming actually and explicitly political, and so both sets of conventions are morally objectionable.

Now, the presumption that every gay person will keep every other gay person's identity secret from the public is a convention and not merely a rule. Any field anthropologist examining the folkways of the gay community would easily notice that among all the variety in the gay community—just for starters divisions of life-styles between lesbians and gay men—The Secret is *the* social convention that most centrally defines the community. That The Secret is *the* gay social convention explains why outing is so highly charged. To those committed to The Secret, which is to say virtually all gay people, the outer is a traitor. Thus is explained outers being called "terrorists" and "cannibals."[35] Outing hits the bedrock of the gay community. To the extent that the convention of The Secret is the structuring element, the DNA, the constitutive convention of the gay community, outing is not simply *a* problem in gay ethics but *the* problem in gay ethics.

Yet what a strange convention The Secret is. That which binds the community together is a commitment to a belief in the community's worthlessness. The very structuring principle of the community functions as a denial that the community exists—indeed, a denial that it should exist. The convention is a complete capitulation to the general social belief that the only good gay is a nonexistent one. In this regard, gays are dissimilar to blacks and women traditionally considered, in that blacks and women have at least had a perceived legitimate presence in traditional society through their roles as slaves and servers. In this respect, gays are much more like Native Americans, about whom society holds the belief, as given voice by General Philip Sheridan, that the only good one is a dead one. The definitional work that gays perform in society is accomplished from their position in Non-being, the fearsome Just Beyond. In this evacuating milieu, for gays to maintain The Secret—the dirty little secret of their socially abject status—is like Native Americans knowingly handing out to their own people smallpox infected blankets provided by General Sheridan. Each time one gay person insists that other gay people, whether open or not, keep his identity as gay hidden in conformity with society's belief that gays are to society what shit is to the body and should, like shit, be eliminated from the body politic—each time he insists that the others go along with society's values in these matters—he is requiring the other gays to degrade themselves as gay, to sink to the level of abjection dictated for gays by the dominant culture.[36]

The Secret's requirement that its keeper degrade himself means that, even if one could argue that the closet is a form of legitimate self-defense against unjust discrimination—could argue, that is, that there is no *duty* to come out, so that I cannot insist that you on your own come out—you still cannot insist that I keep your secret. For to require that keeping is to require that the out person do a double injustice to himself—to degrade himself and to force him to commit his life to the very values that keep him oppressed. The gay person who keeps another gay person's dirty little secret degrades himself, does an injustice to himself by going along with rather than resisting the values that oppress gays.

The web of omissions and commissions entailed in maintaining The Secret does not leave its keeper as an innocent bystander, who merely observes the immorality of others without participating in or enhancing it. The openly gay keeper of The Secret is morally *not* like those who, working the fields, simply observed in the distance trains carrying Jews to the East; rather, the keeper is like those who, while not setting the trains in motion, nevertheless voluntarily serviced the trains on their way to the East.

IX. Dignity versus Happiness

An examination of the types of values variously lost and protected by the closet will show all the more clearly the moral permissibility of outing and the expectation that the gay person, living morally, will indeed out others. The closet case tries to assure his happiness by maintaining his closet. He collects nice antiques, buys nice clothes, drinks nice wines, and takes fun vacations that he might not be able to afford if he were openly gay. And he seeks out the regard of others. Regard feels nice. Love feels nice. But regard is not respect. One can have a warm regard for a painting. One can even love it. But one does not respect a painting. People have warm regard, even love, for their pets, but few people respect them. What the closet case does in maintaining his closet is to barter away his self-respect, his worthiness for respect, his dignity, for happiness, regard, and nonrespectful love.

To accept the closet is to have absorbed society's view of gays, to accept insult so that one avoids harm. Thereby one becomes a simulacrum—a deceptive substitute—of a person. One seems to be a moral agent with ends of one's own and an ability to revise them, but one really is simply a puppet to the values of society—the equivalent of the perpetually deferential "housewife" (of stereotype) who has no views but her husband's and who eventually loses even the ability to see things through any other eyes than his. To accept the closet is to be at best the "happy slave" (of stereotype) committed to the institution of slavery in the way a dog is committed to his food bowl.

Life in the closet is morally debased—and morally debasing. It frequently requires lying, but it always requires much more. Dan Bradley, president of the Legal Services Corporation under President Carter, elaborates:

> Always there was the coverup: Arranging for women with whom I was friendly and had shared my secret to brag about my virility to F.B.I. agents making a routine background check; keeping up a macho front with male colleagues; making sure I had a female escort for parties, and worrying about how to deal with homosexual issues in the legal services program. . . .
>
> The web of deceit I had so consciously and meticulously woven over the years made it possible for me to rationalize whatever I had to do to protect myself. You can rationalize the lies, the deceptions or whatever. There is no end of it.[37]

The life as lie chiefly entails a devolution of the person as person, as moral agent. The whiteness of the individual lies might be forgiven as self-defense, but the dirtiness of the secret that the lies maintain cannot be. The dirt is the loss of self, of personhood, the loss of that which makes human life peculiarly worth protecting to begin with.

The secret that the closet case wants to force on others is not a secret that is unique or peculiar to the individual (say, the secret that he really is the author whose nom de plume graces the dustjacket of many a mystery novel). Rather, the imposed secret is about his status, a status that he views as abject and that he shares with the others who are supposed to keep the secret for him. So, in abiding by the convention to keep the secret, the keeper commits to the view of gays that the convention presupposes: that gays are loathsome and disgusting, to be kept from sight, nauseating if touched or seen, filth always in need of being flushed away.

This abject condition is quite remote from valued privacy. The philosopher Ferdinand Schoeman has pointed out that violations of privacy are experienced similarly to violations of sacred objects and that the sharing of a privacy is like the revelation, in ritual, of a sacred object. Outside their religious context sacred objects may be quite humble, say, mere dollops of flour or a few bound twigs, the commercial value of which may be as little as nothing. Still, their violations are experienced as affronts, defilements, and pollutions.[38] But the closet case inverts this moral structure. The closet case and the society whose values he accepts do not view his violation as a defilement and pollution. Rather, he and society view his very existence—him—as an affront, as defilement and pollution. And his revelation of himself to his sacred band—his blood family—is not a wonderment but (he supposes) a horror.

The convention of The Secret would commit the openly gay person to a similar vision of gay people and so commit him to give up his own dignity for the happiness of the closeted gay person. To do that is the very inversion of moral life, in which nobility of character, as in the case, for example, of Freedom Riders, lies in sacrificing one's happiness so that dignity—one's own or others'—might be asserted. This is what civil disobedience does, yet the inverse does not hold. A person cannot be morally compelled to be debasedly servile, to sacrifice his dignity for the happiness of others. I cannot be morally compelled to eat dog shit even if to do so would comfort the lives of those who otherwise would commit suicide.

There are two exceptions to dignity-based outing. The first is if the outing violates some right of the outee. I cannot legitimately advance my dignity at the expense of other people's rights. But we have seen that there are no likely candidates for such rights that outing purportedly violates. And this is crucially important: even if my actions in outing someone are a necessary condition for someone *else* violating the outee's rights—say, his right not to be harmed or his right not to be discriminated against—still, *my actions* are not violations of his rights any more so than are his great-great-grandfather's siring actions, which were also a necessary condition for the violations. Minus the siring or minus the outing, true, the violation would not have occurred, but the violator of the outee's rights is the bigoted employer, or whoever caused the violation, not those who merely provided some of the millions upon millions of necessary conditions for the violation.

The second circumstance that would make outing morally impermissible is if particular acts of outing objectively cause an overall loss of dignity—if, that is, dignity lost in others is greater than the dignity to be had both by the potential outer living morally and by the increase in overall gay dignity that attends outing's destruction of the code of silence that degrades all gays. This condition will rarely be met. Still, if it were the case (as it currently is not) that the government was shooting gays, I would morally be expected to suspend my dignity temporarily so that the current and prospective dignity of others is made possible.

Notice what will not count here against outing: any assertion of individual dignity that is dependent on upholding or giving effective voice to the prejudices of others or to other forces that degrade gays in general will not count toward an exception to outing. To lose a child in a custody case for prejudicial reasons is, to be sure, to suffer an indignity, but to insist on being closeted to protect one's parenting is simply to give effective voice to those social conditions that degrade gays in general. Or again, to remain a closeted member of a racial or ethnic minority community that despises gays is to avoid an indignity to be sure, but it also gives effective voice to prejudicial forces in the minority community that degrade all gays. A dignity may outweigh a dignity, as a pleasure or measure of happiness may not. But because the indignity bred and maintained by the convention of The Secret is so great and pervasive, it is unlikely that any individual indignity suffered will cancel the dignity gained in the convention's destruction through outing.

34

X. Two Attempts to Defend the Closet

It has been suggested to me that a good reason—one that allegedly does not depend on self-hatred—for staying in the closet and for reasonably objecting to being outed is that one is doing virtuous works (say, for trade unionism) that one might not be able to do if one was out (to the unions). But here the chances that one is self-deceived are great. Why would one want to invest one's energies in institutional arrangements that oppress gays unless one had a less than robust sense of self as a gay person so as always to think it proper to defer one's dignity for The Cause? The following is all too typical: "[The Service Employees International Union's] original contract included a ban on bias based on sexual orientation, but union negotiators abandoned the demand when state officials told SEIU that acceptance of the clause would mean the sacrifice of other arbitration rights."[39]

It might also be claimed that lying by the closet case is a legitimate form of self-defense and so one of the rare justified forms of lying. Indeed, self-defense against injustice provides the star case of justified lying in which *others* in the know ought also avoid telling the truth—to lie to one's captors in a just war. But the lies of the closet invert the moral structure and effect of lies in war. When one lies in war, one puts oneself at risk as part of an attempt to deceive the enemy so that the forces of good may win. But in the closet one lies for one's own self-interest in a way that solidifies the forces of evil. The closet case simply capitulates to the enemy. This capitulation explains why conservatives, who think it unlikely that they can muster national energies for gassing vans, oppose outing: the closet is the next best alternative means of oppressing gays.

XI. Outing as Vindictiveness and Punishment

Although outing is a morally expected activity, still there are a number of bad reasons for outing. When the motivation for outing is something other than the perpetuation of self-respect, the reasons for outing are likely to be morally dubious. When for a cool six-figure sum a has-been

35

porn star outs his alleged ex-lover, a Hollywood movie idol, in the *National Enquirer*, this act does not bestir or enhance the outer's dignity.[40] One can hardly cheer its motives. They are shameless and reflect badly on the outer's character.

Still more troubling is vindictive outing—outing that is analogous to Pete's "outing" of Julie as black in *Showboat*. Indeed, the vindictive outing of gays contributes to the very values that oppress gays. Vindictive outing of gays by straights occurs, for instance, when newspapers print names and addresses of men busted in police raids on tearooms—or when a colleague outs you to higher management because you got a promotion he wanted.[41] Vindictive outing has the same moral structure as the shouting of anti-gay invective, like calling someone a "faggot" or "bulldyke." These are imprecations. Imprecations call down evil on a person or group from an independently existing reservoir of cultural values, as though invoking God or the devil to destroy someone. At the same time, however, imprecations amplify, strengthen, and ritualistically affirm these values by pledging allegiance to them, just as one strengthens the symbolic power of the flag each time one salutes or pledges allegiance to it. Vindictive outing calls on the cultural repository of anti-gay forces to destroy a gay person and at the same time strengthens that repository's power by exercising and admiring its muscle.

Some people have compared outing to McCarthyism.[42] And vindictive outing *is* like McCarthyism: such outing feeds gays to the wolves, who thereby are made stronger. And to the extent that outing is viewed as punishment of any sort and, to be effective as punishment, relies on social hatred of gays, outing seems to pander to the values and punitive instrumentalities of the dominant culture, giving them at least the appearance of credence. But the sort of outing that I have been advocating does not invoke, mobilize, or ritualistically affirm anti-gay values; rather, it cuts against them, works to undo them. The point of outing, as I have defended it, is not to wreak vengeance, not to punish, and not to deflect attention from one's own debased state. Its point is to avoid degrading oneself. The outer who outs as an incident of her gay pride, not shame, does not pledge allegiance to the phobia-driven cyclone of hate that admittedly is sometimes a foreseeable consequence of outing. However, that outing has a foreseeable bad consequence does not make it morally wrong any more than the foreseeable consequence of a reduced GNP would make my taking a vacation morally wrong. What *is* troublesome is the doubt, the possibility, that some outing is indeed motivated by lingering self-hatred on the part of the outer.[43]

XII. Outing as "Living in the Truth"

In not leading a life of lies, in simply "living in the truth,"[44] one will make known the sexual orientation of others because one does not think, and rightly does not think, that there is anything wrong with being gay and because one will not play along with conventions that degrade gay existence, even if they are the conventions of gays themselves as a community of self-hating and self-oppressing persons. Self-hatred is the glue that holds together the convention of The Secret, which in turn generates the shame that underwrites self-hatred.

The core question in the outing debate is, "Whose values shall count?" Are the bigot's values to count—even or especially when bigots are the overwhelming majority? Or are the values of pride and dignity as registered in the lives of openly gay people to count?

Vito Russo puts the core question thus: "What [outers are] saying is that if being gay is *not* disgusting, is *not* awful, then why can't we talk about it? After all, it's not an insult to call someone gay. Is it?"[45] Similarly: "The principle is really very simple. Either being gay is OK or it isn't. And allowing homosexuality to take its place as a normal part of the human sexual spectrum requires ceasing to treat it as a dirty little secret."[46]

Like civil disobedience, outing violates a community's conventions so that the community may come to live more morally. It violates a local or specific community-defining value in order that it may jog to foreground consciousness a community's higher or more overarching values, which it has failed to apply consistently. In this way, the culture's determinate but not fully realized general values are made concrete in the way people live. Outing violates a convention built on self-hatred as *the* lived experience among gays, the internalization of society's viewing of gays as scum. Outing appeals to and banks on a moral bet that, although many gays feel like they are shit and may even think they are shit, still they know they are not shit. Outing begins to show forth, in the proud gay person who refuses to participate in rituals of degradation, models of that knowledge in concrete lived form.

Those who have supported outing have usually done so on the utilitarian ground that those outed—statesmen, movie stars, and the like—will provide positive role models for gays, especially young gays. I suggest that these supporters of outing have picked the wrong models to prize. Outed people will frequently be spiritual basket cases in consequence of the effects of long years in the closet. Other people would not, or at least should not, want these people as models for their soul—however well known, bred, or heeled.[47]

Still, it will tend to be the case that famous people are outed simply because they are famous, not because they are especially worthy of punishment, owing, say, to their being hypocrites, oppressors of gays, whatever. The gayness of the famous is newsworthy. And gays need not feel embarrassed at contributing to the news. Indeed, the news has constitutional import. One of the tests for a group having enhanced rights under the equal protection clause is whether the group is subject to general incapacities that might legitimately be expected to warrant legal distinctions being drawn with respect to the group in general: "What differentiates sex from such nonsuspect statuses as intelligence or physical disability . . . is that the sex characteristic frequently bears no relation to ability to perform or contribute to society."[48] So if presidents, senators, CEOs, Nobel laureates, and such like are gay, that is important news whatever their political leanings, however dirty or clean their hands, and however mangled their self-perceptions.

But the gayness of average people is important news too. The California appellate court that heard Mr. Sipple's case pointed out several ways in which Mr. Sipple—just a typical, unassuming citizen—was newsworthy in his homosexuality. He was a gay ex-marine. That is relevant to military policy. It appeared that a thank-you note from

President Ford to Sipple for saving the president's life was blocked or at least delayed because this man was gay. That is relevant to consider-ations of justice and decency. But further, Mr. Sipple, although just an average joe, had done lots of things to develop the gay community, through his work in Harvey Milk's campaigns, through his support work in the San Francisco drag ball scene, by participating in gay pride parades. And that is newsworthy too: ordinary people can do extraordinary things. Indeed, Sipple's name had appeared several times in the gay press. Those opposed to outing can insulate such people as Sipple from outing only by condescendingly considering them "hapless no-bodies."[49]

Further, when gays do bad things, especially to other gays, that unfortunately too is news, and the evildoers are out-worthy for that reason—to clarify how the machinery of injustice operates—even if not for vindictive reasons. To take a personal example, a closeted colleague of mine voted against me on a fellowship matter in order to distance himself from me in the eyes of our department. Telling a verifiable story that this injustice had occurred would require making the person's sexual orientation known. Indeed, quite generally, it is relevant to know that someone is leading a life as lie, is self-hating, is failing of his moral duties to himself. For such news ought to affect our understanding of the moral texture of the social universe, the dominant strata of which maintain their position in significant part by promoting self-hatred in minority groups while at the same time denying that self-hatred exists so that, in turn, it will not count as evidence that oppression exists. My point then is that, even when vindictiveness and the urge to punish are firmly laid aside, it will still be the case that a person living in the truth will out nearly everyone he or she knows to be gay.

XIII. Outing and Trust

Some have claimed that outing is to be deplored because it is a violation of trust: "It is better to live in a gay community that operates on mutual trust rather than mutual finking. . . . What kind of gay subculture do you prefer to live in—one with an atmosphere of trust, or one of gimlet-eyed suspicion?" Stuck in a *Boys in the Band* mentality, this vision of gay life is drenched with self-hatred and nostalgia for abjection's lure, a hankering for and rationalizing of the closet and The Secret: "Keeping such secrets [of 'our *demimonde*'] is one of the odd pleasures of being [a] member of an outgroup: It makes you a kind of insider, for a change, to know who your co-conspirators are when the rest of the world doesn't."[50] But surely—as even the metaphor here of "co-conspirators" should suggest—whether mutual trust is to be admired or not depends on the moral worthiness of the conventions that the trust uncritically maintains. As we have seen, the convention of which The Secret is the chief engine is one that has gays doing much of the work of their own oppression.[51] He at whom one should cast "gimlet-eyed suspicion" is the person who so openly admires the moral assessments of gays by their oppressors. Just "think," some archly fret, "of the impression outing makes on the general public."[52]

Refuge at the price of self-oppression is not a virtue that people truly in love with liberty can dare afford. Trust in a convention that calls for the obliteration of gays is a virtue that lays the groundwork for the annihilation of gays. Hannah Arendt could as well have been speaking of closeted assimilating "A" gays when, in speaking of another too trusting group in perilous times, she held that what was most beguilingly mendacious was not assimilationism as such but rather "the lying denial of the very existence of widespread anti-Semitism, of the isolation from reality staged with all the devices of self-deception by the Jewish bourgeoisie. . . . The decisive factor in all this was the loss of reality, aided and abetted by the wealth of these classes."[53] And we never know how quickly things can change—change for the worse in a world where, pace Santayana, remembering the past makes not a whit of difference to whether it is repeated.

XIV. Does Outing Thwart the Dignity of the Outed?

Some have claimed that, far from supporting outing, the concept of dignity provides grounds for opposing it. The argument succinctly is that outing someone prevents him or her from achieving the dignity that attaches to the coming-out process. By being outed, it is claimed, "one has lost forever . . . the single thing that makes coming out socially bearable: the dignity one may claim from having at least *chosen* to come out, chosen to be different."[54] Indeed, this argument can be dressed up in the finery of liberal cant: "For many a closeted homosexual, the moment [to come out] does eventually arrive when she steps forward to affirm her own character openly, and thereby becomes the author of it. This rite of passage is far too important to the development of a positive gay identity for someone else . . . to callously preempt it, to steal it away."[55] This argument misunderstands several things: the scope of dignity, the possible materials of liberty, and the complexity of the coming-out process. First, dignity can be achieved in many ways, and it is not a property that can be maximized because the various ways to it will get in each other's way if one tries them all. The relevant question is, Can a person, although outed, still have access to enough dignity to be outstandingly dignified? Second, being free— being the author of one's own character—does not require that a person begin as a blank slate and that every future be indeterminate but for her actions and choices. The relevant question is, Are conditions for the outed person such that she can achieve a richly textured life of her own making given the cussedness of circumstance both social and material? Finally, coming out is not a one-step, single-stage, mechanical process of being publicly known as gay; rather, it is a complex process of self-reflection, self-recognition, and self-acceptance leading to and partly effected by a public presence as gay. The relevant question is, Does the outed person retain the possibility of having a robust, positive, dignifying relation to his sexual orientation? The answer to all these questions is yes.

The evidence is provided by Congressman Gerry Studds. In the summer of 1983, at the age of forty-six, Studds was outed to the nation by a special counsel to the House Ethics Committee for an affair Studds had had with a male page a decade earlier. Unlike many outed people, Studds embraced, rather than denied, his sexual orientation. In its acceptance by him, in his self-acceptance, he found for the first time the capacity to love and a sense of freedom and serenity.[56] In his pride, he has taken up a special role in gay projects, heading up congressional opposition to the ban on gays in the military. In an interview with *The Advocate* soon after he was outed, Studds answered the question, "How do you feel now that you have publicly declared you are gay?" with words that do not sound like those of a man bereft of freedom, dignity, pride, and self-definition:

> Better than I've ever felt in my life. I suspect that's something that would be easy for your audience of gay people to understand. But I've found that in giving that response to the media in general, to folks who have not had this experience themselves, that it requires a great deal of explanation as to how in the midst of what for a lot of reasons appears to be a disastrous situation, one can candidly say, "I've never felt better in my life." Any person who has ever gone through the experience of coming out will understand that. I feel as if the remaining seven cylinders had just kicked in for the first time in 46 years. And that's a powerful feeling.[57]

It is evident from this statement that nothing was robbed from Studds and that opportunity for dignity was not preempted. Despite the fact that his sexual orientation was involuntarily made public, and despite the fact that the circumstances that occasioned the revelation were objectively embarrassing—a sexual affair with an underling in his nonage—Studds still speaks of the "experience" as of his own making, as *his* coming out. And to be sure, in its morally and psychologically important dimensions, it was.

The chief component for achieving dignity in coming out has to do with how one identifies oneself to oneself in light of public knowledge of one's orientation. Many gays will tell straights that they are gay and still be unhealthily self-hating, lacking in sufficient dignity. It is startling and depressing unto sickness to hear the HIV-positive director of the great, 1977 coming-out documentary *Word Is Out*, fourteen years later, make such self-hating statements as "I'm gay, so I deserve it"— AIDS: "There's still a little part of me that, though I don't like it, is just a little ashamed of being gay. It's ground into our heads so strongly, and our culture is so homophobic, that it would take Gandhi to exorcise

42

those feelings from himself. In the same way, there's a part of me that occasionally thinks I deserve this disease."[58] So, on the one hand, coming out voluntarily may lead to loss of dignity for some gay people, and, on the other hand, outing may, as in the case of Gerry Studds, lead to the promotion of dignity for the person outed. Therefore, the argument that outing should be opposed because it preempts dignity on the part of those outed and the argument that allowing each person to come out at his own pace (or even never) promotes his dignity both fail for want of a recognition of reality, even without considering that additional hard fact that the vast majority of gay people never do come out voluntarily.

XV. Outing as Politics

Some people oppose outing because it allegedly "doesn't work"—that is, it does not make for successful politics.[59] But outing on the account given here is not to be understood or justified chiefly in political terms. Rather, outing is a simple consequence of living morally. So whether it has maximally good political consequences is irrelevant to its permissibility. Its point is not to get legislation passed or candidates elected— the usual political fare. So, as far as "working" goes, it is irrelevant that virtually every one of the rich and famous who have been outed have indeed denied the whole matter and thereby contributed to the pitiableness of their own pitiable existence and to the social perception that being gay is shameful to boot. Not one outed celebrity has joined the gay brigade at the barricades. Some have even gone so far as to try to refortify their closet by installing it in a heterosexual marriage. But that such denial frequently occurs does not matter. It is not one's happiness that one is seeking through outing—it is the avoidance of being an instrument of insult to one's own dignity, the avoidance of complicity in one's own degradation.

In a similarly mistaken political vein, many on both sides of the outing issue, but especially those favoring it, have thought that the push toward outing is a political strategy driven, and possibly warranted, by the AIDS crisis.[60] They concur with Sweeney Todd that desperate times

43

call for desperate measures. But on the account given here, the measure is not a desperate one, resorted to only because all else has failed. Outing is living morally. The pacing of outing to the course of the AIDS crisis seems largely accidental. Indeed, gay litigative groups, gay legislative groups, and even many in ACT UP had (unfortunately to my mind) ceased even to treat AIDS as a gay-specific issue long before outing became an ongoing tactical possibility.

Alternatively, it has been suggested that outing has arisen not because things are so bad but because they are so good: "As more of us feel truly comfortable as gay, . . . we forget the pervasive fear and cautiousness that once bound us all. And thus, without trying, we lose the ability to think according to old rules. . . . We [out others] not to be malicious but because it simply does not occur to us to censor what to us seems so mundane. In short, the improving social climate for lesbians and gay men has made outing inevitable."[61] This position is close to being right, but it is not quite right. It is right to think that outing will or at least should become a routine, usual, expected part of gay life. If outing is to have any significant social effects, it will have to be widespread—and widely known. On this score, outing activists have correctly focused protest on the mass media's refusing to speak the truth about celebrities whom it knows are gay and even providing closet cases with phantom heterosexual cover while reserving gay reportage only for sleaze and evil. As Vito Russo has put it: "If you come out proudly and of your own free will, nobody wants to print it. As [recently knighted] British actor Ian McKellan told me about his own coming out, 'If you're not a hypocrite, there's no story for them. They don't care unless it can be used as gossip, as a cudgel to beat people up.'"[62]

But it is wrong to think that outing is occurring because things are so great for gays. Things are not. Outing is not occurring by "oops," that is, by inattentive slip or inevitable accident in consequence of great gay comfort. Outing is occurring now because of an increasing level of gay consciousness. Specifically, there has been a dawning recognition that to uphold the convention of the dirty little secret is to insult oneself and to participate in one's own oppression. A similar rise in consciousness among Native Americans is contributing to the end of their passing as white: "For a long time, Native Americans have been told 'if you can pass, then do it.' We need to be telling our people 'It's O.K. that you're Indian. Make your presence known.'"[63]

It is true that, if outing becomes widespread, those who are tentatively thinking of coming out socially into the gay community may not do so owing to increased fear of what the gay community might do to them—make them more publicly gay than they want to be. In an era of gay radiance, shadows for hiding will be fewer but darker; the price of admission to the gay community will be higher. But only at the higher price is the community one worth joining, one within which, not in spite of which, individual dignity is possible.

Sometimes one can calibrate the progress of gay liberation fairly precisely to that of black liberation. For gays in general the year is 1944, the year when Gunnar Myrdal described blacks' general, but highly charged, acceptance of passing in terms that can easily be transposed to the hesitant but labile consciousness of gays in general about outing now:

> In the American caste order, [passing] can be accomplished only by the deception of the white people with whom the passer comes to associate and by a conspiracy of silence on the part of other Negroes who might know about it. . . . Most Negroes, particularly those in the upper strata, . . . know of many other Negroes, sometimes half a hundred or more, who pass as white. . . . They usually do not expose them. . . . [Yet] they are increasingly brought to the compensatory feeling of race pride: "The Negro community is built around the idea of adjustment to being a Negro, and it rejects escape into the white world. . . . To wish to be white is a sacrifice of pride. It is equivalent to a statement that Negroes are inferior, and, consequently, that the youth himself is inferior." This, however, does not necessarily mean that a Negro becomes willing to disclose another Negro who is passing. The spirit of the protective community will usually work to help the ex-member to pass. If a passing Negro is disclosed by other Negroes, the cause is ordinarily not Negro solidarity but rather

private envy, of which there is a great deal in a frustrated lower caste.[64]

Despite the now quaint language, this passage should ring familiar to gays. Most gay outing now is the result of such frustration, rather than of good gay consciousness. But that statistic is shifting and in a way that will make gay and black history diverge rather than run parallel on the issue of outing passers. Most blacks cannot pass. And even before the black consciousness movement, most of those few blacks who could pass did not.[65] In consequence, by the advent of the black power and black consciousness movements, the issue of passing had already slipped from public discourse.[66] For against the backdrop of blacks in general, passers were a mere speck. At the very point where black pride would overtake envy as a motivation for the outing of passers, the issue was rendered irrelevant. Indeed, the solidification of black identity was, in a twisted way, some comfort to white racists. For solidified black identity meant that both miscegenation and passing would likely decline. And since "to whites, passing is an insult and a social and racial danger,"[67] the passing of passing meant the passing of one major sort of insult and danger *as perceived* by white racists.

With gays the opposite is the case. First, all gays "pass" as straight at least part of their lives, and nearly all gays "pass" all their lives. Second, it is not the passing gay person who is perceived as a major threat (since from gays who pass there is no fear of pollution through undetected miscegenation). Rather, the normal-appearing person being out is a major threat and source of cultural anxiety. For that the normal can be queer means that anyone—father, brother, even you—may be gay. So the gay movement cannot simply leap over or slough off, as did the black movement, the issue of passing and outing since in the case of gays everyone passes and *not* passing is the perceived threat to and imagined betrayal of society.

The comfort that the closet provides society stokes the convention of The Secret, by which in turn gays do most of the maintenance work in their own oppression. It is the shame-inducing Secret that is the chief dynamo of the closet's magnetic attraction. As long as The Secret is intact, the few people who are out are aberrant (even by gay standards) and are easily managed by society through the mechanisms of more and less subtle discriminations (a queer bashing here, a grant not given there, whatever does the trick). Being out, although necessary for gay progress, is nowhere near sufficient to achieve gay progress as long as the machinery by which gays are oppressed is left in place. Being out voluntarily is good. But no substantial gay progress will be made until the shame-enhancing Secret is abandoned. So gay progress requires both being publicly out and living in the truth, a necessary concomitant of which is that closet cases will be outed.

Some have thought that simply ending The Secret will itself usher in the gay millennium.[68] But it is not clear that ending The Secret alone will have the dramatic transformational effect that, say, the media's ending the secret about heterosexual liaisons seemed to have had on divorce and family law reform. For such reform, like currently secrecy-stalled euthanasia reform, provides options that the vast majority of people would probably want as permitted courses for themselves. It is far less clear that the vast majority of people want gay relations as a permitted option for themselves. More modestly, I think that, as a political strategy, outing is a way of getting gay people up to political speed, so that gays may play on an even field with other minorities and interest groups in the mechanisms of democracy. Ending the shame-drenched Secret would free the gay community from having to fight with one arm tied behind its back and much of its soul mired in self-hatred.

It is no accident that the outing movement as shame's destroyer came into being almost simultaneously—in the early spring of 1990—with the coming into being of the social and political movement Queer Nation with its commitment to gay life as visible being. Such visible gay being is best typified perhaps by the design group Gran Fury's T-shirt that pictures two sailor boys in a liplock and commands, "Read My Lips." The realm of gay being is shifting for the better from bars, dungeons, clubs, community centers, second-floor political and professional offices, and concert halls—worlds within walls, lives behind doors—to the bright lights and bustle of public thoroughfares and, I would hope, eventually to a casually Whitmanesque place with cruising and picnics, the American park—that public space and aesthetic in which nature and culture combine and complement each other such that one's private life need not, should not, and will not be a secret.

CHAPTER 2

On Some Words from ACT UP: Doing and Being Done

The worst thing about AIDS is the shame the families feel when their son dies of AIDS.
George Bush[1]

George Bush, you are, pure and simple, a murderer.
Larry Kramer[2]

The chief slogan of ACT UP is SILENCE = DEATH. Vito Russo gives a placard-length gloss on the slogan: "If I'm dying from anything, it's from indifference and red tape."[3] He claims that he is being killed by the government—that the government is murdering him.

Now, sometimes it is true that there is not a dime's worth of difference between killing and letting die. Suppose, for instance, that I hold my hands just below the surface of the water in a bathtub; then a baby, wholly by accident, slips and lodges under them; and I do not move. Have I killed the baby, or did I let the baby die? It is not clear. The AIDS crisis, however, is not such a case of fused or confused causation.

The logic of ACT UP's slogan simply begs off responsibility and misplaces blame, or at least places the wrong blame, on government. The inferential structure of the slogan is the following: if the presence of some thing might (or even would) prevent another thing, then the absence of the former is the cause of the latter; if, that is, the presence of government funding for AIDS research might (or even would) prevent some known person's death, then the absence of the funding is the cause of the person's death. But this structure of inference is absurd.

Just imagine the following parallel case. Terrorists blow up an ambassador's car; however, if it had snowed the night of the bombing, the ambassador would not have gone for the drive on which he was blown up. At trial, the terrorists claim that they are innocent, that the blame lies with clear skies. Why? Because in the presence of snow, the murder would have been prevented, and so, according to the pattern of inference, the absence of the snow—a clear sky—not terrorism, is the cause of the ambassador's death.

Even if maximum government efforts on AIDS would definitely have found a cure for AIDS by now (a dubious premise given the seeming wiles of HIV), it is still illegitimate to say that in the absence of such efforts it is government or red tape or indifference that is killing those now dying.

The sin of governmental inaction against people with AIDS is not murder. Rather, the sin of government here is lack of compassion and lack of equality: government has inequitably written off as insignificant the lives of some of its citizens—those whom it would not have written off were they not members of already despised social groups. Indeed, that any significant government action was eventually forthcoming for AIDS research resulted from fear that those dying and despised would end up killing respectable folk. But that the government should have done more and would have done more if others had been affected by AIDS does not warrant a charge of murder lodged against the government.

My concern in saying this is not the thrill some get from hugging syllogisms. It is a general political and social concern. The mistaken charge of governmental murder blurs the distinction between acts of omission and acts of commission. The charge treats these acts as always of the same moral kind and rank. The error is quite common. It is what lets Larry Kramer claim that "every gay man who stays in the closet is helping to kill the rest of his fellow gay men" and, with even more alarm, that "I have come reluctantly to believe that genocide is occurring: that we are witnessing . . . the systematic, planned annihilation of some by others with the avowed purpose of eradicating an undesirable portion of the population" through AIDS.[4]

Those who commit the error try to bootstrap "rights" as powers or demand-claims (say, "rights" to health care or "rights" to housing) from the nature and strength of rights viewed as immunities against power (say, against police brutality, invasions of privacy, or the suppression of speech). The bootstrapping argument based on the blurring of omissions and commissions runs as follows: if, when one dies from police brutality, the same evil has occurred as when one dies from lack of government-provided housing, then, given that there is a right against police brutality, so too there must be a right to government-provided housing. My concern is that constitutional immunity rights against government power are very fragile to begin with and that, once the equation is made between rights against power and "rights" to power, the result may well be the very opposite of that hoped for by those who bemoan government's omissions. The result will likely be that traditional civil liberties, fragile and now burdened by social work they cannot perform, will be destroyed, without welfare "rights" being significantly enhanced.

We can see how such a devolution of rights has occurred in the women's movement and its relation to pornography. The modern women's movement began as a civil liberties movement, which attempted to increase for women immunity rights against government through the Equal Rights Amendment. The ERA placed limits on how the government might deploy its power, by protecting against governmental discrimination.[5] When in 1982 the ERA failed to be ratified by enough state legislatures for passage, a large portion of the movement quickly shifted from opposing government power to enhancing patriarchal state power. In demanding government censorship of printed materials about and for sex, antipornography activists turned for protection to the very agencies and instrumentalities that had just said to the movement, "We will not protect you." Within two years of the

ERA's demise, feminist-inspired municipal ordinances were passed in Minneapolis and Indianapolis, holding sexual images as actionable civil rights violations. The Minneapolis law was successfully vetoed.[6] In the lower federal courts, the Indianapolis law was swiftly declared an unconstitutional violation of the first amendment; the Supreme Court summarily affirmed that decision without opinion.[7]

The result of the antiporn movement has been no increase in the welfare of women but an increased tendency for government to suppress speech, especially deviant speech, especially gay speech. The 1990 arrest of a Cincinnati museum director for exhibiting Robert Mapplethorpe photographs and the subsequent "obscenity" and "indecency" restrictions on funding from the National Endowment for the Arts are only the best-known examples.[8] Perhaps more telling is the Federal Communications Commission's harassing off the airwaves of Robert Chesley's gay safe-sex radio play *Jerker.*[9] In 1986, the FCC recommended to the U.S. Justice Department that, under federal obscenity and indecency statutes, it prosecute the Pacifica Foundation station KPFK–Los Angeles for broadcasting *Jerker.* Eventually, the Justice Department punted, deciding not to prosecute. But as is frequently the case, gays won the war only to lose the peace. The government's threat of prosecution was enough to stop gay speech. In consequence of the FCC's action against *Jerker,* the heretofore progressive Pacifica Foundation ceased broadcasting any gay sexual materials on its various radio stations. In 1988, the foundation even canceled a broadcast of Allen Ginsberg's classic, gay-laced *Howl.*[10]

Now, what goes around, comes around. In July 1991, the Public Broadcasting System aired in its regular programming Marlon Riggs's video "Tongues Untied" with its visual celebration of gay male bodies and embraces. Only a third of PBS's affiliates braved showing the program. The next month, PBS itself, collapsing under the anti-gay bigotry surrounding the Riggs video, canceled a national showing of the video "Stop the Church," a documentary on a demonstration by ACT UP.[11]

I hope that ACT UP and others involved in AIDS funding and welfare issues will realize that, although they may be protesting the state here and there, at the molar level they are worshiping the state. Government funds never come without strings—as we know from government funding of safe-sex literature. And as the legacy of the Great Society should have made clear, government largess has never been compatible with a robust regard for civil liberties.[12] The loose thinking of much AIDS activists' rhetoric only makes the likelihood of lost rights greater.

CHAPTER 3

Black Law and Gay Law: Do Civil Rights Have a Future?

I. Gays' Past, Blacks' Future

Only once have gays won a constitutional case with a gay content before the Supreme Court. It is sobering to note that the year was 1962—seven years before the Stonewall Riots and the launch of the gay liberation movement. The case held that, even though a photo magazine of male nudes was "dismally unpleasant, uncouth, and tawdry," aimed at "unfortunate persons," and clearly appealed to prurient interest, still it lacked "patent offensiveness" and so could not be considered legally obscene and so further could not be prosecuted as falling beyond the reach of the first amendment.[1]

Equally sobering has been the Court's treatment of gays even in the most liberal of times. In 1967, at the zenith of the Warren Court era, the Court ruled in a case of statutory construction that, even though Congress did not mention homosexuals as an excluded category in the McCarthy-inspired 1952 McCarran-Walter Immigration Act, gays were nevertheless excluded as falling under what the law called "psychopathic personality." The Court took "psychopathic personality" not as a medical concept calling for medical interpretation but as a term of art that Congress meant necessarily to encompass the personalities of homosexuals.[2]

Between 1967 and 1986, the Supreme Court issued no opinions on any gay issue. The silence was broken by a scream that has set the tone of constitutional law for the foreseeable future. In 1986, the Supreme Court held in *Bowers v. Hardwick* that lesbian and gay sex—what the Court coined "homosexual sodomy"—was not constitutionally protected under the Court's evolving privacy doctrine.[3] The next year, the Court dealt gays another blow in what has come to be called the "Gay Olympics" case.[4] These cases (I argue) are providing the Court the instruments by which the development of civil rights law generally and black law in particular is being reversed. Indeed, recent setbacks to affirmative action, to job protections for blacks, and to school integration may indicate that this general trend driven by gay cases has already restricted the rights of blacks.

The gay cases are having this effect because they have inverted the styles of thought that were developed in black civil rights cases. But these styles of legal thought were themselves formed not in consequence of the development and application of neutral legal principles but because the cases affected blacks' interests, especially blacks' political interests.[5] By counterturn, within the peculiarities of gay law, in particular through the courts' extreme efforts to avoid discussing gay issues and interests openly, the courts have discovered the levers and fulcra, the legal "principles" and the will, with which they are able to reverse the civil rights era. I explore several areas of civil liberties—privacy rights, "fundamental" rights, equality rights, first, fourth, and fifth amendment rights—in which retractions of rights have already occurred or are poised to occur as the result of the pivot provided the law by the legal treatment of gays. The general position of the chapter then is that of doubt and justified cynicism. Neither the earlier expansion of civil rights nor their current contraction is the result of the operation of neutral principles.

What is at stake in gay law, then, is not simply the rights of some minority (important as those rights on their own may be); what is at stake is how the nation views itself, how, in particular, it views itself as operating in a principled manner and in accordance with ideals rather than as being guided merely by popular whim and driven by the dictates of power.

II. Black and White and Principles

Palmore and Sidoti are white. They had a child—then a divorce. The mother was given custody. Then she married a black man. In light of this change of circumstance alone, Florida's courts in 1981 transferred custody to the natural father. On appeal, in 1984 a unanimous Supreme Court reversed.[6]

The Court, in its announced analytic, treated the case as a straightforward example of race discrimination, to be addressed by a routine equal protection analysis calling forth the highest tier of constitutional scrutiny: in order to pass constitutional muster, legal distinctions drawn on the basis of race must be necessary means to compelling state interests.[7] But on this understanding—the Court's own understanding of what it was doing—the ex-husband should have won, and the Florida courts were right. His winning claim with the lower courts had been that social recriminations against a mixed-race marriage would damage the child. Now, the Supreme Court itself has repeatedly claimed that the promotion of the welfare of children, even of just one specifiable individual child (say, the victim at a trial of a child rapist), is a compelling state interest.[8] And the determiner of the legally relevant facts of the case had held that the harm coming to the child was "inevitable." It seems, then, not only that the change in child custody would be in the best interest of the child but moreover that, in what is the constitutionally relevant respect, the change would be a necessary means to a compelling end and ought to override any constitutional right.

Acting wisely but randomly and without understanding what it was doing, the Supreme Court paid no attention to the ordinary high-tier equal protection analytic that it nominally had set out for itself.

Instead, the Court framed an entirely different question, a question about whether there are not some means that, even if necessary to

compelling ends, are nevertheless themselves beyond the pale of acceptance—are illegitimate means. Its answer, correctly, was yes:

> The question . . . is whether the reality of private biases and the
> possible injury they might inflict are permissible considera-
> tions. . . . We have little difficulty concluding that they are not.
> The Constitution cannot control such prejudices but neither can
> it tolerate them. Private biases may be outside the reach of the
> law, but the law cannot, directly or *indirectly*, give them effect.

Palmore here gives constitutional status to the following neutral interpretative principle:

> Simply citing the current existence of prejudice, bigotry or dis-
> crimination in a society against some group or citing *the obvious
> consequences of* such prejudice, bigotry or discrimination can never
> constitute a good reason in trying to establish a good faith dis-
> crimination against that group.

The question in *Palmore* was not what enhanced equal protection rights
certain groups have but what the *permissible means* by which the state
may carry out its legitimate goals are—what governments' legitimate
instrumentalities are. The *Palmore* principle holds that the perpetuation
of stigmas is not an acceptable moral cost of the means that the state
chooses to carry out its interests, even if, in being restrained from using
such means, the state likely, or even inevitably, permits harms to befall
known individuals.

The *Palmore* insight entails that the means by which the state calcu-
lates and executes its ends are themselves constitutionally circum-
scribed. More specifically, means are not to be constitutionally judged
simply with reference to their degree of fit to their purposes. Means
that are rationally related to, substantially related to, or even necessary
to their purposes may still be judged unconstitutional. This principle
was a long time in coming, but in a constitutional scheme that puts
brakes on appeals to utility, it ought to be a constitutional principle that
not every end, however important, will justify any means. Indeed, most

of the provisions of the Bill of Rights are just exactly such brakes on procedures, the ways in which government may realize social utility. What is new and important in *Palmore* is a structural advance in equal protection law. The *Palmore* principle adds a third prong to traditional equal protection analyses. *Legitimacy of means* must be added as a third hurdle for a law to leap, in addition to the two familiar hurdles of sufficient *fit* of means to ends and adequate *stature* of the ends themselves.

Note that the *Palmore* principle here enunciated has nothing in particular to do with race. Yet, as the Court's own confusion over what it was doing clearly shows, race alone launched the principle into constitutional orbit. The case announces a principle—a solid one—but the principle was not judicially generated in a principled manner through the operation of neutral legal rules. The principle applies equally well to all cases where government instrumentalities enhance or perpetuate social stigmas. Indeed, the Court has taken the *Palmore* principle out of the racial context of its origin and applied it to discrimination against the handicapped, even when the handicapped are viewed as having no special equal protection rights. In 1985, the year after *Palmore*, the Court in *City of Cleburne v. Cleburne Living Center*, quoting *Palmore*, struck down zoning laws that give voice to mere "negative attitudes" toward or "fears of elderly residents" over having a group home for the mentally challenged nearby, even though the Court held that discriminations against the mentally challenged were neither "suspect" nor "quasi-suspect" in the Court's equal protection analytic.[9] The Court held that, even on the weakest equal protection grounds calling only for a finding of a statute's having a rational relation to a legitimate state interest, the *Palmore* principle—that the law cannot give private biases either direct or indirect effect—is sufficient to bar such zoning restrictions. Negative attitudes and fears "are not permissible bases" for distinguishing the treatment of the mentally challenged from other groups.

However, a legal principle that comes to be at judicial random too can vanish so.

III. Sodomy, Rationality, and Amassed Private Biases

Only one year after *Cleburne* and two years after *Palmore*, the Court was unable to see the import of *Palmore* for gay law. In upholding Georgia's sodomy law, the Court failed even to claim that it is impermissible for a law to give *direct* effect to the mere amassing of private biases against some group.

After more-or-less summarily dismissing the privacy challenge to Georgia's sodomy law in *Bowers v. Hardwick*, the Court still had to find that the law was rationally related to a legitimate state interest so that the law would pass the weak equal protection challenge to which all laws are subject. The Court's sole articulated reason for upholding the law against this challenge was that the law expressed a legitimate state purpose in that it promoted "morality." The Court made clear that what it meant by "morality" was simply "majority sentiments about . . . morality,"[10] that is, simply the positive or merely descriptive morality of the nation—that sense of morality in virtue of which one could say that even Nazi Germany had a morality, a majority sentiment, for instance, of racism and mob rule.

This stance of the Court errs along several dimensions. First, as the four-man dissent in *Bowers* pointed out, the Court, in cases like *U.S. Department of Agriculture v. Moreno* (1973) and *O'Connor v. Donaldson* (1974), had repeatedly rejected the mere expression of raw majority power as generating a legitimate state interest.[11] In *Moreno*, the Court held:

If the constitutional conception of "equal protection of the laws" means anything, it must at the very least mean that a bare congressional desire to harm a politically unpopular group cannot constitute a *legitimate* governmental interest. As a result, "a purpose to discriminate against hippies cannot, in and of itself and without reference to [some independent] considerations in the public interest, justify the 1971 amendment [aimed *sub silentio* against hippies]."[12]

And in *O'Connor,* the Court queried:

> May the State fence in the harmless mentally ill solely to save its citizens from exposure to those whose ways are different? One might as well ask if the State, to avoid public unease, could incarcerate all who are physically unattractive or socially eccentric. Mere public intolerance or animosity cannot constitutionally justify the deprivation of a person's physical liberty.[13]

Yet in *Bowers,* the rationality of a ten-year prison sentence for gay sex was upheld by a simple appeal to public intolerance.

More important, the *Bowers* Court's brief claims about morality are inconsistent with the very meaning of what a constitutional right is. A constitutional right is a justified immunity claim by minorities against majorities, who, but for such rights, get their way through the ballot box. If, as consistency requires, the *Bowers* Court's claim is generalized and "majority sentiment" is taken as sufficient to fulfill requirements for a legitimate state interest, then there is, in fact, no need for a court test of such constitutionality. For *all* laws will have legitimate ends: insofar as laws are made by elected representatives, all laws register majority sentiment—through the ballot box. Further, since the coercive threats that accompany legal sanctions against an activity might conceivably, indeed frequently do, lead to a reduction in the occurrences of the proscribed activity, it turns out that, simply by the very act of making an "immoral" act illegal, legislatures will have established a rational relation between the law and its legitimate purpose—the promotion of "morality." So the *Bowers* Court renders completely vacuous both old-fashioned prongs of the right to equal protection as it applies to all law—a requirement that all laws both have a legitimate goal and, as means, are rationally related to that goal.

The Court's aversion to discussing gays, to articulating in what way legislating against gays is legitimate, led the Court to lose track entirely of what constitutional rights are. If "equal protection of the laws" is a right against majority rule, the determination of its scope cannot be left to the mercies of majority rule. An anti-gay case was used not only to draw into doubt the insight of *Palmore* but also to render entirely ineffectual the already feeble provisions of equal protection as it applies to all law. Even before *Bowers*, virtually every law was upheld against "weak" equal protection challenge. Now even those few types of laws that were stricken down before *Bowers* on weak equal protection grounds are being upheld after *Bowers*'s gutting of the weak equal protection test.

A good example of this *Bowers*-driven weakening of (already) "weak" equal protection is provided by the Court's food-stamp cases. In the 1973 case *U.S. Department of Agriculture v. Moreno*, the Court on a low-tier equal protection analysis struck down a federal law barring food stamps to households of unrelated people, to wit, "hippies." But after *Bowers*'s dilution of the already weak low-tier equal protection, the Court could uphold in 1988 a ban on food stamps going to households that had a member on strike, even though this legislation also targeted a politically disfavored group—strikers.[14]

If the Court, in *Bowers*, could not see that it is illegitimate, even on a weak equal protection analysis, for the state to give private biases *direct* effect in sodomy laws, then one cannot hold out too much hope that the Court and other courts will see the more subtle reaches of the *Palmore* principle on indirect effects of biases, if, indeed, after *Bowers*, *Palmore* is still good law.

In virtually all cases where attempts to discriminate against gays are defended as discriminations in good faith, as, for example, in lesbian child-custody cases or in cases claiming the predominant sexual orientation as a bona fide occupational qualification—say, in teacher cases, military cases, or police cases—the discrimination against gays has the form of an appeal to the *indirect* effects of amassed private biases—the same illegitimate indirect effects the Court so perceptively noted and voided in *Palmore*. Take, for example, military policy. As of January 1981, the armed forces have six official reasons for barring lesbian and gay male soldiers:

> The presence of such members adversely affects the ability of the armed forces [1] to maintain discipline, good order and morale, [2] to foster mutual trust and confidence among servicemembers,

[3] to insure the integrity of the system of rank and command, [4] to facilitate assignment and worldwide deployment of service-members who frequently must live and work under close conditions affording minimal privacy, [5] to recruit and retain members of the armed forces, [and 6] to maintain the public acceptability of military service.[15]

What all these six claims have negatively in common is that none of them is based on the ability of gay soldiers to fulfill the duties of their stations. More generally, none of the claims is based on gays *doing* anything at all. What the six reasons have positively in common is that their force relies exclusively on current widespread bigoted attitudes against gays. They appeal to the bigotry and consequent disruptiveness of nongay soldiers (reasons 1, 2, 3, and 5), who apparently are made "uptight" by the mere presence of gay soldiers and officers and so claim that they cannot work effectively in necessary joint projects with gay soldiers. The reasons appeal to the anti-gay prejudices of our own society (reason 6), especially that segment of it that constitutes potential recruits (reason 5), and to the anti-gay prejudices of other societies (reason 4). No reasons other than the consequences of currently existing widespread prejudice and bigotry of others are appealed to here in order to justify a discriminatory policy. So all six reasons violate the *Palmore* principle and are illegitimate.

Gay soldiers are being discriminated against on current Pentagon policy simply because currently existing bigotry and prejudice are counted as good reasons in trying to establish good faith discrimination. And in every federal circuit where gay military and security clearance cases have been heard (the D.C. Circuit, the Federal Circuit, the Seventh and Ninth Circuits), prejudice against gays or prejudice's consequences have been held sufficient grounds to exclude gays.[16]

Seven years after *Palmore*, out of the dozens upon dozens of cases where *Palmore* was relevant to gay litigation, I am aware of only two cases where a court indeed took note of and correctly applied *Palmore*. One is a lesbian child-custody decision from the Alaska Supreme Court, which, citing *Palmore*, refused to follow the usual pattern and change custody to the father when the mother's lesbianism came to light: "Simply put, it is impermissible to rely on any real or imagined social stigma attaching to the mother's status as a lesbian."[17] The other is a Ninth Circuit case that remanded to the district level a gay military case that had there been summarily dismissed in light of the Circuit's earlier rejection of enhanced equal protection rights for gays in a case that went on to uphold on weak equal protection grounds restrictions on gays getting security clearances. The newer Circuit case held that *Palmore* requires that the gay soldier be allowed the opportunity to challenge the military's use of prejudicial grounds in its rationales for exclusions. But since the Circuit had already acceded to such prejudicial grounds as legitimate in the security case, it is not clear that this case on remand is headed anywhere in the long run.[18]

Instead of following the constitutionally warranted and morally required path of *Palmore*, court after court keeps right on accepting violations of the *Palmore* principle as "common sense" when directed against gays and holding them as legitimate and reasonable grounds for discrimination against gays.[19] Gay law has basically been allowed to put into doubt the continuing validity of even a recent black law triumph and draws into doubt the courts' ability to perceive and apply neutral principles; but then *Palmore* itself was not arrived at in anything like a neutral fashion.

IV. Civil Rights Futures: Privacy

Bowers has already been used by the Court to limit some constitutional rights and has set up others for future whittling or outright reversal. First among such impaired rights are privacy rights. In its sodomy decision, the Court ruled that gays have no privacy right to have sex. The most remarkable feature of the decision is that the Court was able to hasten to this conclusion without even discussing gays or privacy or sex—or indeed any substantive issue. *The Advocate* reports that, during an appearance on May 17, 1991, at Claremont McKenna College, Justice Harry Blackmun, the author of the four-man dissent in *Bowers*, lifted the veil a bit on the Supreme Court's secret conference session on the case and claimed that, indeed, no judicial thinking went into the Court's *Bowers* decision: the majority "decided on the result [it] wanted and then went for it."[20]

Instead of listening to and evaluating arguments, the Court was simply a pawn to society's taboos. The only way the Court was able to live out society's taboo against speaking of gays and sex was to cast privacy rights directly as what are oxymoronically called "substantive due process" rights and then use for substantive due process a test that allowed the mere cataloging of past and current sodomy laws to ground their constitutionality.[21] The Court claimed that the only activities protected by privacy rights are those "fundamental liberties" that "are characterized as those liberties that are 'deeply rooted in this Nation's history and tradition.'"[22] In doing so, the Court set the stage for its 1989 radical restriction and likely future overturning of *Roe v. Wade*.[23] For the nation's history does not leave abortion meeting the Bowers test for what a fundamental right is. In the early history of the United States, abortion laws had been relatively liberal because they had been so in English common law. But by 1868, when the fourteenth amendment was passed, the legislatures of at least thirty-six states and territories had adopted abortion prohibitions. In 1973, only four states had adopted a position even remotely approaching the liberality of *Roe*'s holdings.[24] So at the time *Roe* was decided, abortion was illegal in virtually every state and had been so for over a hundred years—hardly an activity rooted in the traditions and conscience of the nation. Indeed, if *Bowers* is played out consistently, the whole line of privacy cases going back at least to the 1965 marital contraception case, *Griswold v. Connecticut*, would have to be reversed: there is no long tradition even of married couples having legal access to contraceptives.[25] Taboo rather than thought was operating in *Bowers*—and it means that, if the Court is consistent, privacy has been dropped as a freestanding constitutional principle.

Indeed, *Bowers* has already been explicitly used to eliminate one privacy precedent, the 1969 case *Stanley v. Georgia*, which established a right to own and use in one's own home materials that are legally obscene and so not protected by the first amendment—because they are not counted as speech.[26] This right was pendant from a right to control one's emotions and sensations. *Stanley* was cited as a precedent for the right to privacy in the contraception and abortion cases *Eisenstadt v. Baird* (1972) and *Roe v. Wade* (1973), cases that could hardly be considered first amendment cases.[27] Indeed, in an obscenity case that distinguished *Stanley* from first amendment jurisprudence, the Court held that *Stanley* was simply "a reaffirmation that 'a man's home is his castle.'"[28] But in a 1990 case, *Osborne v. Ohio*, the Court, citing *Bowers*, has construed *Stanley* as *only* a first amendment case with no privacy dimension, leaving *Stanley* without a constitutional leg to stand on, and so, ripe for overturning.[29]

Osborne held that privately possessed depictions of children that are *merely* "lewd"—that is, "lewd" without being obscene—are not covered even by *Stanley*'s protection of obscene materials. Justice Brennan, in dissent with Marshall and Stevens, astutely noted that, given the vagueness of "lewdness" and the vagaries of the police, the case's result—although seemingly a neutral rule—would be used almost exclusively to harass gay men:

> The danger of discriminatory enforcement assumes a particular importance in the context of the instant case, which involves child pornography with male homosexual overtones. Sadly, evidence indicates that the overwhelming majority of arrests for violations of "lewdness" laws involve male homosexuals. . . . Such uneven application of the law is the natural consequence of a statute which as judicially construed measures the criminality of conduct by community or even individual notions of what is distasteful behavior. The "lewd exhibition" standard furnishes a convenient tool for harsh and discriminatory enforcement by local prosecuting officials against particular groups deemed to merit their displeasure.[30]

Obscenity law aside, *Bowers* has already been used in the lower courts to rake in privacy rights across a wide range:

> According to a compilation by the Alliance for Justice, a liberal legal policy group . . . , the [*Bowers*] case has been cited in more

65

than 100 state and federal court decisions as authority for refusing to find a right to privacy in a variety of contexts. The decisions have included not only gay rights cases but also challenges to drug testing, seat belt requirements and state laws governing the naming of children.[31]

V. Civil Rights Futures: Fundamental Rights

Bowers has put more than privacy at risk. It has shaken the Court's whole understanding of what constitutes fundamental rights. It has cast doubt on the status of those protections that are so important to the country that, even though they affect the substance rather than procedures of law, and even though they are not mentioned in any of the specific explicit clauses of the Constitution, still have been thought to be covered by the Constitution's broad due process clauses.

Traditionally—pre-*Bowers*—there were two standards for determining whether a claim to a substantial immunity from state coercion was a fundamental right protected by substantive due process. One standard was that an asserted right would be an actual right if it is "implicit in the concept of ordered liberty," such that "neither liberty nor justice would exist if it were sacrificed."[32] This standard calls for reasoned argument about liberty and justice. A second standard for fundamental rights is the test formulated in the 1977 case *Moore v. City of East Cleveland*, which holds that the asserted right will be an actual right if it is deeply rooted in American tradition.[33] This standard calls not for reasoned argument about "ordered liberty," "fair play and substantial justice"[34] but rather merely for historical survey, a project that itself is neither clear nor objective.

Basically, this second standard does away with rights altogether. For it allows entrenched majorities to determine both what the laws are and what one's rights against the force of law are. Tellingly, then, the *Bowers* court fused the two tests, treating the "ordered liberty" test as though it were simply a restatement of the tradition-and-consensus test.[35] In doing so—in casting reason out from determinations of fundamental fairness—the Court undermined the whole understanding of rights that lies behind the Bill of Rights, that is, a justified belief that the country's constitutional scheme warrantedly protects the individual from entrenched majorities. The grounds for such protections are rational arguments presented in the courts viewed as forums for rights.[36] By reducing fundamental rights to historical assay, the Court has left the specific guarantees of the Bill of Rights standing simply as an arbitrary list, a historical quirk, devoid of any unifying understanding of what rights are.

After *Bowers* there have been three cases that have called on the Supreme Court to make a determination of what "fair play and substantial justice" are.[37] Not surprisingly, given *Bowers*, in each case the person pressing the claim of a right to fundamental fairness and justice lost. *Bowers* has produced a chaos of doctrine with a consequent diminution of rights. In one of the cases, *Burnham v. Superior Court of California* of 1990, a technical case about jurisdictional authority, three Justices (Scalia, Rehnquist, and Kennedy, forming the Court's plurality opinion) thought that tradition alone determines what fundamental justice is; four Justices (Brennan, Marshall, Blackmun, and O'Connor) thought that considerations of history are important but not dispositive and that final judgment in matters of fundamental fairness call for independent judicial inquiry; two Justices (Stevens and White) simply punted, giving no opinion about what approach should be used to determine fundamental justice.[38]

In another of the three cases, *Michael H. v. Gerald D.* of 1989, an important decision dealing with parental visitation rights, *all* the Justices seemed to accept the *Moore-Bowers* tradition-and-consensus test for substantive due process, but they could come to no agreement at all about what that test meant in practice. They splintered into incoherence when it came to deciding at what level of generality the historical analysis was to proceed in determining what meets the tradition-and-consensus test. Does one investigate the purported right at the most specific level at which its claim might be formulated? In practice this had been done in *Bowers* where the court framed the question to be investigated as whether a right to commit "homosexual sodomy" was deeply rooted in American tradition. By *that* standard, the

Court rightly concluded that there was no such tradition.[39] But in *Michael H.* only two Justices (Scalia and Rehnquist)—three years after *Bowers* and citing *Bowers*—thought that the investigation ought to proceed at the most specific level possible. Justice Scalia formulated the plurality opinion's test thus: "Though the dissent has no basis for the level of generality it would select, we [Scalia, plus Rehnquist] do: We refer to the most specific level at which a relevant tradition protecting, or denying protection to, the asserted right can be identified."[40] Not even *Bowers*'s author, Justice White, accepted this analysis.[41] Even though all the other seven Justices disagreed with the "lowest level" standard, no Justice suggested that *Bowers* was soon to be reversed. And Scalia was at least right in noting that none of the other seven Justices made clear at what level of generality the analysis should proceed.

The result is amazing. Michael sired a child and parentally reared the child with the child's mother, but *by state statute* Michael was not the legal father of the child because, when the child was born, the mother was legally married to someone else, who by statute was the legal father with complete custodial rights at law. The fractured and confused Court ruled that a parent, although both natural and nurturing, had no constitutional right whatever even to a hearing to determine whether he had any rights under state law to visit his child. And so Michael is forever barred from seeing his child.

Justice Scalia thought the relevant historical question in *Michael H.* was about what the traditional rights of "adulterers" are, while Justice Brennan thought it about traditional protections given family relationships, personal relationships, and emotional attachments in general.[42]

One might have thought that the case would have attracted those conservative sympathies that flow out of the natural law tradition and its claim that moral rights and duties can be read off of natural or biological properties. Such conservatives hold the view that the family is the normative core of civilization and is so because it is society's chief (and possibly only) natural institution. But the result of the case is that, as a matter of constitutional law, the family is entirely a social artifice, one exhaustively constructed and defined by law understood narrowly as statute; so, beyond the law, there exists no source of familial values that can sufficiently form the basis of a critique of anything that statutes might do to the family unit.

As such, *Michael H.*, in playing out *Bowers*, draws into doubt even the "familial rights" cases from the 1920s—*Meyer v. Nebraska* and *Pierce v. Society of Sisters*—that *Bowers* had nominally left intact even while it dismantled privacy rights, cases that are the sole line of continuity between the pre-1937 substantive due process era and the modern substantive due process era that began with the Court's 1965 marital contraception case, *Griswold*.[43] These early family-rights cases protected familial control of children's education. Pierce held that, while states can compel education, they must allow parents the choice of having their children's education carried out in private or religious schools rather than public schools. *Meyer* held that parents have a constitutional right—even in the face of the anti-German hysteria that swept parts of the nation during World War I—to have their children taught German. After *Michael H.*, it would seem that the state could, simply by definitional fiat, hold that education is not an essential function of families, and then traditional familial rights would no longer protect education. Note how ridiculous *Meyer* would appear if framed in *Michael H.*'s "lowest level" standard for tradition and consensus. Has positive law traditionally given American parents a right to have their children taught German? Swahili? Urdu? Although *Bowers* nominally asserted the continued flourishing of "traditional" familial rights, its thinking has rendered them moribund.

The third recent "fundamental rights" case is *Cruzan v. Director, Missouri Department of Health*, the Court's well-known 1990 "right to die" case. The question before the Court was whether the irreversibly comatose Cruzan, as represented by her parents, had a substantive due process right to prevent the state from barring the removal of a feeding tube that is necessary to sustain her biological existence. The Court answered: in theory yes, in practice no. It held that there is a right to refuse medical treatment but that the right's strength is so weak that it is overridden by virtually any state interest, even paternalistic ones. The result is that the state can bar Cruzan's parents from acting as proxies in determining whether she would wish to be allowed to die and can require, before the right to die is engaged, Cruzan herself to have left behind clear and convincing evidence that she wished to die in such circumstances.

Citing *Bowers*, the Court claimed that fundamental rights cases are no longer to be thought of as privacy cases.[44] Privacy as a concept that invokes substantive due process protections is dead doctrine. But in the wake of the chaos of standards for substantive due process flowing out of *Michael H.* and *Burnham*, the Court offered no alternative nonprivacy analysis explaining the grounds of the right to refuse medical treatment. Oddly, the Court even seems to have eschewed the tradition-and-consensus standard for substantive due process when it claimed that American traditions as registered in "state constitutions, statutes and common law" are irrelevant to its constitutional determination. Instead, the Court simply plucked the right to die out of the air, rawly asserting that the right to refuse treatment is a "constitutionally protected liberty interest" but giving no analytic suggesting which of all possible free human actions do invoke constitutionally relevant liberties and which do not. Rather, the Court cites five cases in which bodily invasions by the state, although invoking due process liberty, nevertheless were allowed by the Court to be overridden by state interests. And so too must the fundamental liberty right fail to have effect here. For, once any and all personal actions may potentially invoke fundamental liberty rights—as they may when there is no analytic given for what fundamental rights are—then invariably the rights must be weak and deferential to state interests, lest the state be universally hamstrung. But then further it would seem that, if *fundamental* rights must give way to state interests, all rights must.

VI. Civil Rights Futures: The Bill of Rights

The weakness of the Court's current fundamental rights holdings draws into doubt even the strength of the specific and explicit rights of the Bill of Rights. The Supreme Court's 1989 drug-testing cases perhaps offer the clearest example of this trend. Against challenges based on the fourth amendment's specific and explicit protections against both warrantless searches and unreasonable seizures, the Court has upheld drug searches even entailing bodily invasions, as a condition of employment for railway workers after accidents and for customs officials seeking promotions. The Court upheld these invasions of privacy even in the absence of any individualized suspicion of abuse on the part of the workers.[45] The customs case, in particular, opens an unobstructed path to random drug testing of all government workers. The state interests that the Court accepted as establishing the exemption to the explicit fourth amendment requirement of warrants and probable cause are such weak *and pervasive* interests as avoiding the diversion of valuable agency resources—mere administrative convenience—and the promotion of physical fitness, integrity, and judgment.[46] Such interests in drug testing would apply to any government job.

Although this result perhaps comes as a shock, it should, after *Bowers*, not come as a surprise. For, once the government may invade your bedroom to control your body there, the next logical site of invasion for the ever more ramifying state is your body itself.

Even the first amendment is under attack from *Bowers*. In the Court's 1990 political patronage case, Justice Scalia came within one vote of successfully using the *Bowers* tradition-and-consensus test to determine what rights to free speech there are beyond the rather strict right against regulations of speech based on its content.[47] Any right that called for a balancing test between individual and state interests, like regulations of the place, time, and manner of speech, Scalia claimed, could be sufficiently settled by appeal to tradition: if the regulations have a historical pedigree, then the regulations cannot be unconstitutional. Scalia would have held that, since political patronage laws have had a long history in this country, they cannot be declared unconstitutional restrictions of first amendment rights to political association and political participation.

It would take only one more year before *Bowers* would shift from being cited in dissent to being cited in the main opinion of the Court in a first amendment case. The case, *Barnes v. Glen Theatre, Inc.*, dealt with an Indiana law requiring the wearing of "pasties and a G-string" while dancing nude before a paying audience.[48] Although it might

sound frivolous, the case appears to be a major turning point in constitutional law. In it, the Court paves the way for the elimination of the
near absolute right that protects the content of speech and replaces it
with a right that calls merely for a balancing of state interests against
the interests of those who would speak or express themselves. Even
against an admission that nude dancing (unlike obscenity) is a first
amendment protected form of expression, the Court upheld the Indiana statute, which in fact does not allow the dancer to be nude after
all. The Court thought the ban a negligible infringement on expression, even though it has (as the four dissents pointed out) a maximum
destructive impact on the dancing as conveying a sexual message. On
the sole weight of *Bowers*'s majoritarian understanding of what morality
is, the Court held that the state has not merely a legitimate interest in
protecting morality but a substantial interest as well, one that out-
weighs any interests that dancers might have in expression.[49] As first
amendment tests for speech protections become more and more matters of balanced interests rather than of individuals' rights trumping
state interests, *Bowers* can be used to uphold all restrictions of speech
as promoting a substantial state interest in protecting morality and
"majority sentiments."

VII. Civil Rights Futures: Equality

Still other areas of civil liberties are similarly affected by *Bowers*, in
particular the Court's approach to minorities. I suggest that it is really
Bowers that was standing behind the Court's 1989 affirmative action
case *City of Richmond v. Croson*, which has lethally wounded municipal
and state affirmative action programs by establishing the fundamental
rights of white people.[50] The case held that state and municipal minority set-aside programs are unconstitutional under the equal protection
clause because classifications made with respect to white people are as
"suspect" as those made with respect to blacks.[51]

But white people do not fulfill the criteria for enhanced equal protection rights as developed in either of the two lines of cases that the
Court has used in establishing such rights. A 1938 case, *Carolene Prod-*

ucts, established the principle that groups subjected to discrimination either by government or by society more generally in ways that tend to exclude them from political participation will be given special protections under the equal protection clause.[52] But clearly whites are not politically disenfranchised. Nor do whites as a group have a socially degraded status, which would trigger enhanced equal protection rights under the line of cases that derive from the 1954 school desegregation case *Brown v. Board of Education*.[53] And the same Court that in 1989 established white rights had abandoned any "immutable characteristic" test for enhanced equal protection rights in the 1985 case *City of Cleburne*, as part of a holding that the physically and mentally challenged, even if immutably handicapped, do not constitute suspect or quasi-suspect groupings.[54]

The phony legal formalism of *City of Richmond*'s affirmative action opinion is so sheer, then, as to be transparent: whites cannot have enhanced equal protection rights because they are somehow relevantly like blacks. The Court again is self-deceived about its justifications for its results. Its actual but unstated thinking runs something as follows: if, as per *Bowers*, it is those actions that are by tradition socially averred that are the actions that are performed by right, then it is the people whose privileges are by tradition socially averred who have those privileges as a matter of right. It is the history and tradition of white privilege that converts the privileges into white rights. Thus, the style of reasoning specifically developed to deny rights to lesbians and gay men is now used to restrict legal protections afforded to other minorities and to enhance majority privilege. Substantively, it is from *Bowers*, not *Brown*, that we get white rights and white people's liberation from the oppressive burdens of the tyrannical state. On this issue, one and the same are Sandra Day O'Connor, the author of *City of Richmond*, and David Duke, founder of the National Association for the Advancement of White People. David Duke says:

> I'm not racist like Jesse Jackson. I'm proud of my heritage like Jesse Jackson is proud of his. But I believe the time has come for equal rights for everyone in the country, even for white people.[55]

I oppose any oppression of people. . . . The closest thing that I know to the policies of [Nazi] Germany in this country is the so-called affirmative action or quota system. They had quotas in Germany as well on the basis of race. I don't think you should have racial preferences.[56]

Justice O'Connor says:

"The rights created by the first section of the fourteenth amendment are, by its terms, guaranteed to the individual. The rights established are personal rights." The Richmond Plan denies certain citizens the opportunity to compete for a fixed percentage of public contracts based solely upon their race. To whatever racial group these citizens belong, their "personal rights" to be treated with equal dignity and respect are implicated by a rigid rule erecting race as the sole criterion in an aspect of public policy decision making.[57]

If, per *Bowers,* the Court holds itself as the guardian of fundamental values but views fundamental values as purely majoritarian, then altered will be the Court's understanding of any rule that, although neutral on its face, in operation preponderantly assists minorities. For such rules or laws will then be seen as a deviation from fundamental values and so as grants not of equality but of special privilege and so further as calling for judicial oversight and restriction. I suggest that this chain of reasoning explains the Court's 1989 gutting of every dimension of federal civil rights statutes—restricting to ineffectiveness the who, what, when, where, and how much of civil rights remedies.[58]

The final descent of civil rights' arc can be discerned in the Supreme Court's 1991 school busing case, *Board of Education v. Dowell.*[59] This case suggests that the *Palmore* principle barring both the direct and the indirect consequences of amassed private prejudices is now dead—not just for gays, but for blacks too. The question in the case was under what conditions the courts can dissolve judicial decrees requiring busing as a remedy for proved past school and housing segregation. The

Court held that such decrees can be dissolved even when to do so means that a majority of a district's schools become either 100 percent black or 100 percent white. In the school district in question, the schools—after busing ceased—became totally segregated because housing was totally segregated. The federal district court, as the relevant determiner of the facts in the case, had held that this "residential segregation was the result of private decision making and economics," not of government actions. The district court, in consequence, held that the school segregation and its likely attendant stigmatizing of those at the numerous all-black schools were "simply" the indirect results of amassed private prejudices, not discrimination mandated by the state, and so the district court concluded that the school segregation was okay, was constitutionally acceptable. The Supreme Court agreed, holding that it was all right for the courts to give indirect voice to this amassed prejudice in housing by allowing its manifestation in totally segregated state-run schools, where segregation is the consequence of the seemingly neutral rule that made no explicit mention of race: "Let there be local schools." But this permission to allow prejudice to operate indirectly through court enforcement of neutral rules was exactly what the *Palmore* ruling had forbidden when it held that the seemingly neutral rule that custody is to be determined by reference to the best interest of the child could not be used by the courts if the rule indirectly registered amassed private prejudices. We no longer hear the Court saying: "Private biases may be outside the reach of the law, but the law cannot, directly or *indirectly*, give them effect."[60] It appears that *Palmore* has been reversed *sub silentio*.

Brown v. Board of Education had held that "in the field of public education the doctrine of 'separate but equal' has no place. Separate facilities are inherently unequal."[61] But now racially segregated schools are all right. After *Brown*, Governors Orval Faubus, George Wallace, Lester Maddox, and their segregationist fellow travelers had misunderstood what form of "massive resistance" to integration would be effective. Baseball bats held high at schoolyard gates was not it. What worked was for whites in their day-to-day lives to go right on being prejudiced against blacks—and school segregation returned.

75

The *effects* of *Brown* have now been overturned by the Court's allowing amassed private prejudice to register indirectly in public policy through the actions of the courts themselves. But do not worry that the Supreme Court might overturn *Brown v. Board of Education* itself. For in an inversion of history the oddness of which perhaps only a Foucault or a cynic could fully savor, a purely formalist reading of *Brown* in *City of Richmond* has now become a chief guarantor of white power.

VIII. Of Limp Wrists and Leather Balls

The other substantive gay constitutional case that has been heard by the Supreme Court—the Gay Olympics case—has also had the effect of reducing rights more broadly.[62] The issue in the case was whether the Gay Olympics could call itself the "Gay Olympics." The Court answered: "No. Such a use of the term 'olympics' is a trademark violation."

As in *Bowers*, the Court found no gay issues in the Gay Olympics case. It used two strategies to avoid discussing these. First, at lightning speed the Court claimed that, in contrast to the use of the term "Olympics" by the "real" and (implicitly) noble and honorable Olympics, the use by gays of the same term was simply a crass attempt to make money and so was to be treated as commercial speech rather than political speech.[63] This interpretation of gay speech suggests that the Court simply was viewing gays automatically and stereotypically as greedy, exploitative manipulators. The Court then not surprisingly upheld the government's interests in the existence of trademarks over such perceived evil and tawdry gay interests. But in doing so, the Court more or less terminated a line of cases starting in the mid-1970s that were beginning to give commercial speech the same high standard of first amendment protection as political speech: bars to truthful commercial speech needed to be necessary means to compelling ends. In a 1989 case, the Court acknowledged that ending this standard for commercial speech was in fact what the Court had done in the Gay Olympics case.[64]

Second, although the gay side in the Olympics case was seeking to speak and print a noun both descriptive and normative—"Olympics"—the Court, again hastily, interpreted such speech and press as simply posturing and gesturing and so to be afforded only the comparatively weak protections it gives symbolic actions. This interpretation of speaking and printing "Gay Olympics" suggests that the Court was again viewing gays through stereotypes, taking gays as *poseurs*, frauds, and deceivers, as queer as three dollar bills, but without any message to convey, certainly not any serious political message. Only two Justices saw that the federal government's bar to gays' use of the term denied gays important political means to the important political goal of dispelling one of the most severe of anti-gay stereotypes—that gays, especially gay men, are limp-wristed wimps incapable of prowess or anything noble: "Here, the SFAA [i.e., the Gay Olympics] intended, by the use of the word 'Olympic,' to promote a realistic image of homosexual men and women that would help them move into the mainstream of their communities." Indeed, the Court aggravated anti-gay stereotypes by completely giving itself over to them and giving them its imprimatur. As in *Bowers*, by failing to engage gay concerns, the Court snubbed gays and thus treated them as beneath contempt.

Perhaps the most amazing use of the Gay Olympics case has been in Justice Rehnquist's almost successful dissent to the first of the flag-burning cases of 1989 and 1990, in which a bare majority of Justices ruled that torching the American flag is an expressive activity protected by the first amendment. Rehnquist's dissenting argument had two parts. First, he gave a survey of all the government-enhanced, glorious uses of the flag in U.S. history. Then, citing the Gay Olympics case *and nothing else*, he analogized that, just as surely as Congress can give the U.S. Olympic Committee exclusive proprietary use of the term "Olympics" as thanks for all the good works the committee had done in giving the term meaning, so too "surely Congress or the States may recognize a similar interest in the flag" and so give themselves exclusive proprietary rights to its use as thanks for all the good works they have done in giving the flag meaning.[65] By the same logic, Congress could legitimately give the Justice Department sole use of the term "justice" as thanks for all the good works the Justice Department has done in giving the term meaning. It is now generally thought that, since only three of the Justices in the flag-burning cases' majorities are still on the Court, the cases are ripe for reversal, and the Gay Olympics will offer the decidedly kooky rationale.

IX. The Gay Legal Future

Since *Bowers*, changes in Court personnel hardly bode well for future gay cases. Justice Scalia filled Justice Burger's position within months of *Bowers*. Before his elevation to the Supreme Court from the District of Columbia Circuit Court of Appeals, Scalia had joined Judge Robert Bork's opinion that held that gays have no privacy rights, two years before the Supreme Court reached the same decision.[66] In Scalia's first year on the Supreme Court, he joined the Gay Olympics opinion. He also wrote a heated dissent to a 1988 case that gays actually won, not because the Court was turning over a new leaf, but because in the case gays' interests just happened to coincide with the Court's own interests in maintaining its power. The CIA was claiming that the 1947 statute that established what would become the CIA exempted from constitutional review CIA decisions to fire its employees—in the case at hand, an openly gay man. Had the Court gone along with this claim, the result would have been momentous. It would mean that Congress has the power to say that, at its discretion, the laws it passes are not subject to the Constitution. Congress could simply bar the federal courts from hearing whole ranges of cases. Not surprisingly, the Court balked at this prospective assault on its job and found a way to punt. In an opinion by Chief Justice Rehnquist, the Court claimed that the statute in question was vague enough on the issue in question that the Court could not be certain that the statute meant what the CIA held it to mean and so construed the statute narrowly in order to avert the constitutional crisis of the Court having to decide whether such a law limiting the Constitution was itself constitutional.[67] Scalia in dissent, however, thought that it was perfectly clear that Congress could suspend the Constitution when it came to gays: "Even if the basis of the [CIA] Director's assessment was the respondent's homosexuality, and even if the connection between that and the interests of the United States is an irrational and hence an unconstitutional one, if that assessment is really 'the Director's alone' there is nothing more to litigate about."[68]

After the failed attempt of the Reagan administration in 1987 to elevate Judge Bork himself to the Supreme Court, Judge Kennedy from the Ninth Circuit Court of Appeals was so elevated to replace Justice Powell. Kennedy came to the Supreme Court with a solidly anti-gay record. In all four of the gay cases in which he had a recorded vote as a circuit court judge, he voted against gays. These cases covered military, privacy, employment, family, and immigration law.[69]

In 1990, Justice Souter replaced Justice Brennan. Three years earlier, while a justice on the Supreme Court of New Hampshire, he joined perhaps the most egregious anti-gay court decision of all time. The opinion upheld a ban on gay adoption and foster parenting on the ground that gays would cause the children in their care to become gay. For its rationale, the case appealed to nothing but anti-gay stereotypes, especially the stereotype that gayness is a corruptive contagion. But what is more shocking: the premise that being gay is so evil that it has to be prevented at all costs was taken by the justices as so obvious that the premise was never actually stated in the opinion.[70]

In 1991, Justice Thomas replaced Justice Marshall. During his Senate confirmation hearings, Thomas bobbed and weaved when asked what he thought of the *Bowers* decision. He has been less evasive elsewhere. In December 1986 as a member of a presidential commission on "the family," he joined a report that not only praised the *Bowers* decision but also heralded it as a model for future jurisprudence.[71] And in 1989, as part of his slender legal writings, Thomas explicitly endorsed an article that, for constitutional purposes, compared sodomy to killings by inferno—the shouting of "fire" in a crowded theater and the committing of suttee.[72]

Gays have not done particularly well either by the lower federal courts *even before* these courts became laden with Reagan and Bush appointees. In every federal circuit where gay equal protection cases have been heard at the appellate level—and this has now occurred in six of the thirteen circuits—gays have been held to have no enhanced equal protection rights. In each case too, discrimination against gays has been upheld as being rationally related to some legitimate state interest.[73]

There has been only one area in which gays have come anywhere near to consistent success in the federal courts. And in the grand scheme of things it is a depressingly unimportant and unfertile area— the recognition of gay student groups by state universities. In every federal circuit where these cases have come up, gays have won. The series of cases culminated in a 1988 decision holding that the University of Arkansas not only had to recognize its gay student group but had to fund it as well.[74] But by any count, these are slim pickings.

Nor have gays fared well in the state courts. No state supreme court has held that gays have enhanced equal protection rights either under the federal constitution or under its own state's constitution.[75] Nor, since *Bowers*, has any state supreme court knocked down its laws making gay sex illegal. Nor has any state legislature rescinded a homosexual sodomy law. So, as was the case at the time of the *Bowers* decision, gay sex is still illegal in half of these United States. Still, in consequence of the gloom emanating from the federal courts on gay issues and civil liberties issues more broadly, gay litigative groups and even the national office of the American Civil Liberties Union are now determined to concentrate their efforts on state courts.[76] However, two types of cases already on the books suggest that this shift is probably a heady mix of sour grapes, wishful thinking, and sheer desperation, rather than a strategy likely to have much success in winning cases.

First, consider a pair of gay family law cases from what is generally conceded to be one of the most liberal state supreme courts in the country—the Court of Appeals of New York. In July 1989, in what at the time looked like a major breakthrough in gay law, the Court of Appeals held that a gay life-partner of a deceased tenant in a rent-controlled apartment could not be evicted by the landlord because the life-partner counted as a "family member" under the state's rent and eviction regulations.[77] The Court reached this conclusion by claiming that the term "family" should be given a broad, indeed functional definition, rather than a narrow, merely legalistic definition, because the statute in question was basically a civil rights law protecting a class of people—family members.

However, two years later the same Court left this case standing as an isolated legal incident when it refused to extend its style of thinking to a case where two lesbian domestic partners were jointly rearing a child, who was conceived by artificial insemination. The Court declined to give a functional analysis of the two women and child as a family, such that the two women would both be parents for the purpose of visitation rights on the demise of the women's relationship. Rather, only the most narrow, conservative understanding of the family was upheld. The woman who had been artificially inseminated was declared the child's real, natural parent, while the woman who had shared all the responsibilities and rights of child rearing, but who had not contributed any chromosomes to the child, was dismissed rhetorically and legally as a "biological stranger."[78] The Court seemed to be trying to revert to the natural law position that biology is moral destiny, at least in family matters. But heterosexual couples who adopt children too are "biological strangers" to their children and yet are not thought the least bit less "parents" at law for being so. The Court's curt *per curium* opinion offers no analysis. It is completely conclusory: it merely *presumes* that the functional but nonbiological mother is a "nonparent" and then cites a few cases in which other "nonparents" (say, friends, teachers, distant relatives) have no rights. The earlier gay domestic partners case goes entirely unmentioned, leaving the appearance that, the Court's claim there to the contrary, the earlier case was in fact being treated simply as a property rights case, on a rough analogue to the Supreme Court's 1917 case *Buchanan v. Warley*, which struck down racially drawn zoning laws governing the sale of property, not because race discrimination is bad, but because the zoning interfered with property rights, chiefly those of white people.[79] A few months after the lesbian visitation case, the same Court greatly expanded the rights of grandparents, holding that a grandparent has a legal right to sue for visits with his or her grandchild even against the wishes of both of the child's parents—again suggesting that biology is moral destiny.[80]

Conveniently for the equanimity of the New York court's mind in the gay rental case, the plaintiff was not, after all, in a living gay relation—owing to the death of his life-partner. It is clear from the lesbian visitation case that anything that would require the Court's rethinking familial relations and addressing how gay people live day to day in nontraditional relations would not be tolerated, or even imagined and entertained. The courts may give rights to gays by ones, but they will not give rights to gays by twos. They will not give rights to gays *in relations*, which after all is what it is to be gay—to have relations of a certain sort. So when the courts do on occasion give rights to gays—by ones—they do so in spite of rather than because of their gayness. And in giving rights to gays by ones *only*, the courts, even as they hand out a right, destroy the very basis and idea of gayness, that it is a relation between people. If this sort of treatment is the best that can be hoped for from the most liberal courts in the land, then one cannot have much hope for decisions coming from judges in Boaz, Alabama, Enid, Oklahoma, Wallace, Idaho—or where you live.

The second type of state court rulings that should be giving gays pause are ones that use constitutional rights not to protect gays but to squelch gays' statutory interests and to "protect" the dominant culture from gays. Two recent examples are telling. First, in 1991 a superior court judge in California held that, even though gays are judicially held to be covered under, without being mentioned in, the state's very broad public accommodations law, and even though the Boy Scouts of America count as a public accommodation, the Boy Scouts' first amendment rights to political association trump the public accommodation law and so allow the Boy Scouts to boot out gay scoutmasters. The judge held that, since the Boy Scout Oath and Law address "sexual morality" by requiring Scouts to be "morally straight and clean," and since Scout leaders do not consider homosexuals to be "morally straight and clean," the presence of gay scoutmasters "would substantially interfere with" the organization's "ability to achieve its expressive goals."[81]

Second, in 1991 a Minnesota appeals court allowed the Catholic church to break, without penalty, a rental agreement it had with a chapter of the gay Catholic group Dignity after the Catholic church threw the chapter out of the church. The court ruled that Dignity functions as part of the church, even though church officials in response to Vatican directive have since 1986 expelled more than fifty Dignity chapters from church-owned meeting spaces across the country. The court then claimed that, under first amendment religious rights, the church could enforce "conformity to certain standards of conduct and morals" among its members and so elude the law of contracts.[82] Again, constitutional rights were used to void the few legal rights that gays have at law.

The courts are restless institutions. There is never a time when they do not actively assert somebody's interests as rights. There is never a time when they simply say that there are no rights and then let democratic processes take whatever course they will. In 1937, the Supreme Court ceased advancing the interests of businessmen as rights when it systematically withdrew its doctrine that the right to contract is a fundamental right within due process.[83] But the very next year it set out for itself a new agenda of rights—those of the socially and politically marginalized. In 1938, the Court held that it would begin to examine

> legislation which restricts those political processes which can ordinarily be expected to bring about repeal of undesirable legislation [and so which] is to be subjected to more exacting judicial scrutiny under the general prohibitions of the fourteenth amendment than are most other types of legislation . . . [and begin to examine] whether prejudice against discrete and insular minorities may be a special condition, which tends seriously to curtail the operation of those political processes ordinarily to be relied upon to protect minorities and which may call for a correspondingly more searching judicial inquiry.[84]

This judicial project, which might generically be called the civil liberties agenda, blossomed and was realized to a large extent in the Warren Court and the early years of the Burger Court, although gays were never allowed to be part of it. In recent years, even the uncompleted agenda has become seriously eroded in the Rehnquist Court, and its demise can be dated—June 27, 1991. On that day, in the final case of the term, *Payne v. Tennessee*, the Court reversed a pair of very recent decisions, from 1987 and 1989, that under the eighth amendment had barred at death penalty hearings presentations of "victim impact statements" either about the victim's moral character and social standing or about the unforeseeable consequences of the murderer's actions on the victim's family. The Court's decision was programmatic, setting forth a new standard for when constitutional cases may be reversed. The old standard was that a case could be reversed only if its remaining in the law reduced the coherency and consistency of the law generally, especially in its development after the case. The new standard basically held that, for the sake of proper deference to democratic processes, any past case asserting a *constitutional* civil liberty may be reversed if five Justices now think it had been wrongly decided.[85] Yet the Court held that, given the need for reliability in the marketplace, business cases should not be easily reversed. What is important, it seems, is possessions, not people. Given the current personnel of the Court, the rights of people as people have all been slated for possible termination.

An important, although unstated, gay issue was near the heart of this case and the two cases that the Court reversed. In the reversed cases, the Court had held that, because victim impact statements do not bear on the blameworthiness of the murderer, they can hardly have anything but, in varying degrees, an inflammatory effect on juries, who are supposed to be at their most impartial when sentencing someone to die. The current Court says that inflammation is all right. But what causes varying degrees of inflammation? It is the varying value that society places on those who are the subjects of the victim impact statements. These are, first, members of families as defined by law—which excludes gays as gays, gays, that is, in gay relations—and, second, the victim himself, who—if gay—is typically going to be thought much less of by society as a whole and by its random jury samples than if the victim is a "family man" with wife and children and all the trappings of privilege that heterosexuality bestows. The cases that were reversed had the effect of making a gay person's life of equal value to that of a heterosexual. They carried forth the promise of democracy's ideal that each person is to count for one. In reversing the cases, the Supreme Court promoted the general social view that holds that queer bashing is almost a form of public service and that registers in the following sort of sentencings:

> San Antonio gay, lesbian and Latino activists expressed outrage at the light sentencing of a marine private who brutally beat to death a gay man last year. Nicolo Giangrasso received a sentence of 10 years' *probation* with deferred adjuration, allowing his guilty plea and related court actions to be expunged from his record if he successfully completes probation. Giangrasso pleaded guilty to voluntary manslaughter, saying he beat Charles Resendez because Resendez made "homosexual advances" toward him.[86]

The Supreme Court in its restlessness is unlikely to repose in a position that holds "no rights for anyone." As *Payne*'s talk of business rights might be read to suggest, the Court will likely, in any new agenda, find ways to assert as rights the privileges of the dominant culture.[87] As in the Boy Scouts and Catholic church cases, gays stand to be big losers in any new expansion in the rights that are now likely to be declared by the courts. There is already a hint from the Supreme Court of how this trend might develop. One type of expanded "right" that the Court in 1991 suddenly and dramatically resurrected from the dead was "states' rights." In a series of three opinions by Justice O'Connor dealing with prisoners' rights of appeal, the employment rights of the elderly, and rights of the accused—all of which were diminished—the Court held that a doctrine of "federalism" requires judicial deference to state law and state judges when the Court interprets both federal law and constitutional rights.[88] What this trend means for gays in the long run is that they will be subjected ever the more to local "community standards" without resort to any of the impartiality and uniformity of law that tends to come when laws must be passed by representatives coming from everywhere in the land. Federalism defers to local hysterias.

With the recent changes in Court personnel, nothing is ruled out

85

for the future. There is no limit on what other "rights" the Court might invent. With Justice Thomas aboard, the Court might, for example, adopt a natural law stance to the effect that "the defense of homosexuality offends the nature and dignity of the human person," and so hold that civil rights laws that protect gays are contrary to nature and irrational, and so further void under the equal protection clause's rationality test.[89]

Still, the double prospect not only that gay rights will go unacknowledged but also that the courts will diminish or destroy gays' legislated interests does not mean that gays should avoid the courts. It means rather that, in approaching the courts, gays need to acknowledge that there are some cases and moral causes that are advanced for the sake of such important values that they are causes and cases worth losing. I now turn to an examination of these values.

[ADDENDUM, AUGUST 1992: GAYS AND ABORTION

In June 1992, the Supreme Court revisited *Roe v. Wade*. Four justices wanted to reverse *Roe* outright, claiming that *Bowers* had shown that *Roe* was incorrectly decided. Avoiding *Bowers*, the majority held abortion was still covered by *some sort* of right, though not, as in *Roe*, a privacy right, nor even a "fundamental" right. Like the ineffectual right to die asserted in *Cruzan* (1990), the right to abortion is now loosely tethered to a liberty interest residing in due process. As in *Cruzan*, regulations of such a right were broadly upheld.

Three diverse sources were offered for liberty protected (if feebly) by due process: the family, conscience, and control of one's body. *Bowers* and the "adulterers' rights" case *Michael H.* (1989) strongly suggest that the first source will do nothing for gays or anyone else other than those married at law. The second source—conscience—potentially covers every action and so ultimately protects none. But the last source—bodily integrity—if applied consistently, would protect gay sex and support a reversal of *Bowers*. The Court, though, is unlikely to be consistent here. In *Roe* itself, for example, bodily integrity was explicitly denied as a source of rights.]

CHAPTER 4

Social Lenses, Social Progress: Do Ideas Matter?

I. Call Me Jeremiah

A white derelict calls me "faggot" from the gutter.

A beer bottle—full—ricochets off my shoulder. Its hurler—a black man sitting at the back of a city bus—shouts "suck that queer."

If you want to know what marriage is and look "marriage" up in the standard legal dictionary, *Black's Sixth Edition*, you'll find the definition—"the legal union of one man and one woman as husband and wife"—followed by a citation, the article's only citation, to a gay case, or rather anti-gay case, *Singer v. Hara*.[1] Gayness marks out, defines, what marriage is.

In 1987, Congress dropped communists from classes barred entry into America by the McCarthy-inspired 1952 McCarran-Walter Immigration Act, leaving gays as the sole class of persons excluded from America based on a distinction of status rather than behavior. It would be three more years before the anti-gay exclusion would be dropped. The armed forces continue to exclude gays. Immigration and military policy are nominally intended to *defend* what the country is, but as their racial and gender histories show, they are chiefly institutions by which the nation *defines* what the country is.[2]

In the 1986 case *Bowers v. Hardwick*, the Supreme Court marked out

two worlds of sodomy—a heterosexual one and a homosexual one.[3] Yet
the Court's distinction between heterosexual and homosexual sodomy
could not have been made on the basis of actions or moral agency. For
many sodomitic acts (rimming and fisting, e.g.) do not even employ
genitals and so cannot specify various mixes of biological sexes in their
definitions. And to say that the genital mix of the partners is what in
the Constitution's eyes distinguishes analingus that is necessarily unprotected by the Constitution from possibly protected analingus is like
saying that the act that killed *this* corpse will be considered justifiable
homicide if the corpse and its killer have different-colored eyes but
murder if they have the same eye color. This is absurd. So one is forced
to the alternative that for the Court homosexual acts are ones performed by people of a certain sort, rather than that homosexuals are
those people who perform certain acts. The result is that homosexuals
have fewer rights, less privacy, than other people, not from any failure
of moral agency on the homosexual's part, but because the homosexual
is perceived to have, like animals, a lower moral standing than full
persons have: homosexuals are the degenerate form of life that desig-
nates what full life is—or so it goes.[4]

What the derelict, my assailant, the Supreme Court, lesser judges,
Congress, and the armed forces here have in common is the effective,
if unconscious, belief that the concept "homosexuality"—not the class
of homosexual acts or even the homosexual person (except *per acci-
dens*)—defines what America is and what a person is. Homosexuality
sets the limits and establishes the conceptual structure by which the
nation defines itself to itself—with respect to its internal constitution
from what our politicians (Left, Right, and Center) are fond of calling
the basic unit of society, with respect to its presentation of itself to the
world, and with respect to what it means to meet threshold criteria for
membership in the moral community and national life.

At heart it is the *concept* "homosexual," rather than any act a homosexual might perform, or even the person who is homosexual, that
performs this definitional work in American society and thereby explains why America's definition of itself may be created and propagated
in total ignorance of the concept's extension, that is, in complete igno-

rance of flesh-and-blood lesbians and gay men. This situation in America is similar to racism in Japan and anti-Semitism in Poland. Racism
can define what Japan is even if no blacks live there, and anti-Semitism
can define what Poland is even though virtually no Jews live there—
now.[5]

In this country, as race, gender, religion, and even sport have gradually been dislodged from the national center of definitional gravity,
and as the perception that the Comintern is no longer The Evil Empire
or even much of a threat waxes, increasingly by default this nation-
defining work is performed by the concept "homosexuality." So the
stakes for the nation in sustaining current attitudes toward homosexuality become ever higher, and correspondingly ever lower becomes the
likelihood that the attitudes will change.

When such definitory concepts are translated from idea into reality,
the transformation is effected by rationalizations—usually stereotypes—that most frequently appeal to perceived threats of daunting
harms. Dangerous behavior is retroactively assigned to the instances
(actual or imagined) of the defining concept. This moral and ontolog-
ical retrofitting attempts to "justify" the vicious social treatment of the
members falling under the concept, where the concept itself had made
no reference and need not have made any reference to behavior on the
part of those maligned. Thus, Jews are held in stereotype to be the
murderers of children and messiahs, gays to be child molesters, sex-
crazed maniacs, plague bearers, destroyers of the family and of civilization itself.

Such retrofitting, however, can be considerably more subtle than in
these common instances. Thus, for example, the courts, retrofitting
Singer v. Hara's conceptual work on marriage, have held that, even if
there were a fundamental right for gays to marry, it would be overridden by a compelling state interest in restricting marital relations to
straights.[6] This decision presumes that marriage, like titanium, is somehow a scarce commodity, the possession of which by one person necessarily excludes its possession by someone else—rather than that marriage is, as it is, a common good, like friendship or knowledge, that any
number of people may possess and of which the possession by some

may actually promote its possession by others. So the courts, at the level of brooding *concept*, claim that straights wouldn't really be married if gays were, that the meaning of marriage would be revised beyond recognition if gays could marry, while, at the level of rationalizing *practice*, the courts hold that gay access to marriage must be a form of grand theft. The four Roman Catholic bishops of Massachusetts have taken this charge of the theft of essence one step further. In jointly writing a letter opposing a domestic partnership bill for Boston, they held that the bill was a hijacking that would end civilization itself: "The extension of the title *family* to gay and lesbian couples and the granting of economic privileges to 'domestic partners' on an equal place with true families must be opposed and rejected as undermining the family in our society today. If family life is ignored or despised or undermined, there is no natural foundation for social and civil life."[7]

Now, the bad news is that stereotypes are not defeated by facts. Getting the facts right makes no difference when it comes to the concepts by which society defines itself to itself. This unfortunate fact about facts and reason is forgotten by those who support a "Brandeis brief" approach to litigating gay cases, the approach that would just wow 'em with the facts, as was attempted unsuccessfully in many of the gay-supportive briefs for the *Bowers* case.

Worse still for the prospect of gay social and legal progress is the fact that, when serving as norms, such definitional concepts have the status of sacred values. Now, by sacred values, I do not mean values of divine origin, but rather values for which society is willing to sacrifice its interests in order that its most deeply held beliefs are manifested and advanced and its group solidarity secured. During the early 1960s, the whites of Jackson, Mississippi, with the imprimatur of the Supreme Court, closed rather than integrated the city's swimming pools through a statute that made no mention of blacks. Thus, Jackson's white City Council was telling blacks—no less forcefully for its facial neutrality—that whites view blacks as so disgusting and polluting that white social solidarity would be maintained even if to do so would require of whites the loss of comfort, joy, and pleasures of the season.[8]

Analogously, most coercive AIDS legislation—notably mandatory

AIDS testing—should be viewed as purification rituals. In them, by sacrificing social efficiency, society degrades gays without mentioning them and reconsecrates heterosexual supremacy as its central sacred value and as the inviolate bond of its group solidarity. Policy experts pretty well agree that, as social planning, testing dentists, surgeons, and others who perform "invasive" medical procedures is zany: the direct costs of implementation would be enormous, and needed medical personnel would be pointlessly excluded from the professions, all because a cluster of five patients may have been infected from one incompetent dentist in Florida.[9] Society would do as well to protect itself by requiring that people always stay indoors lest they be hit by stray meteors. What is really going on unacknowledgedly in calls for mandatory testing of medical personnel is that, on the one hand, the doctors and dentists who are to be excluded through testing are overwhelmingly gay men who get fucked in the ass while, on the other hand, the legislators who are passing these purification laws are overwhelmingly heterosexual males who don't like being penetrated by anything, let alone being "invaded" by a passive gay man: to get fucked by the fucked would make one lower than the lowest. That assault on heterosexual male self-definition must be avoided at any cost. In general, then, even if true, appeals to overall social utility and benefit—appeals, for instance, that gay rights are good for everyone—have no force in dislodging or transforming such values.

When a government uses coercion to express society's deepest values and establish or rededicate them as sacred, there will be no stopping it however odious and immoral its acts, for these values already are or come to be embedded in a preinstitutional social knowledge through which all else is viewed, interpreted, and judged. The pairing of sacred values and coercion simply short-circuits the usual procedures that put limits on tyranny. Worse even still, the intensity of gay definitional work in society may be so powerful that, acting like an eddy, it may well draw other things—other people, other rights—down in its whorl. It looks, as I argued in the preceding chapter, that the changes in law wrought by gay cases have already begun to reverse the general course of civil liberties.

Do ideas matter? Yes, all the wrong ones, all the bad ones. Given the structure of concepts, definitions, and values that I've sketched, one cannot be very optimistic that there will be dramatic improvement in gays' social circumstances over the foreseeable future. At the centenary of the Japanese internments, I think it equally likely that a national gay rights bill will have been passed and that all gays will have been put in concentration camps. At a minimum, national gay leaders have been naive when, perhaps with an eye on the collection plate, they have messianically proclaimed: "Gay and lesbian freedom is imminent, and we will be there when it is won."[10]

In 1979, even before the executive and judicial branches of the U.S. government solidified in the hands of the political Right, the French philosopher and novelist Guy Hocquenghem could observe of the American gay scene:

> You know, there was a gay community in Germany before the Nazi period which had all the characteristics of the community we have now—including community centers, balls, newspapers, a scientific research institute—everything. I am struck by the ignorance among gay people about the past—no, more even than ignorance: the "will to forget" the German gay holocaust. That we forgot about these hundreds of thousands of people and about the fact that out of one hundred years of gay life, in thirty of them we had a virtual vacuum—that we forgot in such a *radical* way is, I think, something of a warning. This has happened to no other minority. Even the Armenian genocide was remembered, at least by the Armenians. . . . Our lesson from history, then, is that we can't be sure we won't be suppressed. . . . As long as gay genocide is not officially acknowledged, it *could* happen again. . . . If there really is a social crisis beginning, gays are in a position similar to that of the Jews in pre-Nazi society.[11]

Domestically, lesbian poet and essayist Adrienne Rich is even more pessimistic. In a November 1991 interview, she held:

> If [the nation doesn't come to grips with homosexuality], I think that we're in for one of the most terrible, terrifying periods of

repression, of brutal, vicious repression of large numbers of people that can possibly be imagined—something on a par with Nazi Germany. I feel as if all the monsters of American history are coming home to roost now, and they're monsters of privilege and monsters of repression and monsters of denial. And unless as a society we can face these monsters and look at them and give them names, they're going to take us over.[12]

Call me Jeremiah.

II. But Pray—in Thanks and Future—for Rosa Parks

Although commies keep trying, historians and sociologists have failed to give any convincing account of how society's basic values change, although they do change. Quiz: can you name six pundits—or even just one—who predicted even vaguely the events of the Eastern European summer of '89 or the Moscow August of '91? Similarly mysterious are the forces that brought about the 1990 congressional passage of the Americans with Disabilities Act, which was the first expansion of the 1964 Civil Rights Act to cover a group not encompassed in the original act.[13] This void in predictive powers makes practical recommendations for gay law and gay political life very difficult. Without laws of social change covering basic values, there are no grounds for prediction about what might improve the social circumstances of gays and so for clear courses of action that will bring about hoped-for political, legal, and judicial change on lesbian and gay male issues.

And society's basic values congest even piecemeal social planning. In 1987, the half-a-million-strong March on Washington for Lesbian and Gay Rights immediately and unexpectedly precipitated nearly unanimous congressional censure of gays. Three days after the march, the Senate voted 94 to 2 to cut off all funding for gay-targeted AIDS outreach; the House vote the next week was 368 to 47. No AIDS literature that mentions gay men or lesbians as okay can be federally funded.[14] In consequence, for example, in 1988 my town's Gay Community AIDS Project was blocked from receiving a previously approved twenty-six-thousand-dollar Centers for Disease Control grant—virtually the group's entire budget for the year. If gay men and lesbians were going to assert themselves, be open, act up, and speak up politically, Congress was going to do its best to shut them back up—both substantively and symbolically. The march was surely a good thing, although not if measured by standards of business-as-usual politics.

Now admittedly, political skepticism does not commend itself to those whose salaries depend on others' continued belief in their political savvy. But it may be what reality counsels. Remember that women were included within the protections of 1964 Civil Rights Act as the result of a joke that backfired rather than because of hard-hitting liberal and progressive legislative initiatives: congressional conservatives introduced protections for women as an amendment aimed at defeating the whole bill; the amendment was greeted by laughter on the House floor. Doubts about practical gay gains, however, do not render all actions pointless. For there are important and worthy ideals for which and, more important, within which lesbians and gay men may work even if "experience" rejects us and even if, as appears to be the case, gay law is nothing but politics.

I suggest that, for the foreseeable future, dignity rather than happiness or practicality ought to be the ideal and polestar of gay politics. Now admittedly, dignity is an elusive notion. But the common and clear phrase "adding insult to injury" affords an intuitive grasp of the types of evil that correlate to dignity and happiness. An insult is an offense against dignity, while an injury is something that reduces one's happiness or pleasure, or denies one some benefit, wealth, power, or useful possession, or, generally, reduces one's material circumstances in the world.

Insults are a graver form of evil than simple injuries, for they are of a class of evils that attack a person as a person. The paradigm case of insult is group-based invective—say, calling someone a "nigger," "faggot," or "cunt." This assaults persons as persons in two ways. First, by focusing importance on irrelevant characteristics, such invective attacks persons as repositories of deserved fair treatment and equal respect. Second, such insult views its targets as morally lesser beings, takes them not as failed moral agents but as having—like children or trees—less than full moral standing.

For gays in particular, the avoidance of insult is of paramount importance. For harm directed against gays almost always takes the form of assaults on dignity. The purpose, for example, of unenforced sodomy laws is degradation: they are the chief systematic way by which society as a whole tells gays that gays are scum. When injury *is* involved in anti-gay discrimination, the harm is usually not the intended final aim of the action but "merely" a vehicle of insult. Queer bashing is one example of this; job discrimination another.

If I'm right in the belief that what is chiefly at stake in gay politics, understood broadly, is dignity, then the gay movement primarily needs to take the form of asserting rights by acting in a principled manner. Proceeding in this way itself brings dignity to gays. The process of gay politics itself should be a source of dignity and pride—and it can be. For dignity as an ideal is something (unlike happiness) that lesbians and gay men can achieve to a significant degree independently of the goodwill of the dominant culture: it can be experienced in the very political procedures that gays choose. And it is so if, in asserting rights and attempting to bring about the conditions that make them legislatively and judicially enforceable, gays act as though they already have them, act as though they had equal respect—by respecting themselves to the degree they respect others, even in the face of virtually certain opposition to their doing so. In this way, gays put principle over practicality.

Business-as-usual gay politics does not have the proper form to achieve pride and self-respect *if* it panders and ingratiates itself to the values of the dominant culture, *if* it is nice to those who insult us and who even use our niceness to do that. In such ingratiation, business-as-usual gay politics fails to treat gay experience, feelings, and values as worthy of equal treatment, of consideration on a par with the dominant culture's. Here the hearth and home of gay dignity and self-respect is mortgaged to buy stocks in hoped-for, but improbable, practical gains.

Such moral indenture occurs, for exemplar, when gay professional activists call for the overlooking of a politician's views and practices that insult gays because overall he is a candidate who if elected is more likely to promote the interests or well-being of gays. The misunderstanding here is to suppose that interests and dignity are commensurable when in fact they are not. They cannot be measured on the same scale, they cannot be balanced against each other, and so dignity cannot legitimately be bargained away or made a table on which to cut deals. We cannot support those who, in their policy on adoption, for instance, hold that gays are morally lesser beings, who hold that two gays are worth less than one heterosexual, and who, for their own political expedience, compound that insult by pandering to insidious stereotypes of gays as child molesters.[15] We cannot let our goodwill and efforts be used as instruments in support of the deepest forms of our oppression. It is by adhering to principles and being nurtured by them that a people gets through dark times—and these are dark times. What, more concretely, does putting a premium on dignity over hoped-for direct political gains look like in practice?

First, professional activists must avoid exaggerated claims of likely progress and accomplishment; these simply lead to frustration and burn out all around. Gay organizations should not advance themselves as a business with a product to sell—happiness. They should not be asking for donations as a sign of confidence in their skills at social manipulation. Rather, they should ask for donations as a means of holding gay dignity and rights in trust. And they should be evaluated not by a standard of practicality—Did they get the legislation passed? Did they win the court case?—but by whether they conducted themselves in a way that betokened and preserved gay dignity. Did they, to our shame, sell out, or did they—like Socrates in refusing to obey orders that would implicate him in an unjust execution—simply and nobly go home.

And so, second, the politics of dignity means brooking few compromises. In his stump speech, Harvey Milk correctly asserted: "The first gay people we elect must be strong. They must not be content to sit at the back of the bus. They must be above wheeling and dealing. They must be—for the good of all of us—independent, unbought."[16]

We must avoid legal exemptions or qualifications that reinforce anti-gay stereotypes. We must be wary of seemingly neutral rules that in fact have a radically disparate impact against gays (like the Democratic party's 1984 abolition of its caucus system) or that indirectly but determinately degrade gays (as does virtually all coercive AIDS legislation).

Third, we must be forthright everywhere. We must remember the basic truth of the coming-out process, an experience that itself offers a model for a politics of dignity. Coming out is not chiefly a means to happiness. It is a conscious giving up of power, a subjection to an increased prospect of discrimination, and an opening to a heightened awareness of the ways by which society despises gays—these are not the near occasions of happiness. Yet coming out—even in the face of social interdict—gives people a sense of self, a sense that for better or worse their lives are their own, that their lives have a ground. We must let our love and emotions show publicly; we must resist attempts to make us clean up our act—to live by the standards of others. We must not hide behind lackluster claims that, "Shucks folks, we're just people too." That is to assume falsely that justice is already here—and to do so in a way that virtually guarantees that justice will not arrive.

Finally, we must begin thinking more seriously of civil disobedience as a regular part of gay politics. Civil disobedience stands to law as coming out stands to social interdict. It is the purest principled manner in which to assert dignity in politics, for it necessarily puts self-interest imminently at risk for the sake of what is right. Rosa Parks established and asserted her dignity and self-worth by sitting at the front of a city bus in violation of law so that it would come to pass that other blacks could do so by right. So too, religiously organized gays could show that they have dignity in substance—not just in name—by conducting holy unions at marriage license bureaus in violation of law so that it would come to pass that other gays could marry there by right.

III. Postmodern Politics

How do these views redound on the belief, now much touted by gay political leaders, that the future—the certain success—of gay politics lies in coalition building? Where does all this leave the relationship between various civil rights movements, in particular, the gay movement and the black movement? And where does it leave those who are subject to multiple forms of oppression, say, people who are both black and gay? In an uncomfortable manner and place, I fear, but not an intolerable one—and not one that is going to be remedied by high hopes for unity and alliance between movements. If I am right that gay law and black law have been developing in contrary directions, and that in fact gay law is leading to a reversal of the civil rights era, then at a minimum (although through no fault of gays) blacks in general will (understandably if not justifiably) view gays with resentment.

Further, in legislative attempts to revive and revitalize black civil rights, the black movement and the gay movement will be out of phase with each other. There is a lesson from history that is relevant here. In her 1971 essay "Women's Liberation and Black Civil Rights," Catharine Stimpson traced the history of the constitutional and legislative movements of women and black men in their attempts to secure the franchise and voting rights.[17] She found that the two movements, although ostensibly aimed in the same direction and sharing the same principles, were forever out of synchronization with each other—and in ways that always disadvantaged women. Women were always asked to defer to black men's claims of greater plight and to delay their own concerns—their rights—until black men got what they wanted, but then black men were noticeably absent when favors were to be repaid, their attentions having moved on to other issues, to other pressing needs. The cussedness of political reality made unity impossible.

I think something similar is likely to repeat now in the case of the black and gay movements. The black political agenda currently (at least as I see it) has two chief aims. First, it needs constant legislative vigilance to maintain and solidify statutory rights against ongoing attacks from the Supreme Court and from a White House whose CEO opposed the passage of the 1964 Civil Rights Act and has recently been given almost unlimited power by the Supreme Court to interpret federal laws however he wants.[18] Second, something needs to be done about economic justice and black poverty.

Now, in legislative civil rights efforts, does it behoove blacks to insist on the inclusion of gays within protected classes? As a matter of practical politics in the world of compromises and the compromised, the answer is obviously not. Inclusion would threaten efforts whose success has been precarious at best.[19] The black movement will ask gays to defer their agenda, as it asked women to defer theirs. Indeed, in the legislative effort that eventually led to the reversal of some of the Supreme Court's 1989 anti–civil rights rulings, the congressional civil rights leadership entertained for less than a day proposals for general civil rights reform that would have included gay protections, dropping them in favor of a narrow recuperative strategy for blacks.[20] Should gays sink their necessarily limited energies into civil rights efforts that do nothing for them? That is far from clear.

And how about issues of economic justice? First of all, no one can say for sure what economic justice for gays should look like: even in the AIDS crisis, hardly anyone has given any thought to the issue. But strategies for what are clearly warranted—gay civil rights—will tend to collide with strategies for black social justice. As I've argued, civil disobedience ought increasingly to become the central strategy of the gay rights movement, and more than a few indications suggest that an increase is in the offing.[21] But, as the black philosopher Bernard Boxill has argued, it seems unlikely that civil disobedience will be a strategy effective in achieving black economic justice or what has come to be called more generally "social justice."[22] For in politically successful civil disobedience, the disobedient's sincerity crucially acts as a catalyst in social change. But it will be hard to convince the public at large of that sincerity when it is clearly one's own advantage and self-interest—a larger piece of the pie—for which one is arguing in claims of economic justice.

Once slogans are laid aside for political analysis and political realism, it seems unlikely that the black movement and the gay movement are going to be one and the same movement. It may well be that the metaphor of the rainbow—with its suggestion of tandem parallel trajectories—neither captures the reality of minority pluralism nor acts as a guide for coalition politics. It may be a beguiling, yet false, hope. Between minority movements, there will be conflicts of interest, mixed motives, compromises that sell out each other, betrayals of principles for practicality and of each other, and misunderstandings and biases

99

generated by self-interest.[23] These and all the rest of the gunk of social life will accumulate between and divide movements.

When joint self-interest fails, coalitions come unglued. The best recent example of this dissolution is the collapse of the much-Leftist-touted coalition between the disability rights movement and the gay rights movement over the fate of Sharon Kowalski, a lesbian left brain damaged and quadriplegic in a 1983 car accident and, for years, with the courts' blessings, barred by her parents from even seeing her life-partner, Karen Thompson. The two movements worked together to free Kowalski from the prison-like, disability-aggravating conditions imposed on her by her parents, but once that was accomplished the movements divided. The disability rights movement, with individual self-sufficiency as its goal, declined to help press for Kowalski's lover being given guardianship over her as a spouse would be and instead pressed for having no guardian at all, an achievement that would secure no victories for gay domestic partnership rights.[24]

Similarly, while gay men and lesbians have been pressing for the expulsion of ROTC programs from college campuses because of the military's bar against lesbian and gay male soldiers, blacks have supported the retention of the programs since the military, in which the percentage of blacks is more than double that in the general population, has in recent tradition provided (or been perceived as providing) a path of upward mobility for blacks. In this support, blacks have provided bigoted legislators a seemingly nonbigoted way of overwhelmingly backing a spate of legislation that preemptively blocks state universities from throwing out their ROTC programs. The bigots claim, "We're helping the minorities."[25]

Organized gays, in turn, from their daunting position of power, have snubbed the animal rights movement. At the Seventh International AIDS Conference in Florence, European animal rights activists protested the use of nonhuman animals in AIDS research. American gay activists shouted them down with calls to "Save AIDS patients first, animals second."[26] Now, at first hearing this slogan seems to express some concern for animals and sounds as though the issue is analogous to asking, in a prison break, which political prisoners it would be most efficacious to free first in order to increase the likelihood that they will then be able to free the others. But in fact, given the way research is conducted on nonhuman animals, the slogan is analogous to asking whether it is morally acceptable to force some of the prisoners to be tortured to death so that others may escape.

When coalitions are morally coherent and politically effective, they will properly be topical, local, and tactical rather than structural, global, and strategic. Gays and blacks might, for instance, have very strong parallel interests in getting rid of a certain police chief whose racism and heterosexism permeates his force. But it is not surprising that principled coalition building has not been consistently carried out even among those who see coalitions as *the* path to political success. There are very strong conceptual and moral parallels to be drawn between the polygamists' rights movement within Mormon fundamentalism and the domestic partnership rights movement within the mainstream liberal gay rights movement, but I have yet to hear of outreach efforts from the Lambda Legal Defense Fund and the National Gay and Lesbian Task Force to small-town southern Utah.[27]

No matrix that coalitions build is ever fully annealed. Tensions remain. Coalitions are always subject to fracture. But understanding that this is so has a practical benefit. For understanding why the conflicts and slippages are as they are will tend to lessen the recriminations that invariably follow on compromises and betrayals. Betrayals will no longer be seen, and taken, as personal; they can be seen rather as the expected product of the complexity of political life. Having knowledge of explanations mutes inflated responses to the absence of justifications. With such understanding, various movements need not then tear each other apart as have conflicting groups of the Leftist fringe.

For the individual caught between two oppressions and between two movements, I can only, yet tentatively, recommend an appreciation of our postmodern condition. Our lives are not simple, homogeneous, unidimensional. A paradigmatically postmodern building is one with something pink, something purple, a pyramid, and an arch that doesn't hold anything up. Our lives are a bit like that too in contemporary

America—an integrity of, at best, disparate elements in refracted and splintered array. Our professional lives, for instance, are frequently unrelated to and indeed conflict with our domestic lives—one could do better at the one if one did less well at, spent less time at, the other. Yet we muddle through, without fixed rules or even good advice available about how to balance or decongest the two—and usually without resort to betrayals.

Other values, even basic values, will conflict in their realizations. The quest for the value that is knowledge will tend to conflict with realizing the value of having friends or creating beauty. There could not, then, be a moral obligation to be optimally moral. For values in their concrete manifestations cannot be jointly maximized. Nor is there even a moral obligation to be outstandingly moral. This is not to counsel moral laziness. It is morally expected, as in the case of outing, that one will advance basic values, like dignity, that can be promoted with relative ease and without concomitantly diminishing other basic values. But activists need not feel guilty that they have not done everything, for not everything good is jointly realizable. And anyway, values that politics may realize are not the only values. True, everyone has a moral obligation to do with one's uncommitted moral energies more than simply advance one's own personal interests and avoid harming others. But how this "more" is manifested is for the individual to decide—not society, not a cause, not even a cause of which the individual is a natural constituent. We could all probably do a bit more politically, and gay political success will depend on at least some of us doing so, but we need not burn out either from the disjointedness of our allegiances or from guilt at partial resolutions and achievements.

The blend of idealism and realism that I've espoused here will not guarantee the success of the journey ahead, although I think it necessary and proper if success is to be achieved. The journey itself will, I suspect, have all the tonalities—at once sad and hopeful—and all the varied possible outcomes of Porgy's goatcart setting off on its thousand-mile way to New York.

Culture

Go round about, Peer! Room enough on the
mountain.
—Who are you?
Myself. Can you say as much?

> A Voice in the Gloom, from Ibsen's *Peer
> Gynt* (1867)

CHAPTER 5

Text(ile): Reading
The NAMES Project's
AIDS Quilt

A trestle snaps in Asia. A train, like tangled fishing line, dangles through air and water. The halved and the drowned fall and float.

In the town of my home, a teenager fills a tire. The magnesium rim of its wheel—miscast—explodes. A week later, the youth dies of the shrapnel wounds from his beloved new Corvette.

In the summer of 1988, half the seals of the North Sea die from an acquired immune deficiency syndrome. Scandinavian scientists debate whether the acquisition is caused by a virus or from pollution prompting immune system overload.

In 210 B.C., jets from Iceland's Laki Volcano cause several years of perpetual Northern Hemisphere winter. In consequence, half the population of China dies of dearth.

Mass and arbitrary destruction leads the common mind to look for meaning in things. Everything becomes an occasion for signs and symbols. But when this search fails (as it must), the horror stricken and the desperation driven begin to generate new meanings—the central values by which they live.

Thucydides reports that, at the start of the Athenian plague years, people "naturally turned to the old oracles" and interpreted them in light of the current distress. Yet none of this did any good: "As for the gods, it seemed to be the same thing whether one worshipped them or not, when one saw the good and the bad dying indiscriminately." In the end "people were so overcome by their sufferings that they paid no attention" to prayers and consultations. But their new attentions produced new values. The old highly held virtues of courage, honor, and prudence gave way to "the pleasure of the moment and everything that might conceivably contribute to that pleasure."[1]

In form, the AIDS crisis has had the same effect as the plague at Athens—the transvaluation of values when God is silent. In content, however, the North American change has been just the opposite of the Athenian. Unlike AIDS, the disease of the plague at Athens was not merely infectious but casually contagious, and since no one in Athens even thought of quarantines as a public health measure, each and every person was likely to succumb to its fatality—thus the shift to the pleasure of the moment. The AIDS virus as "merely" infectious—you get it from what you do with someone with it—has predictably had an inverted effect on pleasure. The result has been the death of *Schwung* and sex, as one finds, for example, in the etiolated passions of David Leavitt's post-AIDS novel *The Lost Language of Cranes* and more generally in the emergence of infantile elements within gay male sexuality. Teddy bears as hip-pocket invitations, safety pins as symbols associated with crotches, the polymorphic perversity of safe-sex pornography, the antiseptic purity of safe-sex literature, and, in Leavitt's final moment, the incestuous desire of a gay child for his gay father's ankle—these all take us to the nursery with its diapers, latex, educational toys, Freudian babies, and the fight against shit. In the face of mass death caused by sex acts, it is too much to have hoped that gay men's culture would survive as a sexual liberation movement. The question is what else— what more generally—might be transvalued by the AIDS crisis.

It is here that a right reading of The NAMES Project is crucial, for its quilt memorial to those felled by AIDS is the first institutional statement of what post-AIDS values might look like. The values it expresses are presented in ritualized form and so are neither conscious to their expressors nor patently self-presenting. They call for interpretation. And rightly read, The Quilt asserts values of which gay people and their supporters can be considerably more proud than those that have nested around the death of sex. I will suggest that, as a text, The Quilt is a map of classical liberalism operating at its best: that it asserts the individual, not groups, classes, or society in toto, as the locus of human value and in turn interprets this prime value to be the permission for a person to make plans of her own and to carry them out to a degree compatible with other people having a similar permission. This valuation is new in that it disentangles into a pure sample, one thread, frequently blind stitched, frequently broken, that has run along with other strands that compose American history and culture.

———————

Technically, The Quilt is not a quilt at all. Quilting is a process of vertical lamination, not horizontal piecing. Quilting is the stitching together of a cover, a filler, and a backing. Decoration can be achieved with the addition of stippling, cording, and trapunto or stuffing. The classic quilt is of one color: white. While some few panels of the AIDS quilt incorporate genuine quilted elements, The Quilt has no filling or even a backing, no lamination and none of the painstakingly detailed stitchery that makes quilts quilts and that distinguishes them from comforters (which are tufted) and from nonlaminated coverlets. Technically, The NAMES Quilt is a pieced, nonquilted appliqué coverlet.

Further, if the genealogy of a work helps govern its interpretation, then by this standard too The Quilt is not a quilt. The Quilt's origin was a vision of names written on cardboard placards:

> The idea for the Project originated the night of November 27, 1985, when San Francisco activist Cleve Jones joined several thousand others in the annual candlelight march commemorating the murders of Mayor George Moscone and Harvey Milk, San Francisco's first openly gay supervisor. As the mourners passed by, they covered the walls of San Francisco's old Federal Building with placards bearing the names of people who had died of AIDS. "It was such a startling image," remembers Cleve. "The wind and the rain tore some of the cardboard names loose, but people stood

there for hours reading names. I knew then that we needed a monument, a memorial."[2]

Speech, then, of The Quilt necessarily takes place in the land of metaphor, but this at least is already clear: those who wish to see The Quilt's meaning as asserting the value of some social arrangement or another, based on appeals to traditional cultural associations of quilts (say, with quilting bees, families, and the like), have gained their point only by hijack.

Yet The NAMES Project is like the type of quilt called a friendship quilt or autograph quilt—in which each component swatch contains a stitched proper name. A quilter might send out preformed swatches to penpals or even celebrities, who then would stitch their names on their swatch and send them back to the quilt maker. In piecing the swatches together, the quilt maker would have a complete record of friends' names or a single-"sheet" autograph book. Alternatively, a friendship quilt can be a group project made for presentation. For instance, students might each make and sign a square that will be pieced together with the others and presented to their teacher on the occasion of her retirement. Or parishioners might make such a quilt for a minister moving on to other service. In form but not ritual, The NAMES Project is a friendship album quilt.

At the same time, it is also that quilting invention and parlor favorite of the Victorian era—the crazy quilt. Or, more precisely, it is a *contained* crazy, which has no overall pattern other than that made by the borders that surround component crazy blocks—in the case of The NAMES Project, canvas walkways grommeted to blocks of thirty-two three-foot by six-foot benamed panels. In the crazy, each component part, both micro-level patch and macro-level block, is unique in content as well as position. Although visual themes may repeat from block to block, even in variation, each block is one of a kind. Unlike the simple autograph quilt, the component parts of a crazy quilt are made unique not by the name alone but by their graphic content, which may be either representational or not.

In the crazy quilt, the possibility of narration blossoms to the degree the medium allows—that is, stories told within frames. America's most celebrated crazy quilt was produced about 1896 by the former slave Harriet Powers (fig. 1). Its Matisse-before-Matisse figural blocks juxtapose Bible stories (Jonah, the Crucifixion, etc.) with Powers's own odd and awesome tales of man, meteorology, the cosmos.[3] Powers dictated the following description for the central block of the quilt's three-by-five array: "The Falling of the Stars on November 13, 1833. The People were frightened and thought that the end of time had come. God's hand staid the stars. The varmints rushed out of their beds."[4]

Such telling stories-in-brief are what the panels of The NAMES Project Quilt picture as well. But, unlike the Bible stories of Powers's quilt, the stories of The NAMES Project Quilt do not rely on a cultural stock. Rather, the represented, lightning-quick, single-frame narratives of The Quilt are (one might say) probes of distinctness. They target, seek out, and display the named individual's personality—his center of narrative gravity, the orchestral tone of his being, life as his gesture. The panels are snapshots of the soul as posed in memory. The unique depicted name is itself frequently not merely a label or caption but in its decor the very vehicle of its person's story.

Although formally like a friendship quilt—every unit containing a name—the social posture and valuations of The NAMES Project are different, indeed inverted, from those of a presentation friendship quilt. In a friendship quilt, someone beyond the quilt, the recipient, is honored, and the makers of the quilt (it is hoped) are remembered through their stitched names. In The NAMES Project, those named on the quilt by others beyond it are valued in it by them. And the value in question need not be honor. In The NAMES Project, thanks to the craziness of The Quilt, the focus of moral attention is the individual as unique, as having a life plan of his own making and the opportunity to carry the plan forth come what may—including the right to pave his very own way to hell.

The advertising for The NAMES Project frequently calls The Quilt a celebration of life, and this is true in a sense. It is not a celebration of life in the sense of biological life or genetic life. In this sense, "life" is a mass noun and is elliptical for "having life" or "being alive." If it

FIG. 1: Appliqué quilt by Harriet Powers (1837–1911), ca. 1896, probably commissioned by faculty wives at Atlanta University. *(Bequest of Maxim Karolik. Courtesy of the Museum of Fine Arts, Boston.)*

were this sense of life that The Quilt celebrates, The Quilt would be repellently unseemly in its irony—the named have all biologically died, often horribly so. The sense of life that bears normative weight and of which The Quilt may rightly be called a celebration is the sense in which "life" is a count noun and a person is said to "have *a* life." It is this sense that occurs tellingly in the titles of biographies and more especially of autobiographies: Goethe's *From My Life*, Joe Louis's *My Life Story*, Darwin's *Life and Letters*, Hume's *My Own Life*, George Sand's *Story of My Life*, George Armstrong Custer's *My Life on the Plains*, Ronald Reagan's *An American Life*, Dame Edna Everage's *My Gorgeous Life: The Life, the Loves, the Legend*, or the simple generic *My Life*.[5] Each panel of The NAMES Project says not that someone or another was here. The panels are not refractions of the Tomb of the Unknown Solider. Rather, each panel says that this person—like no other—was here. The moral point of The NAMES Project is the valorizing of autobiographical life, not necessarily because such a life issues in the honorable, but just because it is unique—the working out, even if stumblingly, of a self-conceived plan of life.

There is no social story here to read or tell. The panels do not together make a picture. Collectively, they have no meaning. The craziness of The Quilt keeps the named safely both from merely being a heap—from merely being lots of death—and from being or telling some larger multicharactered tale. The edge-to-edge array of the panels is arbitrary. The pun of my title fibbed: "text" and "textile" have as their common history the Latin term for weaving, *textilis*. But there is no weaving or even plaiting here. The panels are neither visually nor metaphorically woven together, as in some misinterpretations: "The panels [are] sewn together into grids—individual lost lives stitched together, woven into an enormous picture of the effect of AIDS. . . . It is as though the dead are woven together, visually mirroring the networks [that] the living form to create the quilt."[6] Here is a critic blinded by socialist fantasies. There is no actual or symbolic warp and woof in which individual strands are submerged for the sake of some greater strength of the whole, some greater cause or glory.

The contents of The Quilt's crazy patches project the central normative claim of liberalism—that the locus of value in society lies, not in groups or classes or associations or even in society as a whole, but in the individual. In turn, The Quilt's manner of arrangement, its walkway strapwork, images the minimal public life that is necessary for the realization of liberal values. The net of canvas paths between the blocks of panels—the grommeted grid that makes The Quilt a *contained* crazy—does not produce a unified picture out of disparate elements. Rather, it reflects certain public goods, in the technical sense that they are things that everyone wants but that cannot be had, or had efficiently, through voluntary associations (remember private toll roads?) and so require coerced coordinations for their production and use. The type of goods I have in mind includes national defense, water purification, the development of vaccines against contagious diseases, equal opportunity, the rule of law, and, importantly for the purposes at hand, highways and byways—unobstructed passageways to the possible means of production and to occasions for voluntary association. Yet these are goods to which everyone has equal access and the use of which (like that of public parks) by some people does not significantly diminish the prospect of their use by others.

The walkways of The NAMES Project are necessary so that each panel may be seen by all. For this purpose, the panels could not be scattered as each maker willed or sewn into a single continuous sheet, nor could people be allowed to walk on the panels at will. The noble end of celebrating and displaying autobiographical lives required state-like coerced coordination. In The NAMES Project, this necessary coercion is institutionalized in the requirement that, when given over to The Project, panels become its exclusive property. Like the telephone company, The NAMES Project does not negotiate. Uncoordinated voluntary associations or private agreements between panel makers could not have brought the panels' display about with nearly the impact of The NAMES Project, yet the panels are all there equally to be seen by all and undiminished in being so, thanks and thanks only to the minimal monopolistic coercion of their presentation and arrangement. The framing walkways do not then mark the value of The Quilt's panels; they simply make that valuing possible. Similarly, in their concerted communal activity, the organizers, staff, and volunteers of The Project do not establish or determine the meaning of The Quilt any more than the scene changers at the Globe—last night *Hamlet*, tonight *Twelfth Night*, tomorrow *The Winter's Tale*—in their concerted communal activity establish or determine the meaning of a play; they simply make its presentation and meaning possible.

Where the edge-to-edge array of the panels is not arbitrary, that is, where organizations have submitted conjoined panels, one graphically sees the baleful effect of groups on individuals—the extermination of individual worth and dignity. In the group submissions, the individual as unique, as narrative, is destroyed and replaced by the individual as having some social role, as being a group's drone or even its advertisement. The individual is submerged into a cause or kind. The most blatant examples of this submersion are the reciprocally mirroring political Left and political Right. On the Right are the brown and black shirt panels of the San Francisco Police Department. The panels, arranged in phalanges, are identical one to the next, composed of parts of standard-issue uniforms and differentiated only by badge numbers. Here persons are reduced to digits and functions. On the Left are the checkerboard blocks, the imbricated pennants, of the national organization for gay male interracial couples Black and White Men Together. Again, all panels are the same one to the next. Here the individual is obliterated by and for the sake of a cause. In the group blocks, as at the national Vietnam Veterans Memorial, death is the referent of a mass noun, an undifferentiated heap—"so *much* death." Here persons are as fungible as coin.

I do not wish to deny that these group submissions have a certain effect. Even the dizzy and trivializing thirty-two-panel array of the San Francisco Gay Men's Chorus, in which the members' names appear on fluffy pillows depicting clouds and wavelets floating above and lapping below a well-known suspension bridge, punches the sternum and hollows the soul—like the opening measure, the single drum note, the loud muted thud, of the Mahler Tenth finale. But it is mass death, not individual loss, that does the punching—and not so nearly effectively as in the Vietnam Memorial.

The NAMES Project installation does not take one through a unified experience: one may start into it from anywhere and leave anywhere, taking in this part but not that part of it. One has a unified—reading-like—experience only in relation to individual panels. And, finally, the amassed death of The NAMES Project as a whole is presented with so much razzle, and so frequently punctuated with fun ("Is this art? No! It's Fred Abrams!"—with beard and high heels), that The Quilt is en masse largely nonthreatening.

In contrast, the Vietnam Memorial, like the Parthenon frieze, does take its walking perceiver through a unified experience. Its two fifteen-rod triangular name-etched earth-embanked granite walls stretch horizontally away from each other like widely opened compass arms and vertically cut gradually, indeed locally imperceptibly, above and below the horizon from a height of an inch at their outer reach to ten feet where they meet to form a deceptive angle, which when seen from along the walls seems nearly straight (thus the popular name for the monument, "*The* Wall") but which in reality is much more nearly a right angle. A brick path guides one along the planes of the walls, slowly immersing one in and, in turn, releasing one from the dead. At the walls' apex, one feels suddenly boxed in, engulfed by, indeed one is literally overtopped by the dead. The unified experience of the memorial is a descent and resurrection in which one is taken, all unawares until one is there, into cold Hades, dumb, death saturated, daunting, and meaningless. The dead here are not even shades of themselves but are reduced merely to that about them which was most public and ultimately arbitrary, given by others, neither created by nor appropriated to themselves. A name here serves not as a sign of distinctiveness or uniqueness but as a mere place holder. Uniqueness is set aside for the sake of the representation of the massiveness of death. By overwhelming the living with death, the Vietnam Memorial says never again to war. Its author cleverly used the memorial's stark formalism to slip a powerful political message by the judges of the memorial's design competition—by the contest's ground rule that the monument was not to have a political message, was to divorce the dead from the occasion of their dying. Clever, that modernism. The Left has criticized The Wall's stunning formalism as a disguise for the evils of the U.S. involvement in an unjust war, but the Right knew more nearly of what it spoke when it objected (wrongly, I think) to the morbidity of The Wall, calling it "a black gash of shame."

The group panels of The Quilt, amassing death as does The Wall but without the message of The Wall, are failures—artistically, politically, and morally—for they gain nothing yet they pay a high moral price; they end human dignity. Indeed they deny one of the chief ways in which The Project interprets itself, a claim to be saying: "Real people die of AIDS, not statistics."

The Quilt is not then at heart to be read as a political document, although this is how it is usually read—a cheap alloy of electoral politics and pop psychology. One interpreter sees its worth in its ability to "communicate collective power. A political demonstration could not have done the same. . . . One of the most important roles The Quilt has played is as a tool for organization."[7] The Quilt's originator even toured the country making boundlessly naive claims that The Quilt would decisively make AIDS *the* issue of the 1988 U.S. presidential campaign. Or again, various educational claims are made on behalf of The Quilt: it helps get the "message" about AIDS out to a wide audience. "Official" NAMES Project literature holds that one main purpose of The Quilt is to raise funds for the care of people with AIDS. I admit to doubts about political justifications that depend for their results on indirect effects—say, more funding through consciousness raising. Such claims of indirect effects are the foundations of failed utopias. And there is reason to doubt the efficacy of such political proposals for this project in particular. In July 1988, during its first Chicago display, only twenty-five thousand people saw The Quilt over its three-day stay there—less than a third the number who attended the city's annual gay pride parade a week earlier, and in any case, if my sense is correct, The Quilt, whatever it was preaching, was preaching there to the converted.

Interpretations of The Quilt that make it an unusual part of busi-ness-as-usual politics probably mean that The Quilt is a failure. But more disturbing than this (it would not after all be the first failure of politics in the AIDS crisis) is the prospect that taking The Quilt as politics degrades everyone: the dead (who are reduced to causes), the quilters (who have wasted their time), and the audience (who are political dupes). Social interpreters of The Quilt use the dead: as fund-raisers, as consciousness raisers, as salves for the soul, as political stooges.

The Quilt is better understood in terms of concepts that come to us not from political discourse but out of religious traditions. The Quilt expresses sacred values, values that, like religious values in an indi-vidual's system of values, override considerations of prudence or utility. In placing these values above one's happiness and well-being, one both affirms and displays one's deepest beliefs and commitments. These are the values by which people identify themselves to themselves.

Those who make panels give up some of themselves, in a process that is neither particularly pleasant nor socially, politically, or econom-ically efficient, in order to say that what is important to them is the distinctive life plans of individuals. In their efforts, they severally invest some of the moral capital they have simply as moral agents, chiefly through the expenditure of that most illusive modern commodity—time—which registers in the care and concern embodied in the unique panels; thereby, the quilters express (even if unconsciously) and enhance and fix the worth of human uniqueness or individuality.

These expenditures of moral capital are not prudential investments for future gain, a plea to Washington, or an aid to the living. The panel makers, if this were the case, would have better spent their time and effort writing a letter to a senator or helping change the soiled sheets of a person with AIDS.

Rather than serving as prayers of petition, in which one asks for something, the quilters' efforts are more nearly similar, although not identical, to prayers of adoration, in which one gives up something to express one's basic beliefs. Yet, in adorational prayer, the prayer is prayed because of a belief that its object deserves adoration—is worthy of the worshiper's attentions. In this, adorational prayer is like standard war memorial rhetoric, for which Pericles' funeral oration milled for all time the boilerplate. "The Fallen" in these circumstances are *presumed* to be good and worthy of our attentions—no matter what they actually did in battle, whether their cowardice precipitated a rout or their bravery turned one back. Adorational prayer and war memorial rhetoric express value, but they do not create it—the value they affirm already exists and is itself the prompt to adore or honor. The NAMES Project rather is a ritual that not only expresses value but that, more important, creates it. The pooling of the moral investments of the quilters makes something of their expressed values that, unlike the clarity of the value of God to his worshipers, was not so clearly there before, something fragile and recurring in American traditions, something glimpsed occasionally in its constitutional tradition, the belief that the value of the individual is a trump over the utility of efficient social arrangements, that moral life in the first instance is individual rather than social.

The observers of The Quilt make moral investments similar to those of the quilters themselves. One does not go to see The Quilt to be cheered; it is painful to see. Neither is the experience chiefly an aesthetic one. The Quilt admittedly is attractive. It prompts and pays that curiosity which images the awe with which art unqualified ends and first philosophy begins. But the same could be said of hobo art or scale-model carnival midways made out of toothpicks by prisoners. The decidedly minor league artistic pleasures of The Quilt do not outweigh or transform the viewer's pain. This pain is the moral price the viewers are willing to invest disparately in the individual dead. More than like going to a museum, going to The NAMES Project is like attending church where the point of attendance is not to plead to heaven, or to ward off hell, but to invest one's time, care, and concern in what one most truly believes.

The moral dynamics of sacred values in The NAMES Project may be traced farther by asking, For whose sake does one mourn when one mourns? In lopsided preponderance, Western civilization's answer is that in mourning the mourner is the focus of moral attention. One mourns for the sake of, more specifically, for the benefit of, oneself. Mourning is viewed as a sort of Aristotelian tragedy, the purpose of which is to purge its observers of pity and fear—so that they may carry on. The West views mourning as though it were a matter of a person sending a note of condolence to himself. Consider Ecclesiasticus 38:17–21: "Make bitter weeping, and make passionate wailing, and let thy mourning be according to his desert, for a day or two, lest thou be evil spoken of: and so be comforted for thy sorrow. . . . Give not thy heart unto sorrow: put it away. . . . Him though shalt not profit, and thou wilt hurt thyself" (so too, Eccles. 9:5). Here, the ends of mourning are the mourner's avoidance of shame, reception of comfort, and preservation of strength. The focus of mourning is entirely the mourner and its value entirely one of benefit and utility.

For Freud, too, "the work of mourning" is a "work of severance," its benefit the mourner's liberation: "In mourning time is needed for the command of reality-testing to be carried out in detail, and . . . when this work has been accomplished the ego will have succeeded in freeing its libido from the lost object. . . . Mourning impels the ego to give up the object by declaring the object to be dead and offering the ego the inducement of continuing to live. . . . When the work of mourning is completed, the ego becomes free and uninhibited again."[8]

Emily Post has retooled these sentiments for a still more modern audience:

> A greater and ever greater number of persons today do not believe in going into mourning at all. There are some who believe, as do the races of the East, that great love should be expressed in rejoicing in the rebirth of a beloved spirit instead of selfishly mourning one's own earthly loss. It is certain however that the number who can actually attain this spirit are few indeed. Most of us merely do the best we can to continue to keep occupied, to make the necessary adjustments, and to avoid casting the shadow of our own sadness upon others. The sooner that we can overcome our grief and turn our thoughts to the future the better. Because mourning is a continual reminder of the past, it can only delay the wearer's return to a normal life.[9]

Here, the dead have dropped out of the moral picture altogether. Although Post claims the moral high ground for herself along several dimensions, her position—like that of Ecclesiasticus—is, as she virtually admits, one of selfishness on the part of the mourner, a selfishness that is morally relieved (and on this I think she is quite right) in that people simply are hard-wired to grieve. Other animals, like quails and elephants, mourn. It is reasonable to suppose that, in its purely physical dimensions, grief is perhaps simply the curdled effluence of selfish genes—or something.

What Western civilization says about mourning is also what the NAMES quilters typically say about what they do. Their tales are too fragile to quote here without shame, but the same view is expressed by the producers of The NAMES Project: The Quilt is "a symbol of the dignity and strength of those who grieve"; "The Quilt's message [is] of hope and compassion"; The Quilt is "a way for people to express what they've gone through"; "The Quilt is a dramatic symbol of how we can heal the pain of fear and loss." These statements morally undersell The Quilt. These accounts might be persuasive if The Quilt-ing were just a matter of crying and keening, the pounding of chests or even the vengeful torturing of prisoners of war. But these accounts of The Quilt, although not The Quilt itself, simply forget the dead. Mourning, they tell us, is for the sake of the living.

All these accounts and uses of mourning are what the *Oxford English Dictionary* defines as the intransitive sense of "to mourn": "to *feel* sorrow, grief, or regret"—full stop, no object. There is, however, another more profound sense of mourning, whereby mourning becomes a moral activity rather than a mere survival reflex. Grammatically, it is the transitive sense: "to grieve or sorrow (for or over someone)." Note that the implicitly self-reflexive "feel" drops out of the transitive definition and a prepositional phrase introducing the object of grief is customary. However, in common, imprecise English, the usual prepositions for this purpose—"for" and especially "over"—most often are simply flags of the *occasion* for mourning in the intransitive sense, rather than pointers to an *object* of mourning. Ordinarily, "I mourn for John" means not that John is the object of some sort of my attention, but simply that John's death is the occasion for my experiencing some feeling, one—civilization tells me—I would do better without, one I need to get over. In any case, in this corrupted transitive sense, it is *I* who remain the moral focus of mourning. In morally insightful contrast, note the preposition of mourning in the quartet from Thomas Gray's "Sonnet on the Death of Mr Richard West":

> The fields to all their wonted tribute bear,
>   To warm their little loves the birds complain.
> I fruitless mourn to him that cannot hear,
>   And weep the more, because I weep in vain.

Forget momentarily the sentiment here. Note the grammar. Gray's preposition "to" correctly captures the essentially intentional nature of mourning. By "intentional" I mean the directedness of consciousness to an object beyond it, the quality of pointing to, and delineating, an object of thought—the outward thrust of the mind as directed on an object. One mourns *to* a known, specifiable person. Mourning, like love, is a vector of attention pointed from the moral agent to the particularity of another person. The proper focus of moral concern in mourning is he who is mourned, not he who does the mourning. Only through and in the mourner's sorrow does the missing of the dead really count for anything. The mourner's sorrow is not psychological self-help or a way station to it but the sacrifice one makes to say what is really meaningful to one.

Mourning to the dead who were our friends provides an especially pure form of the moral dynamics of transitive mourning. Mourning for family members, like mourning for political figures or kings and heroes, is likely to be congested with associations sublimed from the dead's various social types or roles, or at least from their good deeds—real or imagined. These roles and virtues will tend both to occlude for the mourner the particularity of the mourned and to reintroduce the mourner's relation to the mourned and ultimately again the mourner herself as the focus of moral attention. It is the role or noble deed that is remembered—in the form of honor. But one does not honor one's friends. It was not their good deeds or their roles that made them important in our lives; rather, what mattered was their individuality as developed in their relation to us—a relation that had value just because *we* valued it, had the shape it had just because *we* shaped it. Friendship is the intersection of the private and the morally supererogatory. Unlike marital relations or even sexual relations divorced from marital relations, friendships do not morally circulate around either the claims of need or the duties that correlate to legitimate demands. One does not sleep with one's friends, and one does not legitimately make demands of them; at most, one has expectations of them, and one may un-embarrassedly ask favors of them. It is not with one's friends that one shares the common necessities of life in pledges of mutual support. That is what spouses do. Friendship has the place in our moral life that cut flowers in a well-appointed home have in our aesthetic life.

Yet time and again in *The Quilt: Stories from The NAMES Project*, the stories that gay men tell of their relation to their dead lovers is that "he was my best friend."[10] Perhaps this choice of vocabulary is simply shyness on the part of gay men—an inability or unwillingness, from a consciousness too low or too high, to use the vocabulary of marriage of themselves. Or perhaps in speech to the media they feel that they must abandon the well-entrenched and resonant ways of gay speech and presume that gay culture's term of choice "lover"—"he was my lover"—would be taken to denote chiefly or only a sexual relation. But perhaps, more innocently, they are appealing to the development of the pair as unique and private, a feature often overlooked in marital relations, but one that is distinctive, indeed exhaustive, of the content of friendship. Then, saying that "he was my best friend" at the occasion of his memorialization is not to gainsay whatever else he might have been but to focus the attention of the living on his individuality and to value that.

In the sorrow of the living *to* the dead, the dead are valued as individuals—whatever their goodness or badness as moral agents may have been. Properly understood, even the panel to Roy Cohn ("Bully. Coward. Victim.") has its proper place in The Quilt. Because the panels are not essentially tributes, in the sense of honors paid to the dead, their stories—the dead's—need not have been sanitized, as so many obviously have been. Lies of omission abound. A panel for an acquaintance of mine reported that he helped found a gay organization and that he liked Broadway musicals. This is true enough, but what he loved was to eat shit and get beaten up. No mention was made of these activities. His narrators, out of squeamishness, lost his center of gravity. Aside from some scattered trinkets of leathermen, sex is bleached right out of The Quilt, although sex was what was most distinctive of so many of the dead. This quilt has been too frequently bundled.

Perhaps, however, even the selective lies and the impulse to praise rather than prize, to honor rather than cherish, are not simply prudishness but are pressed on the quilters by the funereal language of our civilization. There is no verb in English that gets crisply and without distracting side senses the activity I have been trying to describe as the essence of what the quilters do. "To honor," we have seen, is interestingly wrong. Even its religious variants are tainted by concern with the observance of values rather than their establishment. The religious sense of commemoration, for instance, is a service in memory of a saint or sacred event. What I have been suggesting of The NAMES Project is that it *is* a sacred event—an act that lays value on something. "To consecrate" might be closer, but its links to geography and architecture are wrong. "To hallow" is perhaps as close as our language will take us to the sacred valuing of the dead, although it too is doubly sensed. Its most frequent sense (that, for instance, in the Gettysburg Address) is "to honor as holy"—because worthy of such treatment. The sense I have in mind, however, is its simpler sense "to make holy" because that is where the living choose to invest their moral capital and therefore, in that very cost, to register what is most meaningful to them.

The reason why the transitive sense of mourning and so the moral dimension of mourning has been largely overlooked in the West is (I suspect) the metaphysical scruple that can be detected in the works quoted above by God and Mr. Gray: "him thou shalt not profit," "him that cannot hear." How, Western civilization might ask (its Christianity notwithstanding), can one mourn *for the sake of* the dead if they do not exist or at least cannot be affected from here to there?

In the *Nicomachean Ethics*'s inquiry on whether a person can be made happy or sad after the last post, Aristotle has both the best answer and as much confusion as anyone on this issue.[11] What Aristotle gets exactly right is that, if some goods and evils can affect a person *even if* she is never aware of them, then, at least in these ways, the absence of any commune with the dead is no metaphysical barrier to our affecting them. Where Aristotle is intriguingly yet profoundly wrong is in his understanding of the scope of these goods. He gives as first examples of these barrier-crossing valuations honor and dishonor. These are on the right track, but not quite right either, for the effect of dishonor (when it does have an effect) is shame. One feels shame from being aware that one is its object. But that shame, in turn, requires a person to be in the picture both as a subject with feelings and as an agent cognizant of his own social circumstances.

What *can* affect a person for the worse without her ever knowing it is not dishonor but insult. Unobserved spying on a person, aspersions cast at her behind her back, and lying to a person are all insults. They assault her dignity—*even if* she is never aware of the insult, and *even if* these acts by others (like paternalistic white lies) actually benefit her, contribute to her material circumstances, her well-being, her happiness. This disjuncture between happiness and dignity eludes Aristotle— probably because he and his culture had no conception of individual rights. He could not detach dignity from honor, which he treated variously as a substrate for and a luster to happiness.

The correct answer to Aristotle's inquiry then is that, no, the dead may not be made happy or sad, for there is nothing to feel or perceive over there. But the dead may be insulted or dignified, for that requires no awareness of our acts here or, indeed, any consciousness on their part at all. They need only to have a narrative—either in nature or only in memory—to which value may be attached to mark its distinctness or, conversely, at which individual-obliterating insult may be directed. The grave, then, although a block to aiding or harming the dead, is no bar to dignifying or insulting them. Desecration is the name given insults cast upon the dead.

For the living, the closest counterpart to this sort of dignifying of human distinctiveness regardless of the outcome of the journey taken is the social rituals surrounding the sacrament of marriage, where value is placed on the prospect of a unique two-character narrative—for better or worse, richer, poorer, in sickness and in health. Even personal failure has its proper pride. Among the dead such hallowing is what The NAMES Project does for the individual narratives denoted and valued in its panels. It dignifies the dead whether the dead are aware of it or not.

The NAMES Project was inaugurated on the Washington Mall as part of the events surrounding the half million strong, but virtually unreported, 1987 National Gay and Lesbian March on Washington.[12] No one was quite sure in advance what The Quilt's effect would be. Although there were two other "official" events sponsored by the March Committee beyond the march itself, The Wedding and A Day of Civil Disobedience at the Supreme Court Building, I suggest that The

NAMES Project turned out to be what these other events should have been but were not—the expression of the value of individual dignity. The Wedding, a (much-needed) celebration of gay relationships, in the unfortunate specific form it took—a cross between new age spiritualism and Reverend Moon's herd weddings—stood to the sacred valuation of marriage as ululation stands to aria.[13]

Worse still was the Leftist-corrupted Day of Civil Disobedience— which produced the largest number of U.S. civil disobedience arrests since the Vietnam War and the largest number at the Supreme Court ever.[14] Now, civil disobedience ought to be an exemplary way in which an individual recoups dignity. But the opportunity for the expression of individual dignity was lost and denied by the very form that this disobedience took. Its organizers obliterated individual agents as individual agents—by insisting that everyone involved in the civil disobedience be part of an "affinity group" that was to operate by group consensus, to be in fact a local community with local community standards, and that would be arrested together like a comforting herd.

The arrests themselves were a Foucauldian ballet of police power diffused and modulated and of citizens disciplined and molded. In the face of advanced negotiations with the police, affinity groups, plastic handcuffs, police-controlled turnstiles to the arrest site, quizzes before actual arrest, and school buses doubling as paddy wagons and holding tanks—in the face of all this, individual dignity did not stand a chance. Interest, meaning, and value were all stifled by and submerged in that which stands to autobiographical life as death stands to biological life—enforced boredom, the great anesthetic of the soul, and the chief phenomenological characteristic of contemporary civil disobedience. Bull Connor, where are you when we need you?

In addition to legitimately targeting the Supreme Court's "homosexual sodomy" decision of a year earlier, the disobedience at the Court was also intended to agitate for more government assistance for people with AIDS. But the Court had quite recently held, in a surprising extension of civil rights, that people with AIDS are protected from discrimination in government-funded employment and programs under the 1973 Rehabilitation Act.[15] The Court could not have been a less apposite target for AIDS funding protests. It was clear, then, that, as its organizers thought of it, the civil disobedience was simply one more form of business-as-usual politics, people wanting more stuff for themselves and trying to get it through political persuasion and media attention.

Although the chief object of the protest was the Court's denial to gays of the right to privacy, many of the component essays in the "official" handbook for the civil disobedience—including even its statement of "principles"—deny the very value of privacy. The personal is political, but it ought not to be. That it ought not to be is what the civil disobedience should have been affirming, and that is what The Quilt does affirm magnificently.

If as an institution The Quilt can be thought of as an analogue to any political form, it is not to business-as-usual politics, or even to the operation of a constitutional system in place, but rather to those rare and paradoxical events by which constitutions are set in place, are established and undergirded. At such foundational events, the majority determines that its own powers shall fail in certain areas—those cast constitutionally as individual rights. The majority there commits a limited suicide. Power sublates into immunity, into that which blocks the deployment of power. Historically, such events are propelled by upheavals of one sort or another, in which such limits to power appear as a calm and compromise, say, following mutual sectarian extermina-tions. Such foundations are conscious actions typically driven by past horrors. However, whether the rights so established are maintained in normal nonhorrific circumstances depends on the unconscious persis-tence of the values that sustain rights among a people. These values must, I think, be held unconsciously and so in a way remain unreach-able, for otherwise the blandishments of social utility, the power of certain persuasions, and the enticements of power itself will sweep the values and their pendant rights away—in effect, even if their formal husks remain. (Remember that the constitution of Stalin's Soviet Union incorporated the wording of the U.S. Bill of Rights.) In unconsciously and ritualistically expressing sacred values, in denying the dominance of utility and communal values, and in asserting the worth of individuals as individuals, the panels of The NAMES Project are an exemplar of the necessarily unconscious commitment that sustains that which is most distinctive of the American genius and for which, at least occasionally, America has served as a beacon for others—human dignity and individual rights.

This lesson of The Quilt as a source of ideals rather than merely a political instrument is one that AIDS activists would do well to take note of. Some ACT UP members have viewed The NAMES Project as objectionable AIDS passivism, disparaging it as an insidious distraction, a narcotic, or at best a sideshow to the legitimate, hard, confrontational work needed to mobilize against AIDS. The late AIDS and gay studies activist Michael Lynch held that, "unless mourning turns to action, its special blessing disappears."[16] PWA and thorn in the side of the National Endowment for the Arts David Wojnarowicz asks what many other understandably frustrated AIDS activists have asked: "Why are we so polite? Why don't we go running into the streets screaming for justice instead of perfecting our eulogizing skills?"[17] The proper response to these activists is that elegy making and mourning are especially worthy activities, for they, perhaps more than anything else, remind us, presses to both consciousness and conscience, why, in a world where suffering regularly dwarfs well-being, life is worth living in the first place. In valorizing, even sacralizing, the mourned person in his individuality and uniqueness, The NAMES Project and elegy in general manifest why the goal of stopping AIDS warrants screaming in the streets and more as means to that end.

My favorite panel of The Quilt (fig. 2), one that I would also like to think is a fine example for my interpretation of The Quilt and that in any case I offer here by way of summary, is the panel from David Kemmeries to his Native American lover Jac Wall, a life-size shin-to-crown outlined body silhouette. At first glance it suggests a police chalk drawing at the site of a car accident or sidewalk murder. But at second sight the figure is clearly standing. And the silhouette is cut in reverse—white figure against a uniform, closely speckled backdrop. I do not

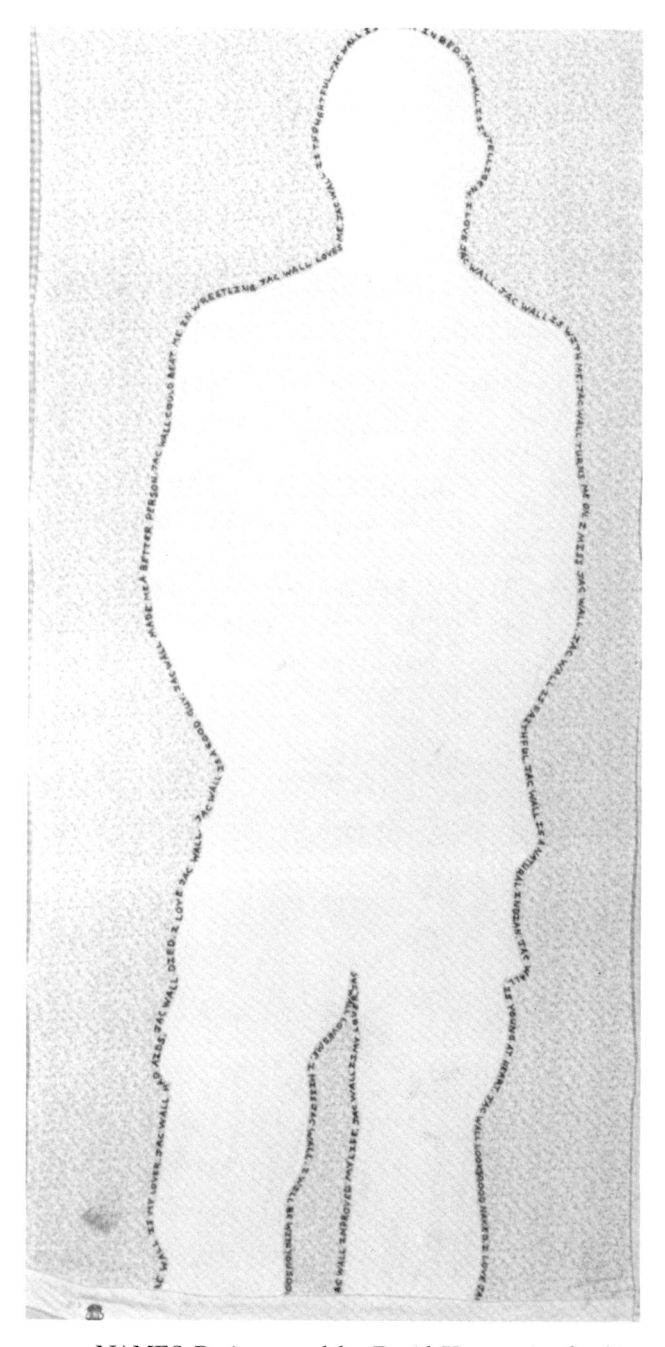

FIG. 2: NAMES Project panel by David Kemmeries for his lover Jac Wall. *(Copyright © 1988, Matt Herron.)*

know whether this was the intended effect, but the panel reminds me of the black rains and white shadows of Hiroshima—where people standing near walls absorbed enough energy as they were vaporized in The Bomb's glare that they left on the wood or concrete behind them permanent shadows lighter than the surrounding areas that were singed and etched by direct rays. The silhouette's outline is a band of text in uncial capitals, a meditation on and droning threnody to the beloved:

> Jac Wall is my lover. Jac Wall had AIDS. Jac Wall died. I love Jac Wall. Jac Wall is a good guy. Jac Wall made me a better person. Jac Wall could beat me in wrestling. Jac Wall loves me. Jac Wall is thoughtful. Jac Wall is great in bed. Jac Wall is intelligent. I love Jac Wall. Jac Wall is with me. Jac Wall turns me on. I miss Jac Wall. Jac Wall is faithful. Jac Wall is a natural Indian. Jac Wall is young at heart. Jac Wall looks good naked. I love Jac Wall. Jac Wall improved my life. Jac Wall is my lover. Jac Wall loves me. I miss Jac Wall. I will be with you soon.

Here, the alternation and confusion of tenses struggle to bind the two men together in a timeless present, the eternal now of love. The white text-ringed cavity makes the lover's absence present to us. We the readers and seers are bestowed an unsettling peace, while the live lover in his pained patient tendance sanctifies the dead.

CHAPTER 6

"Knights, Young Men, Boys": Masculine Worlds and Democratic Values

FIG. 3: The Grail Knights assembled, *Parsifal*, act 1, scene 2, Wieland Wagner staging, Bayreuth Festival, 1951. *(Courtesy of Bayreuther Festspiele Pressebüro.)*

If I say, "I hate not men but what they do," I remain divided against myself, dismembered. I hate myself and not my oppressor. In contrast, when I say, "I hate men," I use language well. I say what I experience: *I* hate men.

    Jeffner Allen, LESBIAN PHILOSOPHY *(1986)*

"Justice" is like a drug, and it keeps us hooked on the structures of patriarchy, and dominance and subordination—the fathers' idea of "cooperation."

    Sarah Lucia Hoagland, LESBIAN ETHICS *(1988)*

Here they come. Lean, hard and fast. The Marines.

    Pentagon recruitment poster (1980)

You know how love flourishes in time of war, women standing on station platforms and waiting for the lines of faces to pull out, men's heads three deep in the carriage windows and arms raised like the front legs of horses on the Parthenon. Men do not want to go to war; they look forward to travel and the warmth of soldiers. . . .

    She had a husband; her husband had been unfaithful; she was looking for a lover. I took her at lunchtime to see the sculptures from the Parthenon; there were the men wrestling with horses as if they were in love. The men and horses were centaurs; they were struggling to be different. I do not think she liked the sculptures.

    Nicholas Mosley, IMPOSSIBLE OBJECT *(1968)*

Many a soldier's kiss dwells on these bearded lips.

    Walt Whitman, DRUM-TAPS *(1865)*

Upon waking next morning about daylight, I found Queequeg's arm thrown over me in the most loving and affectionate manner. You had almost thought I had been his wife. . . .

    At length, by dint of much wiggling, and loud and incessant expostulations upon the unbecomingness of his hugging a fellow male in that matrimonial sort of style, I succeeded in extracting a grunt. . . .

    At first he little noticed these advances; but presently, upon my referring to his last night's hospitalities, he made out to ask me whether we were again to be bedfellows. I told him yes; whereat I thought he looked pleased, perhaps a little complimented. . . .

He seemed to take to me quite as naturally and unbiddingly as I to him; and when our smoke was over, he pressed his forehead against mine, clasped me around the waist, and said that henceforth we were married. . . .

Thus, then, in our hearts' honeymoon, lay I and Queequeg—a cosy, loving pair.

We had lain thus in bed, chatting and napping at short intervals, and Queequeg now and then affectionately throwing his brown tattooed legs over mine, and then drawing them back; so entirely sociable and free and easy were we.

Herman Melville, MOBY DICK, *chaps. 4, 10, 11*

Instantly I felt a shock running through all my frame; nothing was to be seen, and nothing was to be heard; but a supernatural hand seemed placed in mine. . . . I lay there, frozen with the most awful fears, not daring to drag away my hand; yet ever thinking that if I could but stir it one single inch, the horrid spell would be broken. . . .

Squeeze! squeeze! squeeze! all morning long; I squeezed that sperm till I myself almost melted into it; I squeezed that sperm till a strange sort of insanity came over me; and I found myself unwittingly squeezing my co-laborers' hands in it, mistaking their hands for the gentle globules. Such an abounding, affectionate, friendly, loving feeling did this avocation beget; that at last I was continually squeezing their hands, and looking up into their eyes sentimentally; as much as to say,—Oh! my dear fellow beings, why should we longer cherish any social acerbities, or know the slightest ill-humor or envy! Come; let us squeeze hands all round; nay, let us all squeeze ourselves into each other; let us squeeze ourselves universally into the very milk and sperm of kindness.

Would that I could keep squeezing that sperm for ever! For now, since by many prolonged, repeated experiences, I have perceived that in all cases man must eventually lower, or at least shift, his conceit of attainable felicity; not placing it anywhere in the intellect or the fancy;

but in the wife, the heart, the bed, the table, the saddle, the fire-side, the country; now that I have perceived all this, I am ready to squeeze case eternally. In thoughts of the vision of the night, I saw long rows of angels in paradise, each with his hands in a jar of spermaceti.

MOBY DICK, *chaps. 4, 94*

Genet wasn't very interested in gay lib, but he did march in a gay liberation march in 1972, and he signed a few petitions and things, but he almost never had sex with a gay man. He was once in love with a gay hustler in Rome, but generally, he only liked straight men. . . .

So in France, for instance, a lot of gay men in the 1940's, when Genet was first becoming famous, approved of the way the Nazis looked, so they became fascist. Some of the gays that Genet met in the 1940's were extreme right. The whole crowd around Cocteau was extreme right. And Genet was a communist and a militant one while admiring the Nazis—he got off on them sexually and condemned them politically. . . .

And what is great about Genet is that he had these sexual fantasies—but they didn't lead him anywhere politically. And in fact he was able to have quite a decent, human, and, I think, honorable sense of politics while entertaining these so-called fascistic sex fantasies.

Edmund White, interview, OUT/LOOK *(Fall 1990)*

I was fifteen at the time and lived in a small attic room among the soldiers. I will never forget the smell of the Wehrmacht, a compound of tobacco and boot polish. For me, this was the fragrance of happiness.

Michel Tournier, THE WIND SPIRIT: AN AUTOBIOGRAPHY *(1977)*

Whoever designed the Nazi uniforms had to be gay. Those were the sexiest men I have ever seen in my life, and it was mostly because of their uniforms—the high boots and the close-cut jackets. . . .

Yes, I consider my work pornography. Pornography means to stimulate people's sexual feelings, and I'm always very aware of that. I always want to make them come. My motive is lower than art.

Tom of Finland, interview, CHRISTOPHER STREET *(April 1980)*

Here is adhesiveness, it is not previously fashion'd, it is apropos;
Do you know what it is as you pass to be loved by strangers?
Do you know the talk of those turning eye-balls?
  Walt Whitman, "Song of the Open Road" *(1856)*

I confidently expect a time when there will be seen, running like a
half-hid warp through all the myriad audible and visible worldly interests of America, threads of manly friendship, fond and loving, pure and
sweet, strong and life-long, carried to degrees hitherto unknown—not
only giving tone to individual character, and making it unprecedentedly
emotional, muscular, heroic, and refined, but having the deepest relations to general politics. I say democracy infers such loving comradeship, as its most inevitable twin or counterpart, without which it will
be incomplete, in vain, and incapable of perpetuating itself.
  Walt Whitman, DEMOCRATIC VISTAS *(1871)*

We two boys together clinging,
One the other never leaving,
Up and down the roads going,
North & South excursions making,
Power enjoying, elbows stretching, fingers clutching,
Arm'd and fearless, eating, drinking, sleeping, loving,
No law less than ourselves owning, sailing, soldiering, thieving,
    threatening,
Misers, menials, priests alarming, air breathing, water drinking,
    on the turf or the sea-beach dancing,
Cities wrenching, ease scorning, statutes mocking, feebleness chasing,
Fulfilling our foray.
  Walt Whitman, CALAMUS *(1860)*

Finally, by expounding these paradoxical ideas, I wanted to grant to the
professors of philosophy a small favor, for they are very disconcerted
by the ever-increasing publicization of my philosophy which they so
carefully concealed. I have done so by giving them the opportunity of
slandering me by saying that I defend and commend pederasty.
  Arthur Schopenhauer, THE WORLD AS WILL AND REPRESENTATION, *(3d
  ed. 1859)*

So far it's only my brain he's interested in.

—The minute I saw you two at *Parsifal* I said to myself, "He's with a trick."

Knowing you, you probably said it to the people you were with.

—Well, Stephen, it was kind of obvious: two grown men at a performance of *Parsifal*.

What's so obvious about two men going to *Parsifal* together?

—Face it, Stephen, ice hockey at the Garden it's not.

Terrence McNally, THE LISBON TRAVIATA (*1986*)

FIG. 4: *Parsifal,* act 3 close, Wieland Wagner staging Bayreuth Festival, 1951. (*Courtesy of Bayreuther Festspiele Pressebüro.*)

I. Singing Soteriology

In the closing moments of Wagner's last opera *Parsifal*, knights, young men, and boys—some with their soprano-ranged voices sounding angelically from the cupola—sing to music that swells and dreams toward eternity and ecstasy: "Wonder of highest holies. The Savior is saved." As in Wagner's *Ring* cycle, the problems in need of solution in *Parsifal*, the figures in need of saving, are divine, not human, and the needed salvation comes about only through the workings of mankind.[1] Wagner calls his obscurely plotted, densely suggestive *Parsifal*, not an opera, but "a sacred dramatic festival." Yet, between the coverleaf and close, the sacred values that are affirmed in ritual are those of men, not gods.

As the knights, young men, and boys of Monsalvat sing that the Savior has been saved, the only distinct female in the opera—sempiternal witch, reincarnation of Herodias, sensualist extraordinaire, and mocking witness to the Crucifixion—dies. In contrast to Brünnhilde, who, in the *Ring* cycle, spectacularly commits suttee to the tune of some of Western civilization's most stirring music, *Parsifal's* Kundry passes from the scene and life wordlessly, silently, virtually unremarked, and entirely unnoted. As the boys sing of the Savior's salvation, there is

> *A ray of light: The Grail [held high by Parsifal] glows intensely. From the dome a white dove descends and hovers over Parsifal's head. Kundry, looking at Parsifal, sinks slowly to the ground before Parsifal and dies. Amfortas and Gurnemanz do homage, kneeling before Parsifal, who waves the Grail gently over the adoring knights. The curtain slowly closes.*

The music with which Kundry, like swirling lightning, enters act 1 launched the structured atonality through which Wagner made possible serialism and the pinnacle of Western civilization reached in the secular cantatas of Anton Webern.[2] The octave and a half plunging sigh with which Kundry enters act 2 would reverberate through the death screams of Alban Berg's Lulu fifty years later and from there refract into all the forms, good, bad, and dreadful, of expressionism, ending in the very worst of Western civilization, the pulsing anadiplosis of musical minimalism. Yet, although Kundry gave handsel to the twentieth century, at opera's close the music does not even acknowledge her passing. Why does Kundry die—and so vanishingly so?

The standard, liner-notes reading of her death is that "Kundry released, at last, sinks happily into the sleep of death and the redemption she has so much desired." But this frisky reading is warrantless. The stage directions say nothing of happy release. We do not even know Kundry's expression. She has been saved in an earlier epoch of the opera, and after she is saved, we hear not a word of her former desire to die. Others who have sought and found salvation do not die, and it is not Kundry's death wish but that of the failed and maimed leader of the Grail knights, Amfortas, that moans through the final scene. The answer to why Kundry dies is far more complex and has to do with men—and their worlds.

Kundry dies because the opera calls out for masculine closure. Kundry does not die for the sake of men in the way Brünnhilde dies for their sake, even if Brünnhilde, in the end, accomplishes what men could not do—effectuates the needed end of the gods. *That* simply makes her a heroine. Nor is Kundry like Elsa, who also "slowly sinks lifeless to the ground" at the close of Wagner's much earlier Grail opera, *Lohengrin*. Kundry does not die for want of a man or in consequence of some punishment, as does Elsa on losing Lohengrin through her own doing. Nor is Kundry a used and dismissible body over which anxious meetings between men are negotiated and connections between men are made possible and safe. To the end, she acts independently, injecting herself into things, for good or ill, but at her own behest and initiative. She, more generally, is not an instrumentality in men's projects; she is not used, oppressed, manipulated, killed, or discarded. But she is excluded.

Kundry's presence breaks the radial symmetry of the end, the equality of men. At the close in Wieland Wagner's brilliant 1951 staging, men are arrayed spoke-like around and are focused on the phallus—the

Spear of the Crucifixion (fig. 4 above). In an inversion of the knightly military order, fluids now flow not onto the spear but from it—all bathed in a white radiance. In concert with the other Grail knights, Parsifal gazes fixedly at the Spear, which he lofts as he announces the miraculous: "I see the holy blood flow *from* it." For Parsifal and the other Grail knights, *the* Spear, unlike *a* spear but like a cock, ejaculates male bodily fluids worthy of worshipful adoration. And here, too, the Spear, unlike a spear but like a cock, does not produce holes by rending flesh asunder but rather closes holes by filling them: Amfortas's gaping wound is healed by its touch, his physical need satisfied. Male sexuality and its desiring gaze have shifted away from a feminine object; its lure and penetrations are for men alone. Kundry's absence is required so that the values of masculine worlds are realized.

On the path to this sexuality of men and men, a more standard variety of sexuality was in fact the rule. Only two males have been able to withstand Kundry's sexual enchantment. The one is the failed Grail novice turned sorcerer Klingsor, who, vengeful at his expulsion from Monsalvat, plies the Grail knights with heterosexuality through his thrall Kundry and her siren assistants, the Flowermaidens, thereby winning the Spear—power in the old order—when Amfortas succumbs to heterosexuality's temptation. Klingsor can resist and even control Kundry, but only because he has castrated himself. Yet even his castration at Monsalvat—his asexuality—did not give him the requisite "purity" for the Grailhood. He was still rejected.

Parsifal, too, successfully resists Kundry because, well, he is in the end not interested. After the young Parsifal is initially rejected by the Grail knights as being too naive for admission to Monsalvat, he sets off to wrest the Spear from Klingsor. On his approach to Klingsor's ramparts, he expresses interest in the sexy Flowermaidens only as a means of eluding them ("If I am to play with you, give me room!"). After their blandishments fail, Kundry's own attempt to seduce Parsifal takes a more subtle tack. She gets as far as she does with him by making him think that she is his "dear beloved mother." Although she has correctly sensed that his sexuality is out of the ordinary, she undershoots the mark. Parsifal rebuffs her kiss at the very moment his thoughts shift from women to potable male bodily fluids—the "holy blood" in the Grail—which "thrill" him. In consequence, Klingsor's powers and plyings fail. The Spear is Parsifal's.

His passivity and impassivity, rather than the usual knightly fare of battle and killing, gain the Spear for Parsifal. In his subsequent long years of errancy, Parsifal completely demilitarizes the Spear. Although his years of knightly wandering are spent in "countless battles and conflicts," Parsifal never uses the Spear: "This itself I dared not wield in battle; undefiled I've borne it at my side." On chancing again into the environs of Monsalvat, he plants the Spear—now not a spear—erect in the ground and kneels in silent prayer before it, "reverently lifting his eyes to the spear-head." This reverence—which one critic calls "one of the famous imponderables of *Parsifal*" while in the same breath admitting that the Spear is "indisputably a phallic symbol"—is obviously a homoerotic act.[3] And it bestirs the opera's most famous musical passage, the Good Friday Spell, with its wondrous depiction of spring's unfurling and of birth in nature, for which various types of asexual, vegetal reproduction provide the models of splendor. The day on which Christ is penetrated is the day in sacred time on which not even Mary is needed for procreation.

Only Parsifal, now with his obversely limned potent chastity acting as a close marker for homosexuality, can untangle the cosmic mess caused by the last vestige of heterosexual production and of dynastic hierarchy among the knights—Amfortas, sired by the prior chief Grail knight. The "pure" Parsifal alone can restore the essentially masculine to the completely masculine—the now-ejaculating Spear to an all-male world.

Difference, power, and killing within the old order become transformed into affinity between like and like in the new. Sacred beyond trading yet of human origin, the fundamental value ritualistically enacted and advanced in this "sacred dramatic festival" is equality between persons, for which institutionalized homoerotic attraction between males serves as the sign. Salvation is saved in *Parsifal* only when the "pure" replace heterosexuals in a social form in which knights become priests.

II. Three Theses

In this chapter, I will first ask after the proper relation between gender and biological sex for men, where gender—in this case masculinity—is what is socially made of, layered over, imposed on, or even (as some claim) what creates biological sex—in this case maleness—and where man or the manly is the combination and showing forth of the male and the masculine.[4] I argue that gender's appearance, its phenomenological presence, and so in part its social significance, is to a degree biologically determined.

Second, I will ask whether there is something morally objectionable, specifically whether there is something sexist (or even misogynist), in the creation of a male-identified male, that is, a man whose central self-conscious identification is as a masculinely male man and whose *private* moral and erotic concerns and energies are directed toward men with a similar identification. Further, I will ask whether one could build a morally nonobjectionable separate world of such men in closed relations to each other. Is male separatism in some forms morally acceptable or even praiseworthy? I will suggest that such people and structures are not patently immoral and indeed can be found lurking in admirable forms at the fringes of contemporary gay male culture.

Finally, I will try to move beyond both the general perspective that the gay good lies in simple liberation—the allowing of the previously repressed—and the general perspective that minorities are social creations with some powers of self-re-creation,[5] and I will try to advance tentatively an idealization of gay male experience—to position it beyond mere tolerance, beyond acceptance, and even beyond aesthetic celebration. I attempt to recreate for our time a counterpart to the social significance of the facts turned myth of the lovers, tyrannicides, and cult figures Harmodios and Aristogeiton, whose ritualized story and magic names helped stabilize Athenian democracy for over one hundred years.[6] I suggest that male homoerotic relations, if institution-alized in social ritual, provide *the* most distinctive symbol for demo-cratic values and *one* of their distinctive causes. They will help stabilize the always teetering basic structures of democracy, by serving as a model for the ideal of equality.

The Christian metaphysical myth of the immortal individual soul with responsibility for its own destiny has done more to advance the cause of liberty and to undermine the specific thou shalt nots of Chris-tianity itself (and of illiberal governments) than have all the splendid philosophical arguments of John Stuart Mill's *On Liberty*. In parallel, I suggest that a metaphysical myth of male homoeroticism might have a similar benefit for the more elusive concept of equality, clarifying it and causing it to become embedded in social practice more thoroughly than it could ever be through argument and reason.

Although I draw an idealizing picture of male homosexuality, I do not suggest that it is or should be an ideal for everyone or that those who are excluded from the ideal are thereby diminished. For not all ideals can or should be accessible to everyone. Not all ideals are rights. Consider the high end of Catholic sexual morality: the lives of priests are held to be superior to the lives of those who are not priests, and celibacy, as practiced, for example, by priests, is a mode of sexuality morally superior even to reproductive sex; yet no one is held to be a lesser creature for not being a priest, and if every male *were* a priest, the world would be a moral catastrophe, just as would be the case if all farmers grew only cotton because cotton is a fine thing.

Still, *some* ideals should be available to, indeed possessed by, all people. Equality is one of these. It is an ideal to be had as a matter of right. I am, then, suggesting that, when serving as a model of equality, male homosexuality, although limited to some, promotes the likelihood that equality as an ideal will be had by all.

Democracy will not become entrenched by passing out ballots in Bulgaria or through prayers for improved child rearing among white liberal Americans. Democracy will be grounded only when male homo-sexuality is not just tolerated, as something begrudgingly given rights; and not just accepted, as something viewed as an indifferently different life-style; and not just prized, as one admirable thing among many. Democracy will be firmly grounded only when male homosexuality is seen and treated in social ritual as a fundamental social model, when male homosexuality is, as it is in some cultures, treated as a priesthood.

III. Male Bodies

In revolt against natural law theory, which assigns different moral destinies to men and to women by appeal to purportedly morally invested physical properties, feminism, on reasonable strategic grounds, has shied away from placing importance on biological sex. If gender roles could be unlinked from biological differences, then, as social fabrications, gender roles could, at a minimum, change as societies change. In some societies men farm and women weave, and in other societies men weave and women farm, even though in both societies gender roles are thought to be assigned by nature. Gender roles, in this view, could be improved or even abolished by society. More important, such a position holds out, at least in theory, the possibility that, quite independently of one's biological sex, one individually could select or reject for oneself, as from a smorgasbord, various attributes and activities traditionally thought of as strictly tied to just one of the sexes, for example, fire fighting and knitting. Biology need not be social destiny—or so the sloganizing went. And biological sex, in this way of thinking, became usefully restricted at most merely to the designation of genitals.

Roger Brown wittily summarizes this position: "Sex is what's between your thighs, while gender is what's between your ears."[7] Strategically, this *mot* does two things. First, it effects separation. Here sex and gender are as remote from each other as the Cartesian body and soul, operating in different hermetic metaphysical spheres, the soul being, of course, what matters. Second, the *mot* effects erasure. It simply forgets and leads us to forget the vast expanse of the body as we usually think of it—this fleshy thing with organs, senses, nerves and their endings, holes and protrusions, contoured surfaces, and features whose descriptions invite the language of design and intent.

The *mot*'s message—the sexual body is nothing, the sexual mind is all—is helped along by the neo-Idealism of Foucauldian thought. For Foucault, a person's body is a blank slate on which society writes scripts that the person then reads off to find out what sort of person the person is and in that very process becomes that sort of person.[8] The body is merely a barren field across which social forces, operating chiefly by induction and lure rather than pushing and shoving, are exercised. These forces and scripts together are the "true" body, real substance, even the soul itself. The purely physical body is an unrepresentable and ineffective thing, while the "true" body is entirely unnatural, a plume-like emanation or a pod-like excrescence budding forth from but not detaching from the gas cloud–like social mind—or whatever it is that speaks social "discourses"—as it brushes across the tabula rasa of the body. The Idealism is rank: "true" bodies are whatever bodies are thought to be.

Although Foucault does not extend this analysis of the body specifically to sex and gender, others have. Yet it seems to me that only those who had not actually seen anybody's body would be inclined to these currently academically popular views of Foucault and his followers, who take the body as at most an unchalked blackboard or an empty stage fit for any genderal performance. That the body is patterned sexually all over in ways significant to its presence in the world, to its phenomenology, and so to its social significance, even if not its social *role*, can best be seen on a tour of it. Let us begin with hands.

Consider the March 12, 1990, cover of *Newsweek* announcing a feature spread on the current status of gays in America and picturing two bared forearms holding hands (fig. 5). Subsequent letters to the editor on the article harangued that the article and especially the cover photograph constituted a perversion and corruption of youths by gay men.[9] But how did the letter writers know that the image was an image of gay men, rather than, say, lesbians portrayed in stereotype as mannish, sporting rolled sleeves and squared nails? Well, the answer lies in the hands, especially the far-from-limp wrists, especially the hair and veins breaking across the wrist bone. The hands are each unmistak-

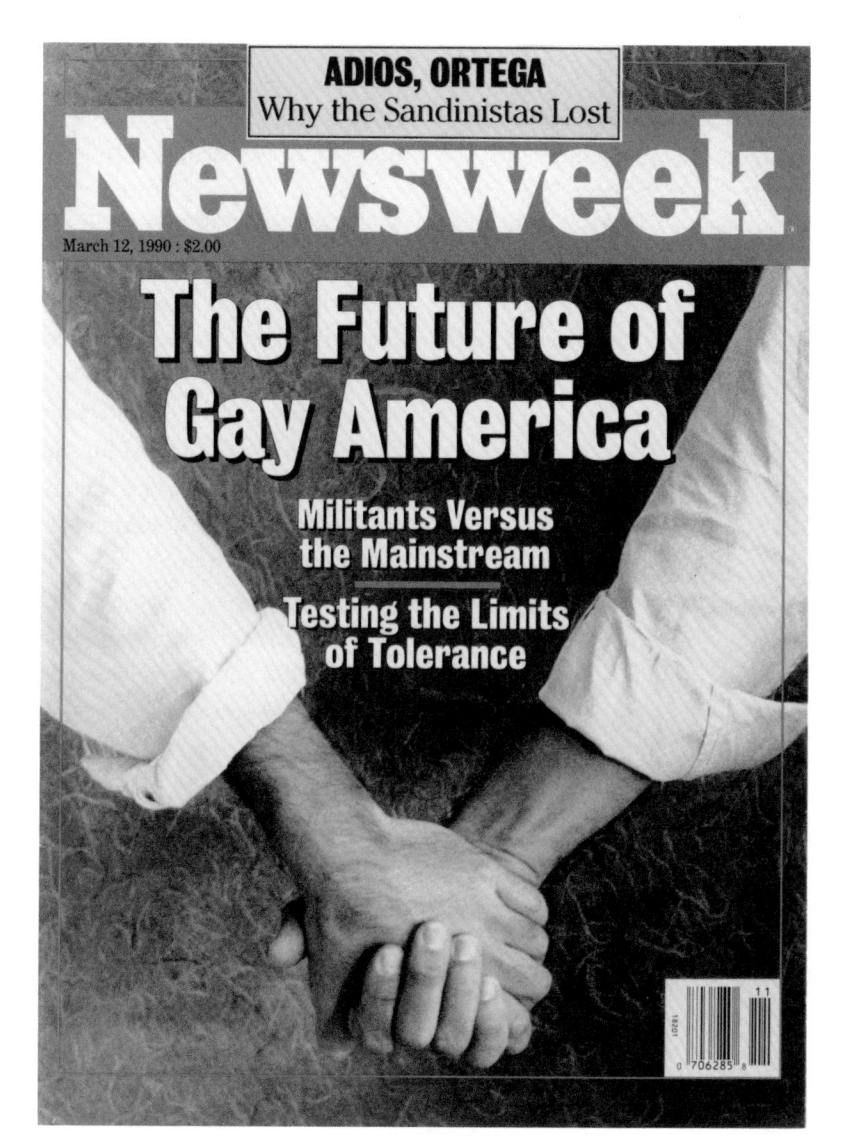

FIG. 5: *(Courtesy* Newsweek, *Newsweek, Inc.)*

ably—rawly and by nature—male. It was not some coded gesture—surely not hand-holding—that gave their sex away. Cock and balls do not alone a male make. The very means—organs—by which we chiefly engage the world (possess it, have it, touch it) are sexed by nature.

Indeed, there is a trick to determining whether someone is a drag queen or not. Don't look at breasts or pereniums. Look at wrists. Even if shaved, their size, shape, veins, musculature, and bone will reveal them as male—if they are. Neither gestures nor even gloves do any good as disguise. For one's wristbone and the width of one's palm cannot be so easily masked. There they are: the hands presenting the queen to the world—throwing kisses, accepting dollar bills, and accompanying with exaggerated gesture a lip-synched song. Sometimes by trade convention, the drag will do something, wear something some way, that is supposed to give the illusion, give the secret away—say, sequining rather than shaving a moustache—as though without that bit of artifice—the giveaway—one couldn't really tell and he really would appear, in toto, female. But this mind-comforting stratagem is as self-deluding as that of the Persian rug weaver who intentionally introduces a flaw into his rug to guarantee that it is not as perfect as Allah—as though without the controlled flaw there would be no others, thus recuperating for the weaver the arrogant and false belief that he does after all control the perfection of appearances. Through the stratagem of the giveaway, the drag arrogantly and falsely supposes that he controls the perfection of appearances when in fact, if it could be said that nature has intentions, nature makes the drag's sex an open secret. It is nature, not the drag, that gives away the drag's sex. Gender cannot be an artifice perfected contrary to nature—contrary to what is given in nature. Gender for the drag is an artifice pierced and undercut in its metaphysics by nature. Structurally, all drag is gender-fuck. The two are just different political readings of the same arrangement of images and materials. Gender-fuck—hairy guy wearing jackboots and a chemise—sends up the politically oppressive roles attached to gender, while standard drag panders to those roles. Gender-fuck challenges by resisting the socially compelled identification of a gender with a sex. It does this, not by presenting gender as a performance, but by presenting a false, because inverted, matching of natural sex and social gender. Gender-fuck says one can be free of the gender roles that have been socially assigned to one's sex. Drag simply affirms the social validity of gender roles by ritualistically pledging allegiance to them.[10]

Now, what is true of hands is true of feet. Even in the absence of any glimpse of genitals, facial features, or chest, do we have any doubt at all of the biological sex of the figure in George Platt Lynes's 1936 photograph *Cyclopes* with its bare feet thrust toward the camera? It is obviously male (fig. 6). Or take the bronze Charioteer at Delphi. Its angelic face is nearly sexless in its fixed, staring intensity, but jutting out from under the severely formal Doric pillar of a chiton are feet so gnarled, so roped with veins, so closely modeled on nature that they could only be the feet of a man.

So in general, that with which we reach out from the typically clothed sectors of the body—that with which we touch the world and on which we stand with it—come, in natural part, without gesture, performance, or decor, as male.

What of the typically clothed body, the realm of the "nude"? What, say, of chests? Consider Joel-Peter Witkin's 1982 photograph *Canova's Venus* (fig. 7). In it, Witkin works a double transubstantiation. There is a Galatean transformation of the marble of Canova's 1804 *Venus* into the flesh of the photo's Venus. And there is another change of substance. Witkin tinkers with voluptuous Venus herself. Witkin's subject is voluptuous for sure, but has changed sexes. How do we know this? Well, if you look very closely at Witkin's Venus, Venus has a penis—plump and tucked in the V shape of the swaddling draperies. But this aside, the figure is obviously male because of the accentuated tuft at the sternum and fronds of hair, luxurious and patulous, reaching across the upper chest—not a rug or piece, but the figure's own natural fur.

Body hair, however, gives a clear example of the way gender *roles* as social assignments float independently of biological sex. (I have not been denying this.) Given that furriness is a natural attribute of maleness—not all, but *only*, males have chest hair—at first appearance a

FIG. 6: George Platt Lynes, *Cyclopes*, ca. 1936. (*Copyright © Collection Jack Woody.*)

FIG. 7: Joel-Peter Witkin, *Canova's Venus*, 1982. *(Copyright © Joel-Peter Witkin. Courtesy of Pace/MacGill Gallery, New York, and Fraenkel Gallery, San Francisco.)*

certain oddity arises in gay male porn. Even though contemporary gay pornographers decidedly emphasize the masculinity of their models—hunkiness and muscle are all the thing—very rarely do gay pornographers use hirsute models, indeed so rarely that hairiness is noted as a "specialty item" on a par with bondage or watersports in porn catalogs. This inversion of expectation shows that gender-typing in social projects is largely independent of biological sex. Hairiness is dropped from gay male porn, for while it is naturally male, it socially connotes age, and the typical consumer of porn does not want age in his fantasies unless he is specifically looking for a daddy or bear type. Here, biological distinctness is neutralized by an overlay of social gender on the body.

On the other hand, completely unsexed parts of the body have traditionally been sites of extreme gender polarity, most noticeably ears and their lobes. Until quite recently, for a male to wear an earring was to run the risk of being labeled a homosexual. Even now, with new wave and new age gestures in the direction of gender-bending, virtually never does one see a male with a single set of matching earrings—the mark of the Eisenhower woman—and even then, as in a famous George Michael video and a not so famous Marlene Dietrich film, the matching hoops code to safely masculine pirates and "gypsies." So gender customs can both diminish (even neutralize) bodily differences between sexes and also create and demand social differences where no bodily difference exists. We do not then even need drag or gender-fuck—one needs only perception—to know that at least *some* social dimensions of gender must be a matter of, have their source in, artifice, not nature.

––––––––

There is another natural truth, natural disclosedness of chests and maleness, one suggested by Robert Mapplethorpe's 1986 photograph *Chest* (fig. 8) and a unique version of the photo that Mapplethorpe produced with the image divided into jointly framed quadrants.[11] There is no doubt that the image is an image of a male. But, moreover, the

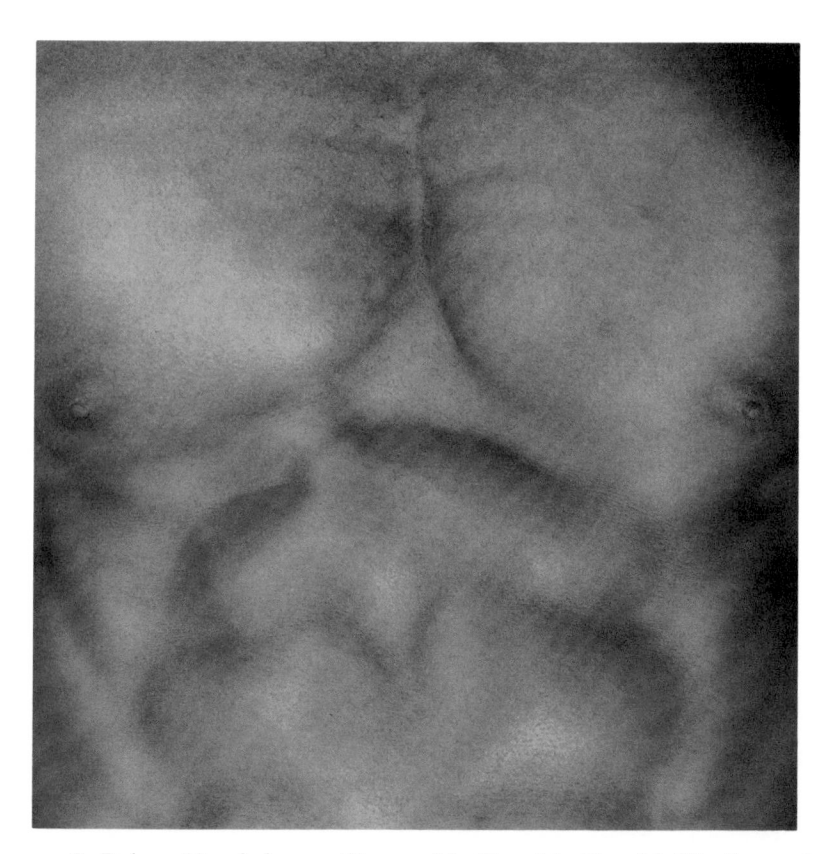

FIG. 8: Robert Mapplethorpe, *Chest*, 1986. *(Copyright © 1986, The Estate of Robert Mapplethorpe.)*

two-by-two layout of the framed photograph's four panes and the attention the layout draws to itself in its one absence—one pane is blank—broadcasts a four-squareness that echoes the natural rectilinearity of male chests and male bodies more generally. The male is rectilinear, not curvilinear. Modernism is essentially male. Henry Richardson's severely rectilinear 1885 Marshall Field Wholesale Store (fig. 9) is perhaps the launch of architectural modernism, especially through its influence two years later on Louis Sullivan's Auditorium Building. Sullivan captured the feel of the Marshall Field Wholesale Store, the only building, not his own, that he ever liked, and at the same time tipped the hand of his own sexuality, when he described the building as "four-square . . . the structure is massive, dignified and simple. But it is much more. . . . Here is a *man* you can look at, . . . a real man, a manly man; a virile force—broad, vigorous and with a whelm of energy—an entire male."[12] Richardson's cubic building achieves this distilled masculinity without appeal in any way to genital sexuality, either cock simpliciter or the socially indicated cock—the phallus.

Some butts are naturally male too, and those that are, like male chests, tend to the rectilinear—as captured magnificently in Lynn Davis's 1979 photograph *Dancer* (fig. 10). It is not still to wonder whether this cropped naked backside is male or female. Other parts of the body are sexed as well: the clavicle, throat, and pores. Biological sex is determined by a single chromosome and, indeed, if I understand recent developments in genetics, is the result of a single gene.[13] The effect of this root biological difference "patterns"—gives differentially distinguishable forms to—the entire surface of the body. Even without reference to genitals, humans are sexually dimorphic, are so all over, and so at least phenomenologically are gendered by nature.

We know this natural engendering as well from the fact that disguising biological sex is extremely difficult, especially if the tool of disguise is a camera. What makes photography such a threatening medium for art about sexuality, the camera's immediacy, its "pitiless glare," is also what makes it a difficult medium with which to disguise biological sex. When using photography to mask, make ambiguous, or invert the

FIG. 9: Henry Hobson Richardson, Marshall Field Wholesale Store, Chicago, 1885–87. Demolished 1930. *(Courtesy of the Art Institute of Chicago, from* The Inland Architect *12 [October 1888].)*

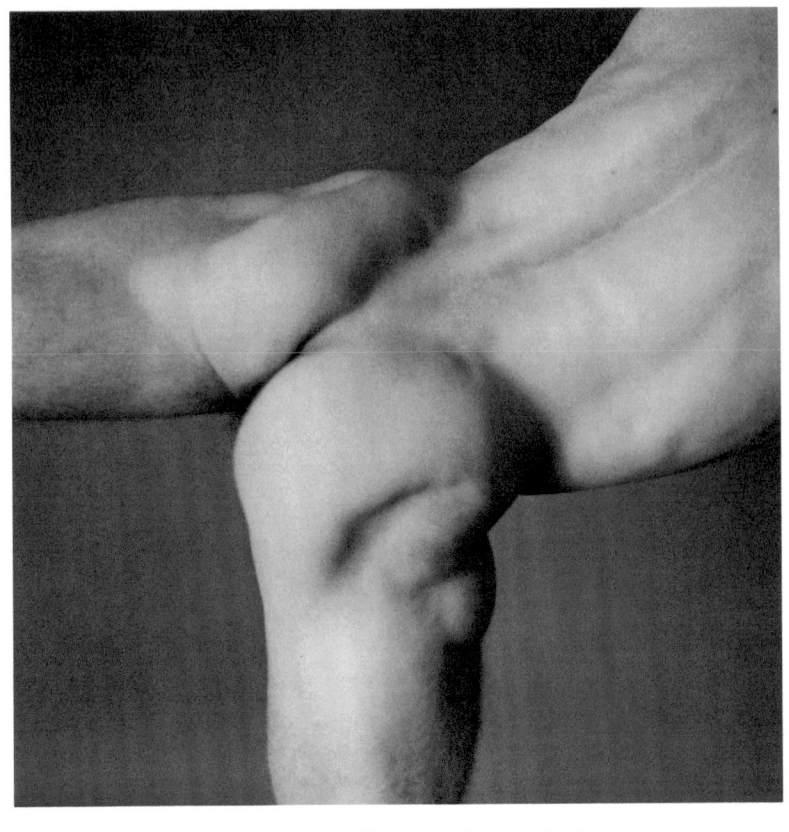

FIG. 10: Lynn Davis, *Dancer,* 1979. *(Copyright © Lynn Davis.)*

perceived biological sex of whole and wholly naked figures, extreme measures must be taken.

Here is a pop quiz. Figures 11 and 12 show two persons of the same biological sex. What sex is it? Each figure is contorted and oddly posed both in relation to itself and against its background. In figure 11, the figure is so contorted and lying atop such a confusing swirl of cloth that it is difficult even to know which side of the image is properly "up." It takes all this (plus probably ignorance of the photographer) successfully to blur the figure's sex without actually blurring the image. In both photos, "successful" sexual erasure requires that the face is occluded.[14]

The attempt to turn naked men into something that reads as female also requires contortion to eliminate the natural pattern of the male body. This attempt usually takes the form of trying to bury the male body under feminine codes. There is the use, of course, of such gendering presentation techniques as maquillage, as in Mapplethorpe's 1980 *Self Portrait* (fig. 13) and the use of makeup together with gesture, as in the belly gesture that is socially coded as feminine captured in Lynn Davis's 1977 photograph *Logan* (fig. 14), whose subject the *New York Times* in 1978 either disingenuously or blindly referred to as a "hermaphrodite," even though the figure's arm veins reveal that it is just a man.[15]

Or again, one can use smoke and mirrors and soft focus to mask sex, as in Mapplethorpe's 1984 photograph of a back, *Vibert* (fig. 15), or one can use drugs, like the figure in Joel-Peter Witkin's 1981 photograph *Androgyny Breastfeeding a Fetus*, who, after one adjusts to the shock of the representation and notwithstanding the photograph's title, is clearly just a pre-op male-to-female transsexual.[16] It is as much the jaw as the genitals that tell us this. Indeed, the face is what gives away the biological sex that Man Ray attempts to mask with socially coded apparel in his 1921 photograph *Rrose Sélavy, alias Marcel Duchamp* (fig. 16). Again, all drag is gender-fuck.

Perhaps the most informative site of the body for understanding the complex relations between sex and gender is not genitals but nipples. Allan Bloom grounds in nipples his whole theory of natural law and its

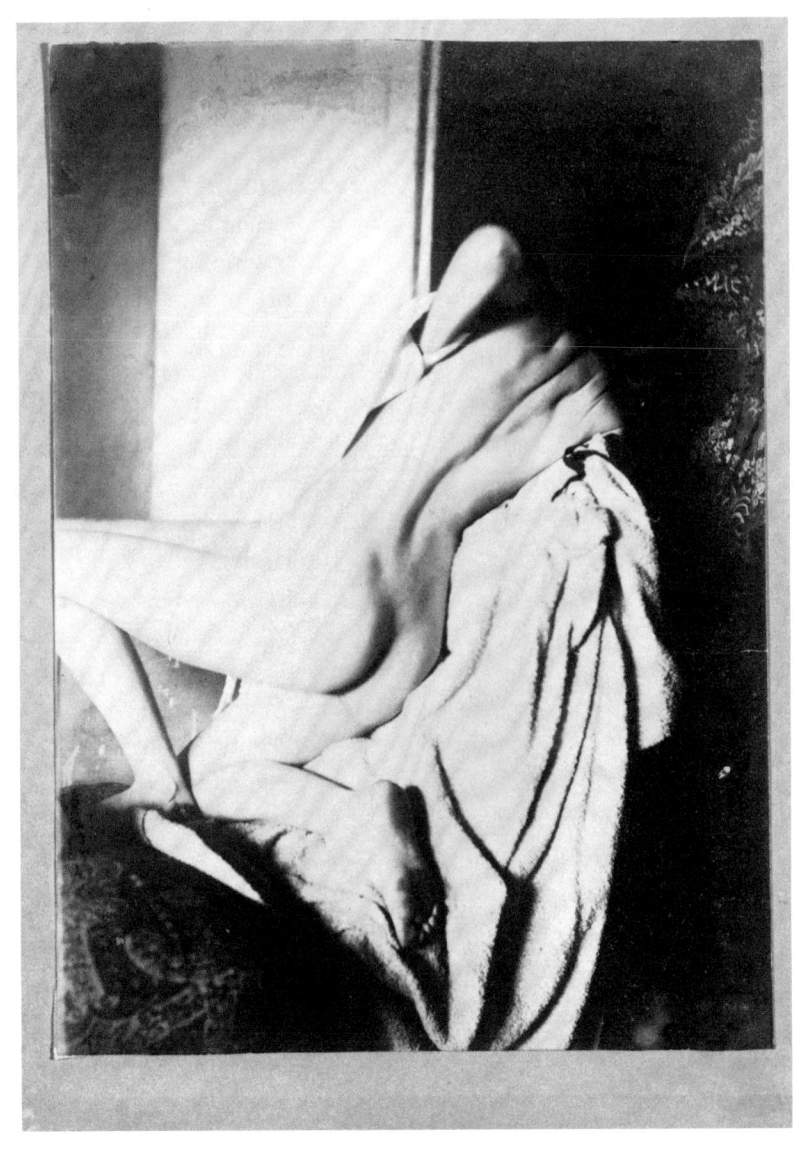

FIG. 11

154

FIG. I2

FIG. 13: Robert Mapplethorpe, *Self Portrait*, 1980. *(Copyright © 1980, The Estate of Robert Mapplethorpe.)*

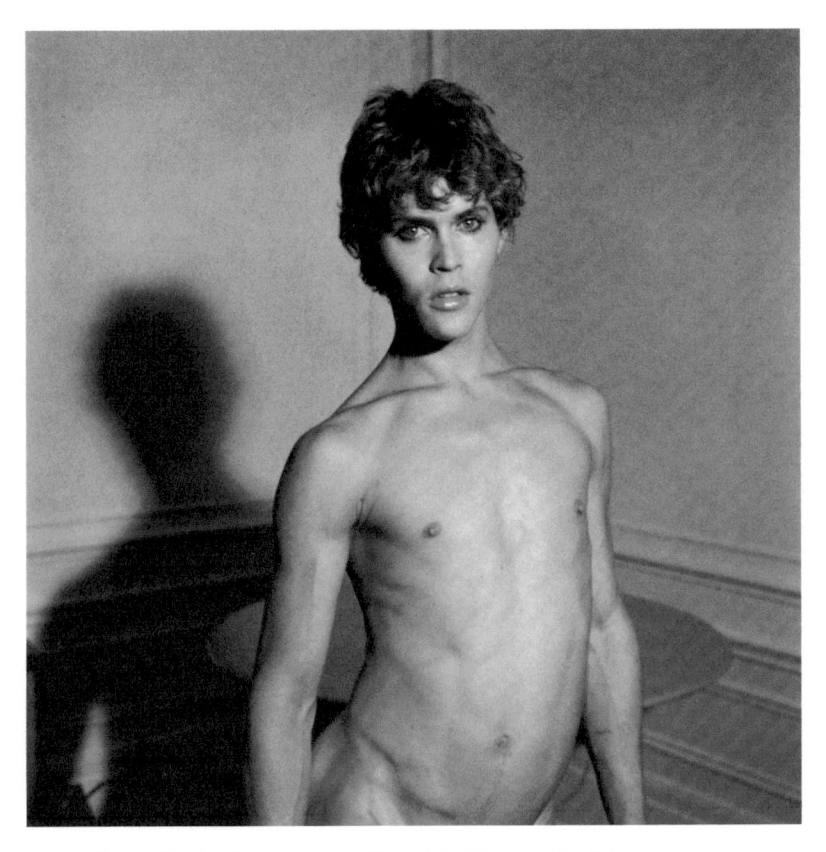

FIG. 14: Lynn Davis, *Logan*, 1977. *(Copyright © Lynn Davis.)*

FIG. 15: Robert Mapplethorpe, *Vibert*, 1984. *(Copyright © 1984, The Estate of Robert Mapplethorpe.)*

FIG. 16: Man Ray, *Rrose Sélavy, alias Marcel Duchamp*, 1921. *(Courtesy the Philadelphia Museum of Art, the Samuel S. White III and Vera White Collection.)*

gender corollary that men and women have different social obligations because they have different physical natures:

> Biology forces women to take maternity leaves. Law can enjoin men to take paternity leaves, but it cannot make them have the desired sentiments. Only the rankest ideologue could fail to see the difference between the two kinds of leave, and the contrived and somewhat ridiculous character of the latter. Law may prescribe that the male nipples be made equal to the female ones, but they still will not give milk. Female attachment to children is to be at least partly replaced with promissory notes on male attachment. Will they be redeemed? Or won't everyone set up his own little separate psychological banking system?[17]

It all comes down to nipples. And from them, Bloom concludes: "The attachment of mother and child is perhaps the only undeniable natural social bond." In turn, from this purportedly nipple-grounded "natural teleology of sex," Bloom generalizes: "Nature is prescriptive."

As with all natural law theorists of my ken, Bloom here falsely presumes that "is necessary for" entails "exists solely for the sake of": females (but not males) exist for the sake of nurture because (absent culture, at least) females are necessary for it. But it would be as good to say that solids exist for the sake of nuclear explosions for without solids there would be no nuclear explosions. No morally obligatory social role can be *legitimately* tethered to biological sex by this style of reasoning.

Still, nipples *are* socially freighted with considerable gender roles. The association of breasts with reproduction and perhaps the association of mother's milk with sperm (certainly in some cultures) prompts some cultures (e.g., ours) to place over the female breast the same obligations to privacy as are placed over the genitals of both sexes. Having mammary glands only vestigially, male breasts are not treated in our culture as linked to reproduction and dissemination and so are not placed under the same conventions. Thus, a woman's naked breast is nude but a man's naked breast is not. Here, society has built up a gender convention that is morally objectionable, in the first place, because the covering of women's breasts serves no function in relation to its biological site yet reduces the liberty of women compared to men. More important, it is also objectionable because the convention's all but unshaken continuation in our culture, like the convention of sex-segregated washrooms, appears to legitimate a whole range of other gender-role discriminations.

The conventions of natalism give physical differences in nipples morally different weights that are unwarranted. Conversely, current convention creates moral differences in nipples even where there are no biologically relevant differences. Male and female nipples have the same very high number of nerve endings and respond similarly to stimulation—and that pattern of response is linked to the erotic stimulation of the genitals. Nipples, like the clitoris and penis, become erect with stimulation; this stimulation is both enhanced by and enhances erotic stimulation of the genitals—the more pleasurable the stimulation, the greater the potential both for further pleasure and for pain. This heightening of sensitivity, paired with the ever closer proximity of pleasure and pain in the process of stimulation, even to the point where the one can prompt the other, makes the nipples, by nature, not convention, a prime erogenous zone and an excellent site for the initial explorations of sadomasochism. When I spell this out to classes on sexual morality, female and gay male students know what I'm talking about right off, but the straight guys just look dumbfounded. The explanation of the different student responses is obvious: in order to distinguish themselves genderally from women, straight men in our society overlook or avoid a determinate natural capacity of their bodies for pleasure. As Masters and Johnson found:

> The techniques of nipple stimulation varied significantly between committed male homosexual couples and married heterosexuals. . . . Only 11 of the 42 committed male couples failed to include some form of nipple stimulation at an early stage of sexual interaction. . . . If penile engorgement was not present before the stimulatee's nipples were approached, it invariably developed during this activity. . . . Rarely did a woman approach her husband's nipples, either manually or orally. . . . No more than three or

four in 100 married men were so stimulated by their wives. . . .
On the few occasions when nipple stimulation did occur, it was
always of brief duration and, with one exception, did not create
an erective response similar to that elicited by homosexual
males.[18]

Tit-play is a regular part of gay sex and gay porn, but for straight men
it is hedged around with all the machinery of taboo: denial and self-
sacrifice for the sake of social values and socially drawn distinctions by
which one invests one's life with significance. For these guys, to have
one's tits played with would be to be a woman, and so these men are
willing to forgo the intense pleasure of tit-play and its syncretistic
interaction with genital-play to solidify their genderal identity as non-
feminine.

Such forgoing of the development of a natural capacity that produces an inherent good—pleasure—is a normative failing of a certain
type. It is analogous to the normative state that would hold if people
failed to develop their natural capacity for language and communication, with an attendant failure to develop knowledge. We have here a
normative failing that rests somewhere between an aesthetic failing and
a moral failing. It has the same unclear status as if one were consciously
to choose ill health. To do so is not a failure to fulfill some duty yet
also not simply the creation of ugliness. It is, however, clearly a failing,
a falling away from an ideal. Consider that domestic cats have virtually
the same natural capacity for color vision as do humans. We have a
ratio of cones to rods of one to twenty; for cats it is one to twenty-five.
Yet color vision is a natural capacity that cats do not use *at all*.[19] The
actualization of that cone-based capacity is "sacrificed" for greatly improved rod-based night vision. The two capacities cannot be mutually
realized. But there is no comparable compensation in those people who
fail to realize their natural capacities for pleasure—rather, the capacity
for pleasure is repressed for the sake of an objectionable ideology. This
repression is, in a quite precise sense, contrary to nature: not a failure
to obey law (allegedly) scripted in nature, but a falling away from
realizing a natural capacity that generates an intrinsic good.

Nature is not prescriptive. Nature is suggestive. Nature does not oblige. Nature hints.

The proper alignment of biological sex and gender, then, would have gender realizing the different capacities of biological sex—which for the most part, as we have seen, have nothing to do with reproduction but have a great deal to do with sexuality, erotics, and arousing attractions.[20] Since biological sex pervades the whole appearance of a male, the male body, sexed all over as a subject, provides a highly determinate natural substrate with specific capacities for development of the male into a nonarbitrary masculine. When masculine presentations build on or actualize natural male capacities, the scents and forms of man, rather than being merely an array of arbitrary conventions and signs, they issue in the hypermasculine—a threshold-crossing intensification of the masculine. This natural but developed masculine body provides, in turn, a natural object for possible symmetrical erotic attractions, to wit, male homoeroticism.

IV. Morality and the Hypermasculine

I now wish to suggest that the hypermasculine is not necessarily morally objectionable, that a male-identified male need not be sexist.[21]

At the turn of the century, one branch of the early German homosexual political movement, the Community of the Special, argued that male homosexual relations were superior to heterosexual relations and did so along fairly straightforward sexist lines. The argument went to the effect that men are better than women, so that men, in admiring and being attracted to what is best, will naturally be attracted to each other, and so too, in pairs, be superior to pairs of one man and one woman and far superior to pairs of women: "Echoing [Benedict] Friedländer, [Hans] Blüher [in 1917] argued that the family was the institutionalization of heterosexual desires while the political state arose from equally natural male homoerotic relations. The true *typus inversus*, as distinct from the effeminate homosexual, was seen as the founder of patriarchal society and ranked above the heterosexual in terms of his capacity for leadership and heroism."[22] I hope to avoid such a layered schema in this project. If one admires the hypermasculine as that which dominates, then one contributes to that which dominates. But there are other possibilities.

As long as the hypermasculine is simply the development of natural capacities, it is justified easily along the quasi-moral, quasi-aesthetic lines mentioned above concerning various nonmoral or at least non-obligating goods (like health and knowledge). It should be noted, however, that these nonmoral goods are trumped by moral obligations and moral rights. The value of their development does not constitute a legitimate excusing condition for failing to carry out one's moral obligations and does not override legitimate claims of rights. For instance, although leather enhances the smell of males, the production of leather may itself be immoral as a violation of the rights of animals. In that case, the nonmoral interest in developing the masculine in this way must give way to the higher claim of rights.

The prospect for moral problems arising in the development of the hypermasculine will loom threateningly when the manly—the blend of male and masculine—alludes to and draws for its force on social tropes that are traditionally associated with domination over women or with the exclusion of women in ways that degrade them, either by denying them equal worth as persons or by prejudicially limiting their liberty. Such problems lour even when women do not appear in specific representations of the hypermasculine, as in fact they usually do not. Now, I would be the first to admit that hypermasculine gay culture is awash in images that are frequently used to promote the admiration of masculine domination and that even mentally fix this admiration through orgasmic inducements. And much of gay culture is at least problematic in the way it portrays power. Here fall Mapplethorpe's sexy photographs of black men sitting, posed and perched, on pedestals and George Dureau's sexy photographs of male nude cripples, midgets, and amputees. Do Mapplethorpe's photographs of nude black males parallel the cultural positioning of women as at once princesses and whores? Or do they instead send up that objectionable positioning while at the same time, in their severe formalism, deeply and authentically admire black men? Similarly, George Dureau's photographs may be read either

as affirmations of the physically challenged as sexual agents or as dep-
redations of them as one-man freak shows. What, for instance, is one
to make of a photo of a gay-coded crippled midget in Nazi regalia
posing and posed as though dreaming of the Hitler Youth? I think that
there is no easy moral assessment here.[23]

What I want to suggest generally, however, is that, when the gay
hypermasculine appeals to objectionably stereotypical masculine
tropes, it can and typically does do so in ways that undercut the tropes'
possible uses in the oppression of women. The gay hypermasculine is
not, on the one hand, the product of a trade in or over women's bodies.
Nor, on the other hand, is the gay hypermasculine a flight from or an
avoidance of the womanly.[24] It does not get its charge, its sense of self,
by distancing itself from women and from the derivative slur that gays
are nellies, queens, inverts. Nor does it get its charge, its potency,
through attempting to assimilate to the dominant culture as an effort
to gain acceptance from that culture and thereby indirectly degrade
women. All this can be so even though the gay hypermasculine does in
fact exclude women—from such private and discretionary spheres as
sex, romance, marriage, and religion. The architecture, the temple, of
the hypermasculine is not the Bohemia Club, the Cosmos Club, the
New York Athletic Club—Clubland generally—but the gay bathhouse
and leather bar. Let us look at hypermasculine men first by ones, then
by twos and more, to see my point. My examples are drawn chiefly
from the gay erotic draftsmen Tom of Finland and Rex.[25]

MEN ALONE STIR MY IMAGINATION

Take Rex's 1983 drawing of a kneeling pantless leather-jacketed fellow
with thighs spreading, cock dripping, and finger beckoning the viewer
(fig. 17). Does anyone think that this example of hypermasculinity
could pass for and enjoy the privileges of a straight man, not be taken
as "queer" but as a man of the dominant and dominating culture—a
General Haig or Colonel North figure? Obviously not. Although his
heavy leather jacket might code to the objectionable, oppressive manners of, say, Hell's Angels, he could not, does not choose to try to, pass
himself off as part of biker culture. For, his pose aside, the chain at his

FIG. 17: Rex.

right shoulder says he wants it, wants it from a man, wants it hard from a big man. He is not someone running away from culture's hatred of gays by first embracing manners and tropes from the dominant culture's arsenal of oppression and then enhancing the oppression by making its tropes sexy. A Rex man wants to have sex with hypermasculine men—men like himself.

Frequently, the iconography of gay male dress will blend and crisscross masculine images that, if taken severally, might suggest domination but, when taken collectively, undercut each other, so that no one could suppose that they draw for their charge on an identification of the gay wearer with the dominant culture. Take, for example, Tom of Finland's 1976 hitchhiker (fig. 18). He is nearly naked, yet he is studded all over with diverse signifying adornments. His leather hot pants and popper cartridge code directly to gay culture. But the rest of the outfit is a panoply of accoutrements from various traditionally male trades: a pirate's earring, a biker's tattoo, a gladiator's cuff, a policeman's cuffs, a cowboy's hankie, and engineers' boots. Another such configuration might include the distinctive apparel and signs of soldiers, sailors, aces, punks, lumberjacks, hardhats, roustabouts, truckers, carnies, and stevedores. Yet, clearly, no one would think that in reality our hitchhiker occupied any one of these coded roles: policemen do not wear earrings, and gladiators went extinct before motorbikes were invented. The figure is probably (socially speaking) a lowly barback in a gay bar: his tattoo reads "Tom's Saloon." Here, the masculine is eroticized, but not in a way that affirms the oppressive features of traditional masculine roles. The various roles' iconographies undermine each other. In pinning these uniformly gendered but clashing images on himself, the fellow cannot plausibly be taken to assume the privileges of any—not even one—of the roles to which his adopted postures allude. Indeed, the hitchhiker's total presentational package exposes the stud to the charge "faggot." Far from endowing him with privilege, his public hypermasculine posture exposes him to violence.

Stereotypes are here used homeopathically. The hitchhiker's motley outfit enacts a creative adorational playfulness, a playfulness with a serious message, one threatening to some people. It says: "I sniff, fuck

FIG. 18: Tom of Finland.

with, and love males." Such a figure is an articulation of a male-identified male who is not "one of the boys" and never could be a member of Clubland.

Hypermasculinist imagery can even challenge the heterosexual presumptions on which much of sexism is based. Consider the most famous of the "Cincinnati Seven"—Robert Mapplethorpe's 1978 *Self Portrait* in which the artist lightly holds a whip whose handle is stuck up his chaps-framed, camera-facing ass (fig. 19). The artist's torso, although prone, is so twisted horizontally that his face can leer in three-quarters profile at the camera. Is the photo's subject, or the photo itself, sadomasochistic in some bad way? Does the photo ritualistically eroticize violence? Does it promote violence? Is it on its own, independently of any possible effects on behavior, a humiliation or degradation of someone or some group of persons? Hardly.

The picture is self-consciously but tweakingly political, at once humorous and serious. It is humorous in that the whip is being perverted. The normal function of a whip is to enforce slavery, mete out punishment, and inflict pain. But here it is used as a dildo, an instrument of pleasure. Robert is massaging his own prostate gland—a uniquely male ecstasy, which registers in his happy leer. But his leer is also serious. It aggressively mocks: "Look straight guys, you impenetrable males, tens of thousands of you die each year because you are so fucked up about your assholes and about protecting yourself from appearing the least bit feminine that you won't even let your doctor stick a lubed finger up your ass to find out whether you have the indices of prostate cancer. So just die, fuckers, die."

Gender stereotypes and their daunting consequences for social roles, especially employment roles, derive from the basic structure of heterosexuality: penetrable woman, impenetrable man. In embracing male penetrability, Mapplethorpe attacks the central cultural symbol that maintains the system of gender stereotypes. Far from contributing to sexual and genderal exploitation, Mapplethorpe's photograph challenges the heterosexist basis of such exploitation.

The picture is also humorously political along another dimension. It mocks a recurrent contemporary idea espoused in a 1990 *Esquire* article

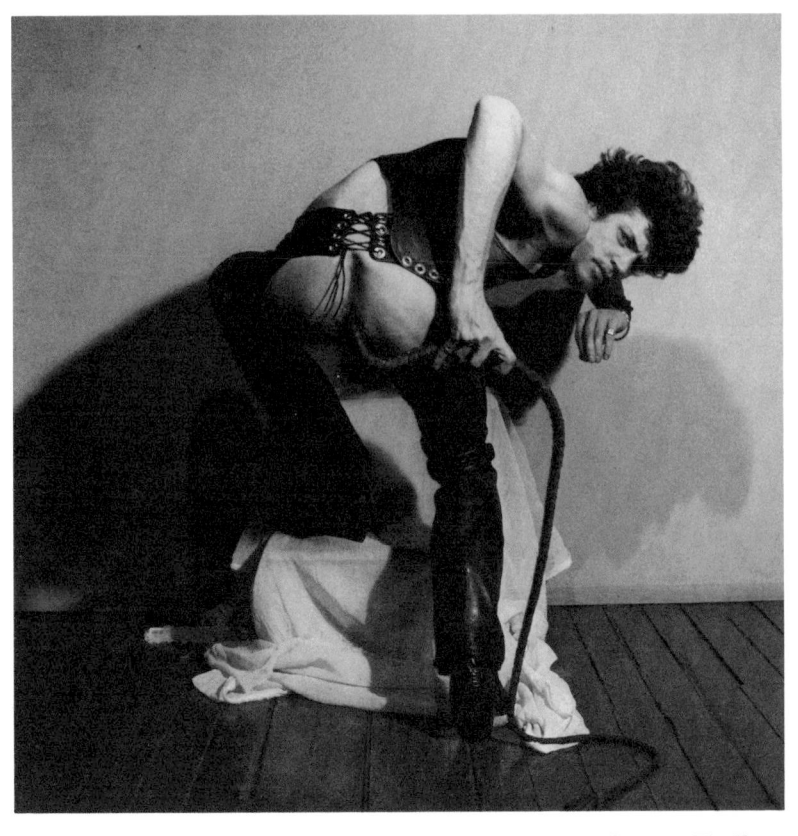

FIG. 19: Robert Mapplethorpe, *Self Portrait*, 1978. *(Copyright © 1978, The Estate of Robert Mapplethorpe.)*

bemoaning a perceived decline in Western letters and claiming that there is a natural animal hierarchy concerning the asshole. The article claims that humans have risen, by 100,000 years, above sexual uses of the asshole—so that (it continues) fags are just AIDS-deserving animals, not human beings.[26] In the self-portrait with whip, Mapplethorpe embraces the animal basis of sexuality. He does this in part by laying on himself the animal, by laying on himself male-identified hides (chaps, bar vest, cowboy boots, bullwhip), not as clothing—as protection or discretion—but as an identification with animality. He further turns himself into an animal by giving himself a tail, a tail so long as to suggest a scorpion, although surely there are touches of satyr and Satan here too. In the context of this sexual lycanthropy, Mapplethorpe's leer challenges, by embracing and twisting, another anti-gay stereotype, that of the gay male as threat to civilization. This aspect of the photo says: "I'm a destroyer, a sexual killer. So there." The current variation of this self-asserting, other-diffusing attack on social definitions of gays is Queer Nation's slogan: "We're queer. We're here. Get used to it."

Far from eroticizing violence and indirectly putting down women by celebrating domination, Mapplethorpe's hypermasculine self-portrait is a dismantling of the conceptually incoherent but socially firm alloy of anti-gay stereotypes, a mix that holds that, on the one hand, gay men are supposed to be passive wimps and nellies and yet, on the other hand, they are the gravest molesting threat to society.

Does all this suggest some understanding of what might count as liberation? Sarah Lucia Hoagland has noted that liberation is not chiefly or simply a throwing off or overturning of the oppressors.[27] On that model, even if the structures of power allowed for such an overturning, the oppressed simply become the new oppressors—a lesson of applied communism in the twentieth century. But I do not think that Hoagland's own metaphor of liberation as "a moving out from under" oppression is quite right either. For this model fails to take into account the all-too-lasting effects of life under oppression. It is naive to suppose that one can just leave oppression behind and not carry along its effects, especially its effects on and in one's thinking and self-perceptions. After

171

decades of society's flickering the gaslights, one must be cautious about one's ability to evaluate what is there to free and what it is to be free. Rather than taking the overturning of oppression or the evading of oppression as models, I suggest that, in the face and under the burden of inherited sexual typographies, liberation is to be found in a *working through* of past oppression, a working through in which the constituents of oppression become morally diffused by being incorporated into and transformed in the self-creation of an oppressed minority's development of a positive ideology of and for itself.

One is liberated, not (simply) by coming to see that the constituents of oppression are artifices, but in the making of something new out of the old evil ways in a manner that defuses what was evil about the old ways. That minorities do in fact adapt and transform social tropes and stereotypes shows minorities as self-creating, self-constituting communities rather than creatures created or constructed by others or by society as a whole. As far as minority identity goes, stereotypes, like the elements of language, are given materials with which to work, not determining social forms. Liberation is not achieved by trying to jump over stereotypes. They do not go away simply by our willing them away, or through our knowing that they do not map reality, or even through our imagining finer worlds, past or future, without them. Rather, liberation must work back through them and only then get beyond them. James Baldwin has made a similar observation about the role of the socially received past in the black liberation movement:

> In order to change a situation one has first to see it for what it is: in the present case, to accept the fact, whatever one does with it thereafter, that the Negro has been formed by this nation, for better or for worse, and does not belong to any other—not to Africa, and certainly not to Islam. The paradox—and a fearful paradox it is—is that the American Negro can have no future anywhere, on any continent, as long as he is unwilling to accept his past. To accept one's past—one's history—is not the same thing as drowning in it; it is learning how to use it. An invented past can never be used; it cracks and crumbles under the pressures of life like clay in a season of drought.[28]

MEN TOGETHER, MOVING TOWARD EQUALITY

The same structures of liberation—liberation through overcoming rather than overturning or eluding—can be found in the interactions of hypermasculine males. Indeed, such compounded masculinity can serve as a test case for the structure. For the doubling up of the hypermasculine might be expected to intensify and so more easily reveal the dynamics of oppression and subservience if in fact such evils are there lurking in, entailed by, but hidden within the hypermasculine. The stakes are high, but I will argue that hypermasculine interactions hold out the possibility of serving as models of equality.

Yet a mere similarity of hypermasculine appearance between two males is not enough to convey a social ideal of equality. At first thought, an equality of the appearances that mark out one's identity might be taken to suggest an equality in meaning, significance, social role, and status between the partners portrayed. And some striking gay images seem to have this point as their point. It is suggested in the sinuous formalism of the cupped bodies in Mapplethorpe's 1985 *Ken and Tyler* (fig. 20), whose sublimity of parallel lines harks back a century to Thomas Eakins's paintings of racing scullers. Formalist equality appears in humorous shape—humorous because so intentionally over-done—in the hourglass symmetry of two Tom of Finland leather boys of 1963[29] and in a whimsical form in Arthur Tress's terrific 1979 photograph *Bikes and Lovers*—whimsical because the two guys portrayed are so alike that even their bicycles can pair off as they do.[30] Formalist equality can take a more explicitly political form, as in David Hockney's 1961 painting *We 2 boys together clinging*. Here, clutching male figures kiss in a red and blue storm, which sweeps their hearts disparately away from them, writes, like a lightning strike, the word "never" across their lips, and decapitates them jointly with the words that make up the painting's title, an ironic adaptation of the title line of one of Walt Whitman's sunniest poems of carefree, buoyant camaraderie.

None of these images suggests any differentiation of roles or actions between the male pairs; in their press toward equality they rely merely on parallelism, repetition, and unstressed symmetry. As humorous, sublime, or politically correct as they may be, they are too simple.

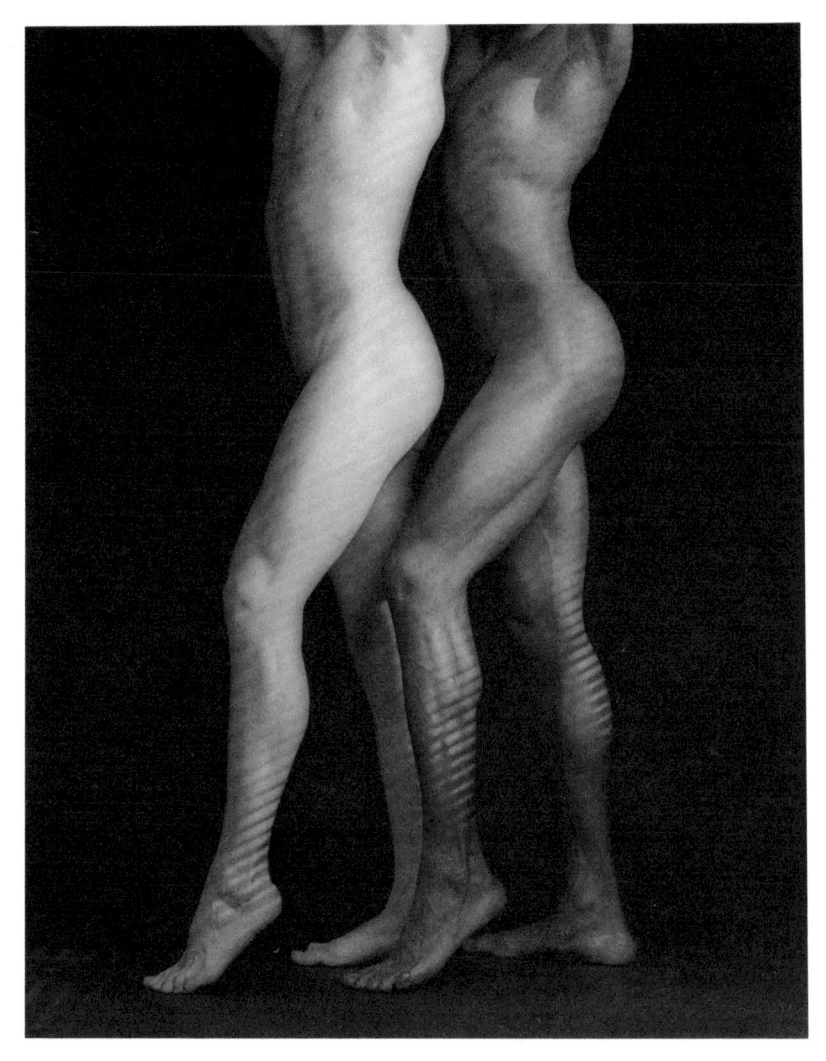

FIG. 20: Robert Mapplethorpe, *Ken and Tyler*, 1985. *(Copyright © 1985, The Estate of Robert Mapplethorpe.)*

More interesting as probes of equality are the stressed symmetries of what might be taken as the first homoerotic paintings in America: George Bellows's boxing pictures (1907–24) and the somewhat earlier Thomas Eakins and George Luks scenes of nude youths wrestling, paintings in which naked or near naked men touch and engage for the first time (figs. 21 [Bellows], 22 [Luks]). This touching, intertwining, and frottage all proceed under a ruse that pornographers would use even through the 1960s to avoid prosecution—the military's anxiety-driven self-deception that, if two men are fighting, they can't be fucking. Unlike armies at war, the figures in such athletic contests, although in competition, touch each other both on the basis of a presumed generalized equality of resources and in social roles that view them as equals. However, the problem with viewing an athletic contest as a model for the ideal of equality is that, although players start in equality, they end in inequality. Someone wins, someone loses. At most the model could serve as a symbol for the operations of independence or freedom. An eroticized athletic competition could not properly serve as a symbol for the equality of respect that democracy presupposes.

In contrast to Bellows's pugilists, take Duncan Grant's drawing from the late 1950s *Two Nude Figures, Embracing* (fig. 23), which erotically desublimates the work of Eakins, Bellows, and Luks. Here we have equality achieved, not through formalism and symmetry, but through a complex operation of interpenetrating and reversing roles—strikingly imaged through a judicious use of the techniques of cubism. But for the men's kiss, the tangled figures could almost be viewed as wrestling. The drawing is electric with the statics and dynamics of engaged struggle. Does the drawing convey, however, the structures of competition, of domination and submission, of winning and losing, of greater and less? At first glance, it might appear that the figure on the right is dominant. His head is higher, his arms engulfing and more thickly limned than those of the figure on the left. The drawing might even appear to be an imitation of a Hollywood kiss and embrace; indeed, Grant did at least two (not very successful) heterosexual variations of this drawing.[31] But look again. At a minimum, the dominantly drawn thighs of the figure on the left engulf the figure on the right and form the base for

FIG. 21: George Bellows, lithograph, *A Stag at Sharkey's*, 1917. (*Courtesy the National Gallery of Art, Washington, D.C., the Andrew W. Mellon Fund.*)

FIG. 22: George Luks, *The Wrestlers*, 1905. (*Courtesy of the Museum of Fine Arts, Boston, the Hayden Collection.*)

FIG. 23: Duncan Grant, *Two Nude Figures, Embracing,* ca. 1960. *(Copyright ©
Collection of Douglas Blair Turnbaugh.)*

the pyramidal structure of the whole drawing. And though the left-most arm, graphically the most dominant feature of the drawing, would at first appear to belong to the large fellow on the right, it is really too long and sprouts from the wrong shoulder for that to be the case, or at least exclusively the case. Rather, drawn twice, the left-most arm can be seen in cubistic displacement as (also) belonging to the guy on the left, who then, as one would expect in affectionate erotic embrace, reaches to and controls the crotch of the figure on the right, who is presenting his genitals to that very end. An electron cloud of lines forming the ambiguous placement of arms and shoulders obliterates into mutuality any trace of dominance and submission and wraps the two men in the cosmos and privacy. Here we have equality achieved not through bland similarity but through a diffusing working back through of the structures of domination and submission.

A more blunt working through of oppressive roles can be seen in the work of Rex. Consider a gloryhole scenario (fig. 24). Its stud hero is laden with images of masculine dominance—leather jacket, Stanley Kowalski T-shirt, boot socks, jockstrap, and well-cured raunch. Yet he has taken the middle of three booths linked with gloryholes. This post, together with his seated position, is the typical posture taken by those seeking insertee roles in washroom sex. The surface geography of the scene would have him be the cocksucker of common parlance and give him the passive, submissive, "womanly" role of common thinking. Yet, twisting roles again, here, as at many a gay blowjob site, it is the sucker who is in control calling the shots. He attends in the first instance to his own pleasures, not giving in to the demands of his hole-piercing boothmates, not assuming a self-conception as servicer of and for others, a conception that would diminish his own agency. Indeed, in his studly "passivity" he has even induced desire for him as agent in the manhandler on the right, while putting the cool on the assertive guy on the left, whose posture—stiff dick wholly pressed through hole and twitching in open air—is difficult to maintain for any length of time unattended. The gloryhole neutralizes the insertor as dominator. There is cocksucking, but no facefucking, in traditional gloryhole sex. Thus, the geography of the gloryhole site, with its occluding of the tradition-

179

FIG. 24: Rex.

ally active posture of the penetrator, allows our stud, despite his glazed-over mind and intense oral fixation, to maintain a comprehensive sense of his own agency and to see himself completely on a par with those who would seek his services. Here, tropes of domination are taken up and reinscribed into a whole that asserts equality of persons. Raunch and sleaze—solvents of hierarchy—are two of life's great equalizers.

Or take a two-frame sequence of a Tom of Finland trio on a fence (figs. 25, 26). Two men are simultaneously fucking a third in the ass. This logistically tricky scenario is a gay fantasy more thought about than enacted. Its fantasy appeal for the gay fucker is that, while fucking, he is also stimulated by that which chiefly defines the object of his desire, the male signifier, the cock. It is a hypermasculine enhancing of the masculine with the masculine.

Still, the image is fraught with two possible heterosexual associations—the double fuck and gang rape—that might, in an objectionable way, provide some of the image's high charge. The double fuck—one cock in her cunt, another in her ass—is a staple of heterosexual pornography. But unlike the scenario of Tom's trio, in the double fuck the two fuckers do not touch each other sexually; the thin membrane between their cocks provides miles of ideological distance between them and homosexuality. Socially, they can reach each other in ideological safety only through or across the woman. In the double fuck, the woman is totally possessed, compressed, sandwiched, and immobilized between the men penetrating her. They bond with each other by bonding against her, like unfriendly nations drawn together by a common enemy.

By contrast, in the Tom of Finland sequence, the third person, the fuckee, is in the open. In his squatting position, he controls the fucking. He is not "topped," and, indeed, as we learn from the second frame, which shows the fuckee's orgasm, his pleasure comes first—ecstasy for everybody, but especially the fuckee. And, surprise, as we also learn in the second frame, far from being an aggressor or some counterpart to an assailant, the backward-leaning fucker is in bondage. Indeed, that his wrists are bound to the fence rail is what makes the topologically tricky act possible in the first place. The gay trio represents a building

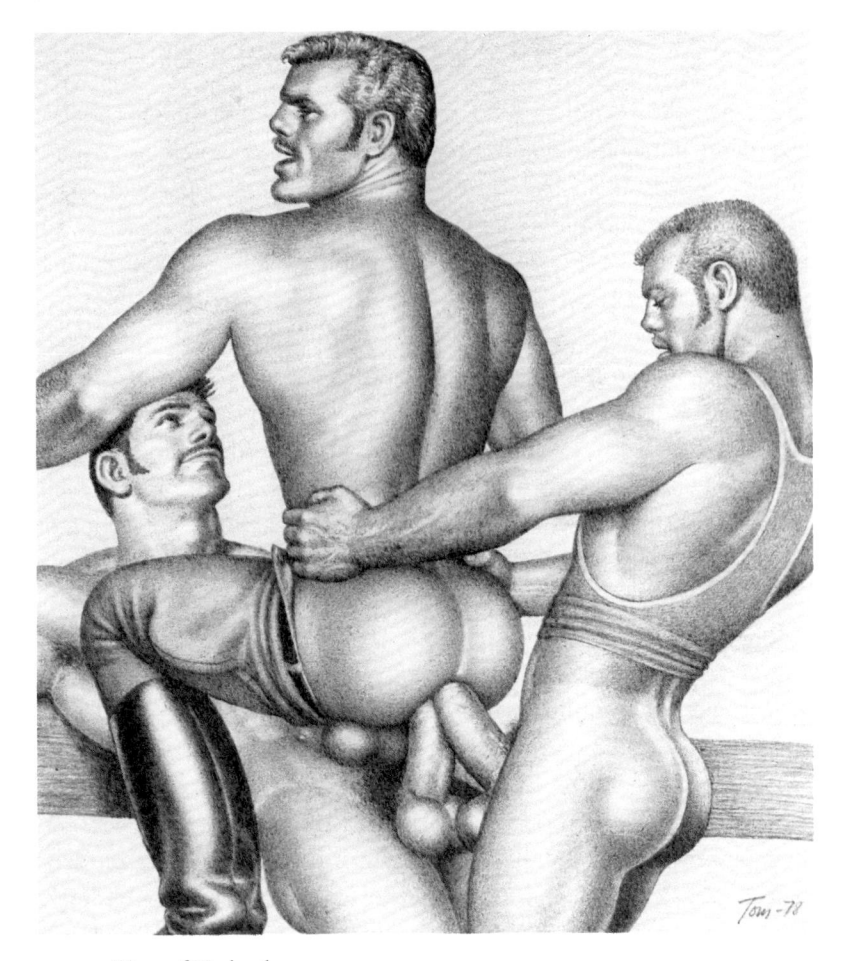

FIG. 25: Tom of Finland.

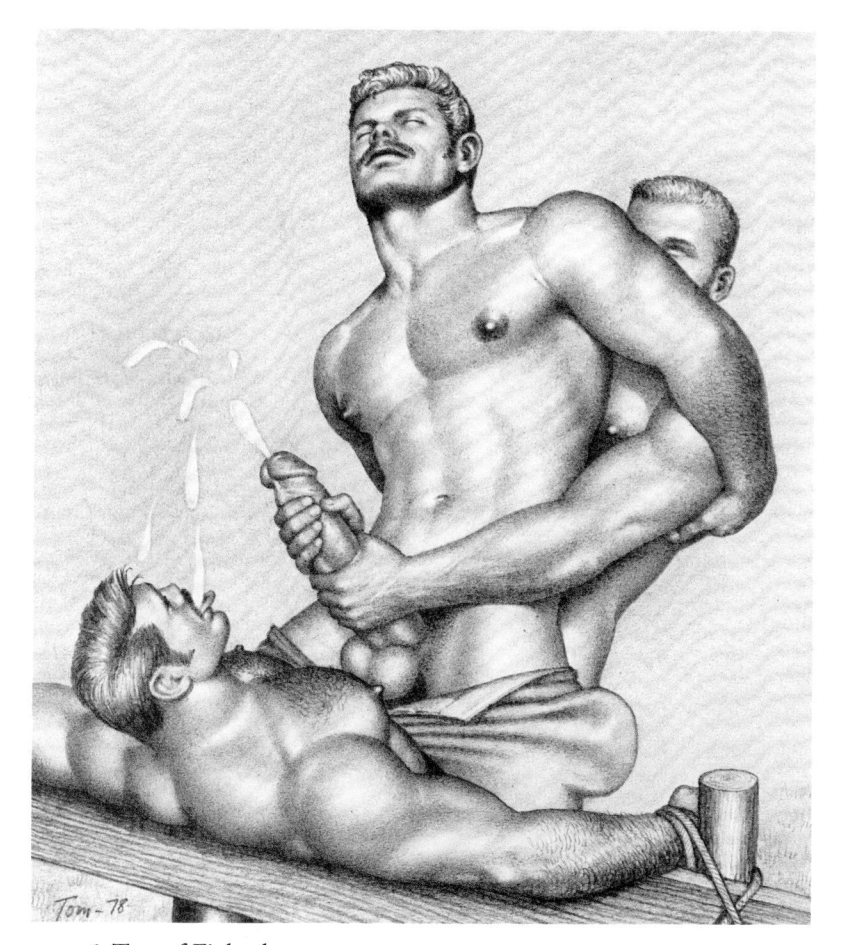

FIG. 26: Tom of Finland.

of community and a commonality of interests; the heterosexual double fuck is raw physical exploitation for refined but objectionable ideological comfort.

The fence series too provides a moral and sexual desublimation of heterosexual gang rape. Who, it needs to be asked, has sex with whom in gang rape? The typical gang rape is perpetrated by men in closely bonded groups: fraternity brothers, team members, street gangs, military personnel.[32] And in the typical gang rape, far more force is used against the woman than is needed to assure her possession by the raping cohorts. If the act of trapping her itself does not cause catatonia through battery, the first few sexual assaults do. In gang rapes, women pass out—if they are not knocked out first. The rapists neutralize her. Without her resistance or fear, the rapist can hardly be stimulated by the thrill of power, of domination, and the woman herself is reduced to nothing more than a masturbatory aid.

With whom are the rapists having sex? Where is the object of the rapists' arousal? It is in each other. Physically, the rapists are quite literally having sex with and in each other's cum. Cum, the masculine essence, is the excited excitable presence in gang rape. Mentally, the rapists project onto the woman the consent that they themselves bring to the rape, so that, "as a gang rape proceeds, . . . as each successive man takes his turn the woman is increasingly viewed as 'a whore' who deserves to be raped."[33] It is each other as sexual agents whom the rapists find sexually exciting: "It is extremely common for sailors to form pairs of buddies, who really love each other though they won't have sex except by having a threesome where they both make it with another person (a woman or a gay guy), often at the same time and watching each other. It's not unusual for a group of sailors or Marines to all fuck the same girl, and occasionally also have sex with the same gay guy."[34]

In gang rapes, men have sex with each other, sex that is ideologically rehabilitated by the presence of a woman. In gang rape, then, we see *not* how sexism generates anti-gay attitudes, how, that is, views about women are used to put down gay men viewed as "the womanly." Rather, the dynamics of gang rape show how anti-gay attitudes—the blockages to men fucking each other in masculine worlds—lead to the annihilation of women. But hatred of women is not the motivation for gang rape, as is claimed on some analyses.[35] No hatred of women is required on the attackers' part; rather, society's hatred of women is taken by them as a permission to attack.[36] In pack rapes, the victimization of women is the *practice*, but dread of gays is the *theory*, even while homoeroticism is its *motivation*. The hatred present in gang rape is hatred of possibly being identified as gay. Far from pandering to the clotted dynamics of heterosexual sociability, then, the gay trio series shows what is wrong with them and offers a positive alternative for the establishment of comradeship.

The erotic desublimation and moral untangling of structures of exploitation can be found even in the sexual pairings that seem to upset the most people—gay sadomasochism. Thus, in Mapplethorpe's 1979 photograph *Elliot and Dominic* (fig. 27), the iconographic allusion to the Roman martyrdom of Saint Peter ceases to be an eroticizing of death, and the pictograph of the expression "having someone by the balls" ceases to portray a cool act of violent coercion. Rather, both actions— inverted crucifixion and clutched balls—are taken up into what I take to be a kindly, caring, uniquely gay, classic marriage portrait. The marriage portrait is a genre that in its hypermasculinized, leather-clad version is a fixture of Mapplethorpe's portrait work, for example, his 1979 photograph *Brian Ridley and Lyle Heeter* (fig. 28).

In the traditional heterosexual marriage portrait, the husband sits on a chair; the wife stands somewhat behind and to the side of the chair and places her hand on his shoulder. Variations are possible: some other instrument, for example, can replace the chair, as in Grant Wood's *American Gothic*. In *Elliot and Dominic*, the four spokes of a cross of chains have replaced the four legs of the traditional husband's chair, abolishing the possible suggestion that "Saint Peter," now in the "husband's" role, is a subservient member of the pair. Similarly, it is the seated "husband" who is chained up in *Brian Ridley and Lyle Heeter*. Whatever is stern in these pictures—and it is certainly not "Saint Peter's" face—is exactly the stiffness and intensity that one expects from

FIG. 27: Robert Mapplethorpe, *Elliot and Dominic*, 1979. *(Copyright © 1979, The Estate of Robert Mapplethorpe.)*

FIG. 28: Robert Mapplethorpe, *Brian Ridley and Lyle Heeter,* 1979. *(Copyright ©
1979, The Estate of Robert Mapplethorpe.)*

the overly posed nature of marriage portraiture: no one looks natural, no one looks relaxed, friendly, or themselves in such photos. So too here. Marriage portraits are public renewals of vows, renewals of the public sanctifications that constitute wedding ceremonies. Elliot and Dominic, centurion and saint, here gazing at the general viewer's gaze, are publicly sanctifying their relation, although, for them, the ritual is a renewal without antecedent. It is a dateless eternity.

One of the more frequently remarked of the Cincinnati Seven, Mapplethorpe's 1978 photograph of a fistfucking, *Helmut and Brooks*, in its stunning, contrived formality and impassivity is also probably a marriage portrait (fig. 29).[37] In keeping with the genre, the image consists of two people and a chair. One person is on the chair; the other person nearby touches the person on the chair, while both stare in the same direction. But here all the elements are intensified into a particularly hypermasculinized form. The chair is the butchest piece of furniture ever designed by God or man—the throne-like, oak-piered, through-tenoned, leather-bolstered Morris chair of Gustav Stickley. And here a hand in the ass replaces the traditionally passive hand on the shoulder.

In fisting, the fisted party is almost always on his back, frequently in a sling, legs raised and approached from above. Mapplethorpe's studied substitution of an unusual prone position for the supine and the placing of the men in the same plane has several important effects. This positioning is the main vehicle of the photo's contrived formalism and impassivity. It distances the fisting represented from fisting's frequent cult associations with birthing manqué. It further dissociates the act from roles of "tops" and "bottoms" and from a sense of risk and danger. The fisted "husband" is cradled by the chair. Indeed, the positioning dissociates the act from sex quite generally. Yet the positioning emphasizes the act as ritual and as ultimate connection. In this gay marriage portrait, the "husband"—the touched one—is at once as butch as can be yet as "passive" as can be, thus blurring and challenging the traditional power roles in heterosexual arrangements.

Now, I am not claiming that gay men are not sexist, only that

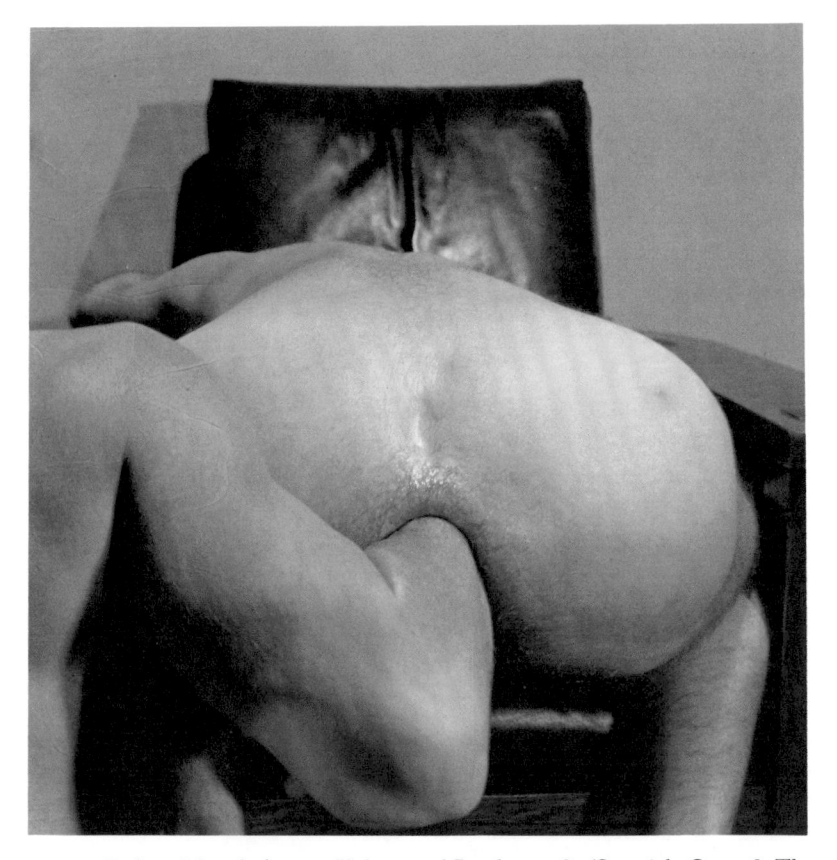

FIG. 29: Robert Mapplethorpe, *Helmut and Brooks*, 1978. *(Copyright © 1978, The Estate of Robert Mapplethorpe.)*

hypermasculinist packaging and interactions do not automatically entail sexism. Some hypermasculinist iconography, I have argued, even provides models for equality. But some gay iconography admittedly is quite objectionable and sexist. One need think only of that great icon of gay male culture, the famous publicity still for the movie *Giant*, in which a genuflecting Elizabeth Taylor plays a long-suffering, all-admiring Mary to James Dean's diffident, self-martyring Christ, who is sexily slumped crucifixion style from a shotgun that he totes across his shoulders. Here, male sexuality—supported by and supporting the iconography of violence, enhancing and enhanced by the iconography of death—is portrayed as the power and the glory that infuses women's lives with such meaning as they are capable of possessing but that also maintains and enlarges itself through its insistence on service, obedience, adoration, even worship from women.

The vast bulk of Tom of Finland's drawings play against stereotypes. But, of the 113 drawings that make up *Tom of Finland: Retrospective*, seventeen appear clearly to make scenes of rape or involuntary domination, usually bondage sex, stirringly erotic—scenes in which the bottom is not getting off on the goings-on but rather is dazed, apprehensive, or even broaching terror. In some ten other images, it is hard to tell whether violence is eroticized. And the only drawing in the *Retrospective* that shows a woman is a classic example of males bonding with each other at women's expense (fig. 30). A woman, in an immaculately domestic setting, watches that locket of domesticity—the home movie. Her husband wittingly uses her as a front for his closeted gay sex life. While he manipulates her vision with images of domesticity, the family vacation perhaps, and while she is taken up into the fantasy world of film, he is quite literally fucking around behind her back. The picture honors his daring and makes fun of her ignorance. There is no end of this sort of refusal on some gay men's part to take responsibility for their sexuality, a refusal frequently achieved at the expense of women, an expense here debited on the ledger of cognition.

On the other hand, there is much that is (probably unwittingly) anti-gay in the representation of men by people who, I think, would

FIG. 30: Tom of Finland.

consider themselves feminists. Joanne Leonard's late-1960s photo collage *Of Things Masculine* pictures a wholly naked, self-indulgently languorous, totally sensual man (fig. 31). Given the received backdrop of cultural signs, his sexiness can hardly but be iconographically taken as gay. Moreover, he dreams on high of cum. His heaven is a celestial river of spermatozoa, the actuality of which in the real world below his feet, however, is mass murder, massacred Vietnamese children. Even before AIDS, John Wayne Gacy, and Jeffrey Dahmer, this photograph managed to equate gay sexuality with mass murder.

Or consider a poster designed by the mixed-gender design group Gran Fury for ACT UP's Women's Committee (fig. 32). It pictures a huge erect cock and bears the title "Sexism Rears Its Unprotected Head." The poster is nominally directed toward straight men: "Men: Use Condoms Or Beat It. AIDS Kills Women." But the poster's iconography completely undercuts its intended result. It is fanciful to suppose that straight men are going to contemplate a magnificent erection poking its way ball-lessly into the frame, as though through a gloryhole, and think that it is anything but a fag's cock. It is "fags" after all who are thought to flaunt their sexuality in our culture—plastering it around everywhere like posters on hoardings. More generally, given the social convention of a presumed male viewer and presumed male creator, any representation of male sexuality is presumptively going to be taken as gay sexuality by mainstream culture, the poster's hoped-for target. But then, since the cock's head is the only head in the picture, the title caption directly calls the erect cock—now gay sexuality incarnate—sexist and, through the caption's play on the stock phrase "rears its *ugly* head," indirectly but determinately calls the gay cock ugly. Then, just to top things off, the poster (what with culture already accusing gays of being the cause of AIDS) accuses gay sexuality of killing women and, perhaps more generally, innocence: "AIDS Kills Women." The poster turns a knife-like gay-coded cock into Jack the Ripper's blade. The poster's advice to straight men—"Use Condoms or Beat It"—is lost in a blizzard of (I hope inadvertent) anti-gay messages. Everyone needs to do better than this.

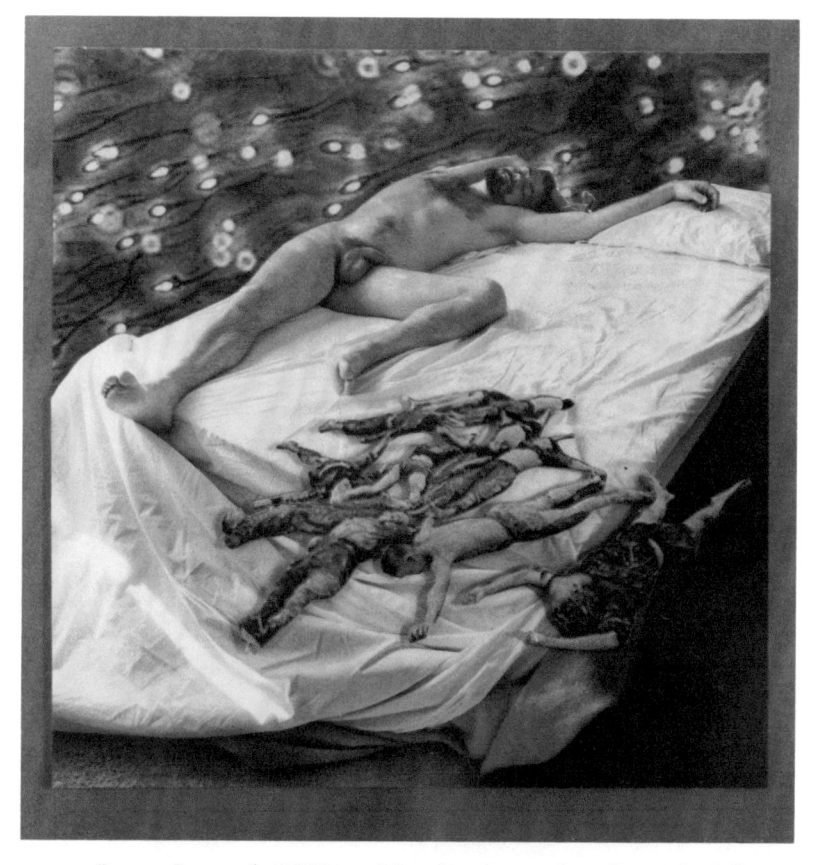

FIG. 31: Joanne Leonard, *Of Things Masculine*, late 1960s. *(Copyright © Joanne Leonard.)*

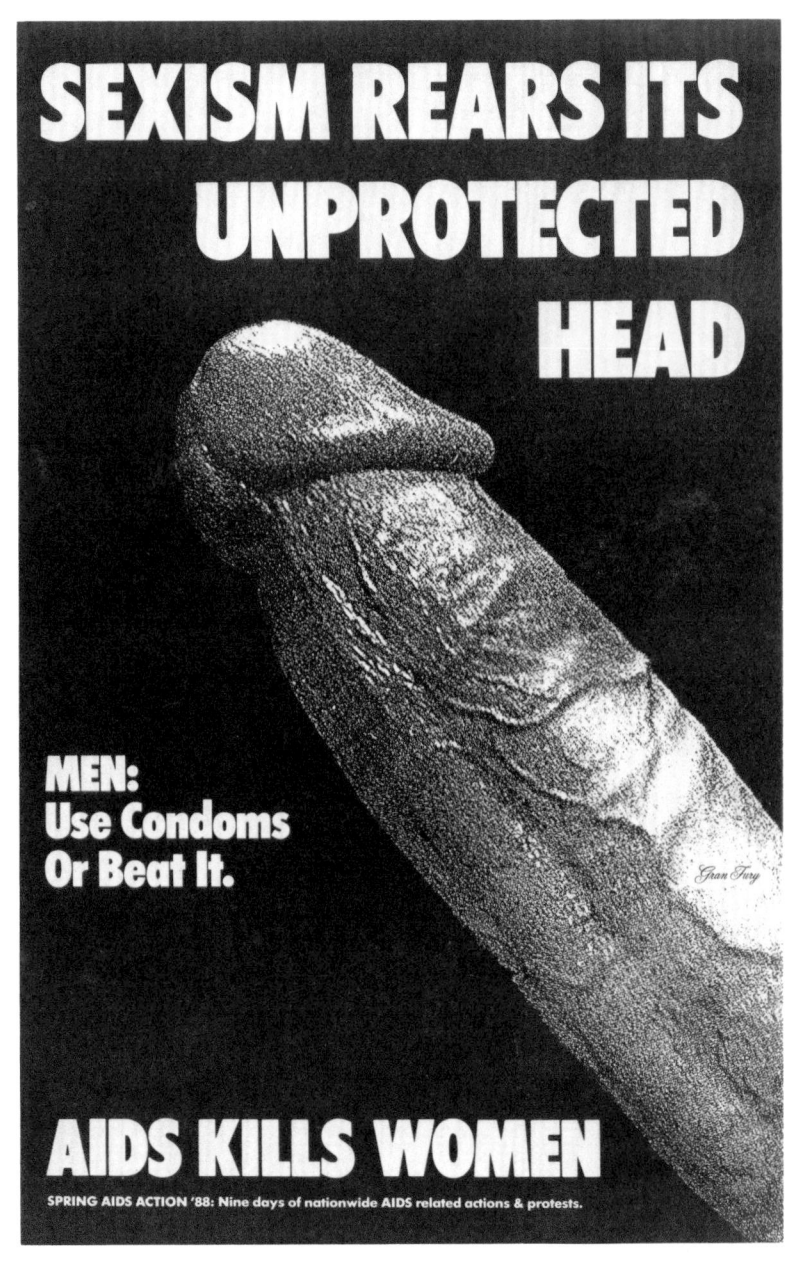

FIG. 32: Gran Fury, Poster, 1988. *(Courtesy Bay Press, Seattle, from Douglas Crimp,* AIDS/DEMO/GRAPHICS *[1990].)*

V. Gay Life and Democratic Equality

Usually, it is thought that gay men's possible contributions to society are at best nugatory, that gays' possibly heightened appreciation and manipulation of appearances—both as erotic source and as self-defense through disguise—have led to contributions in the visual and aesthetic aspects of culture. Some of these "contributions" have been pretty awful, as when gay culture made running wear and gym clothes acceptable street apparel. And, about 1988, fashion hit a low when straight people, aping gay men's masculine eclecticism, started wearing biker jackets with foot-long leather cowboy fringe. On the other hand, the Australian National Ballet successfully, indeed strikingly, drew a bit of gay male culture into the mainstream when it used that staple of the leatherman's wardrobe, the body harness, as the main costume and advertising graphic for its 1990 U.S. tour of *Spartacus*.

This sort of contribution to culture is slight, however, compared to what gay males' contribution might be. The usual defense of gay male sexuality is just that—a defense—usually an appeal to tolerance through the concept of independence or privacy. Gay sadomasochists, for instance, are virtually all libertarians, claiming that, just as capitalism is justified by a general principle of independence, so too are sadomasochistic acts justified—since they are consensual. But even if such libertarian defense could be turned around from apologetics to honorifics—say, by successfully advancing gay male sexuality as an especially glistening exemplar of people taking charge of their own lives—it would still undersell the way in which gay male sexuality might serve as a model for society. Gay male sexuality provides an even better model for equality than it does for freedom. Hypermasculine pairings provide a model for the background sense of equality—mutual respect—on which all other values of democracy depend.

If gay sex is as I have interpreted its representation, then it can serve as a generative symbol for equality. By "generative symbol," I mean a symbol that in part generates or causes to come into being the very thing for which it serves as a symbol. For example, the sun is a generative symbol of light in general, for the sun is both a symbol and a source of light. Gay sexuality of the sort that I have been discussing both symbolizes and generates a kind of fundamental equality—the sort of fundamental equality that stands behind and is necessary for justifications of democracy.

Why democracy? What equality? There are two standard justifications of democracy. In one view, democracy is justified as in some way pooling preferences and so, in the policies generated from it, pointing the way toward optimally satisfying people's desires. This view presupposes that everyone's preferences are equally worth taking into account—one person, one registered preference. Alternatively, democratic processes are valued as being the sites where fundamental human dignity is registered, whether or not the policies that democracy generates end up producing the goods and services that people want. So, for example, at Athens, no matter what one's wealth, talents, or station, each full citizen nevertheless got to vote—voting was what registered individual dignity, registered that each citizen was, at some fundamental level, of equal worth. But for that registration to be warranted presupposes that all indeed are, deep down, equal in dignity. Democracy, then, whether justified by reference to the satisfaction of preferences or the realization of dignity, presupposes that each person is worthy of equal respect.[38] Yet democracy in action, democracy deployed, tends not to respect individuals equally but to degrade some individuals since it exerts power by mere majority counts in which biases go unscreened. Thus, the justification for democracy and the practice of democracy are always in an unstable tension with each other. What would convincingly establish that each person *really is* fundamentally equal to every other and so both socially ground democracy and cut against the tendency of democracy unbridled to degrade some people? By what sort of rituals could needed mutual respect be established as a central social value?

A model for equal respect can be found in erotic, even promiscuous, filiation between males. Such filiations, especially when ritualized, illuminate and preserve equal respect as an ideal, which can then be put into practice universally in democracy. Equality is the ideal, male homosexuality its model, and democracy the realization of the ideal in practice.

Now, lest women and straight males take offense at their exclusion from this model, consider the following analogy, which distinguishes ideals, models, and instances of ideals. Livability is the ideal of a house; a blueprint is the model for the ideal of a house; your nice house is an instance of the ideal in practice. The blueprint, or model, both helps us understand what it is to be a house, that is, understand the ideal of house, and helps us build houses. But your nice house is not a blueprint or a copy of or even an instance of a blueprint. So I am not suggesting that, when, as the instance of the ideal of equality, democracy is put into universal practice, this practice requires that everyone participate in or instantiate the ideal's model, male homosexuality. And no one's life is the worse off or morally diminished by not being part of the model. Everyone—gay, straight, male, female—can have, in the terms of the analogy, equally nice houses. I am suggesting only that people other than gay men might have something useful to learn about the ideal of equality and about its realization from gay men understood as models, although not models merely to be copied or imitated, any more than in building a house one makes a copy or imitation of its blueprint. And I do not mean to suggest that other forms of human experience cannot serve as additional models for democratic liberalism. However, if one leading lesbian social theorist, Sarah Lucia Hoagland, is to be believed, lesbian experience will not provide such a model for liberal individualism. Hoagland has argued that, far from suggesting liberal individualism as an ideal, lesbian relations provide a basis for attack on this ideal and point toward the desirability of communal or communitarian social structures.[39]

Since the idealizing gay filiations that I have in mind as a model are limited to a minority, the realization of the model may require the creation of something like a priestly class of homosexuals, an institutionalized and ritualized social structure frequently found in shamanistic societies.[40]

A GOODMANESQUE MODEL OF GAY EQUALITY

The text for my sermon on gay equality is an autobiographical essay that Paul Goodman published in 1969, toward the end of his life and just at the start of the gay liberation movement. The essay is variously titled "Memoirs of an Ancient Activist" and "The Politics of Being Queer."[41] He writes: "In my observation and experience, queer life has some remarkable political values. It can be profoundly democratizing"—by which he means equalizing or equality making.

First, homosexual relations cut across all social classifications but gender, "throwing together every class and group more than heterosexuality does. . . . Its promiscuity can be a beautiful thing. . . . I have cruised rich, poor, middle class, and petit bourgeois; black, white, yellow and brown; scholars, jocks, Gentlemanly C's, and dropouts; farmers, seamen, railroad men, heavy industry, light manufacturing, communications, business, and finance; civilian, soldiers and sailors, and once or twice cops." A later gay author would make a similar point, describing the neighborly life of urban fellow citizens and using a distinctly gay male metaphor for things more general: "He liked the chat: good basic village chat about the drought or the wind, the graffiti problem, the roses in bloom, the ugly new house that looked like a Ramada Inn. What he had with the people on the block was an unspoken agreement to exchange pleasantries without exchanging names. It wasn't so different from the thing he'd enjoyed at the baths, the cordial anonymity that made strangers into equals."[42] Just as gay sex acts can work back through, splinter, and neutralize roles of domination and submission, so too homosocial circumstances that surround such acts draw into doubt the fixedness of social strata.

Importantly, this sponsoring of equality does not just last for the sex. It is typical for a gay man to draw a substantial part of his coterie of friends from what began as tricks. And friends of one's gay friends are far more heterogenous than the friends of one's straight friends. Goodman remembers: "Many of my lifelong personal loyalties had sexual beginnings. . . . My hunch is that homosexual promiscuity enriches more lives than it desensitizes."

And so a second equality emerges, not just the "negative" equality of social types disregarded, but a positive, filiative equality: gay sexuality generates friendships, which are relations that can hold only among people who are basically equals; the "friendships" of master and slave, and of husband and wife in role-divided marriages, are shams and phantoms. In addition, friendship makes equality, makes things more equal. The things of friends are common—not by conventions that bind, but through intimate understanding that prompts sharing.

Yet another, a third, democratic equality emerges from gay sexuality as a mode of cognition. Goodman writes:

> In most human societies, of course, sexuality has been one more area in which people can be unjust, the rich buying the poor, males abusing females, sahibs using niggers, the adults exploiting the young. But I think this is neurotic and does not give the best satisfaction. It is normal to befriend and respect what gives you pleasure. St. Thomas, who was a grand moral philosopher though a poor metaphysician, says that the chief human use of sex—as distinguished from the natural law of procreation—is to get to know other persons intimately. That has been my experience.

First, from the way a person presents and bears his body to you, from the way he touches and attends your body, you learn immediately what the person's values are; one learns whether his concerns extend beyond himself, whether he is patient, whether he is inventive, whether he is attentive and caring or whether he is manipulative and self-centered, whether he can rise above social expectation, and, importantly, whether he respects himself. And when we know something moderately, at a minimum we tend to be tolerant toward it, even if it isn't our cup of tea, even if it's a little disgusting.

Second, the values likely to emerge cognitively during sex are still not entirely up for grabs, not entirely neutral or random. For in sex acts, as at once open and binding, and as pleasurable, there is a general force in the direction of affection. "It is normal to befriend and respect what gives you pleasure." This truth about sex is part of the reason why high blazes of passion can arise so quickly in the gay male world of multiple sex partners. When things click, they click. And when opportunities to click are great, actuality follows. Love—the real thing—at first fuck is not unusual. Masters and Johnson's study of gay men found that gay men are more attentive in lovemaking than straight men: there is a "higher level of subjective involvement of committed homosexual couples in sexual interaction compared to that evidenced by married couples."[43] Masters and Johnson conjecture that this is so because gay men know each other's bodies better, know better what to expect from each other, are more able to enjoy their partners' pleasures, are more varied in sexual technique, more communicative during sex, and bear less social baggage about sexual performance than straight men. All these are characteristics that hold of gay men generally, not just men in committed relationships. Masters and Johnson also found that gay men have more violent sexual fantasies than do straight men. Yet, as their committed couples study showed, this fantastic violence does not translate into reality. Surely one of the striking features of gay bathhouses is that, despite the megawattage of the sexual currents and tensions running through them, they are completely peaceful, quiet, nonviolent spaces. This lack of violence in gay male sexual institutions and acts, despite fantasies to the contrary, and despite the trappings of S&M styles, both betokens and generates respect and equality between gay men.

Third, male homosexuality diminishes possessive jealousy. When one is both self-confident in the control and completeness of one's body and able freely to give it to others, one has no need to own someone else's body like a prosthetic device or to worry about what others are doing with their bodies. This is not to say that one does not run into all of jealousy's bile and putrefaction in many a closed gay male relationship. It is on the basis of such self-control and completeness of body and freedom from Aristotelian and Christian notions of physical and functional complementarity in sex that gay men approach each other as equals in sex and life.

Fourth, and finally, after mansex—well, at least mansex in a bed or in a park—people don't light cigarettes and stare blankly thinking, "What now?" Rather, gay men tell each other their stories. It is the intimacy and the equality-generating nature of gay sex, I think, that prompts the stories, which in turn generate a new kind of equality. For in these stories, typically, life stories, a person shifts from being perceived as mere congeries of types—of virtues and vices, actions and sufferings—and emerges as a personality—the product of chance and choice, of pluck and luck, and of responsibilities taken. The uniqueness of personality is what makes life, morally understood, valuable and perhaps indeed should replace practical and abstract reasoning as the criterion of the human.

In their recognition and promotion of personality and material completeness, self-sufficiency and attentive independence, in rankless friendship and intimate knowledge, and in their nonpossessive valuing wrought of robust mutual pleasure, gay male relations serve as a general model of equal respect.

OTHER MODELS OF GAY EQUALITY

To clarify, it is not—or not particularly—in the bondings or mutual attractions that constitute or flow from homosexual pairings that I find a model of equality. My Goodmanesque model is not a model of two people glued together into some whole better than the both of them. Such relations of bonding and attraction better lend themselves as metaphors for a model polity of a communitarian or civic republican stripe. And as far as I can make out, this latter type of polity is what Walt Whitman has in mind when he seeks to model "democracy" on homosexual relations. He does not seem to be thinking of democracy as majoritarian political decision making when he holds that the very possibility and hope of "democracy" lies in male homosexual relations or in what he, absent the later coinage "homosexual," called "adhesive" relations between males. Whitman claims that the "special meaning" of his "adhesive" poems—chiefly the *Calamus* cluster from *Leaves of Grass*—rests in their "political significance": "In my opinion it is by a fervent, accepted development of Comradeship, the beautiful and sane affection of man for man, latent in all the young fellows, North and South, East and West—it is by this, I say . . . that the United States of the future, (I cannot too often repeat,) are to be most effectually welded together, intercalated, anneal'd into a Living Union."[44]

The emphasis here on unity and collectivity far outstrips any possible hint that what he is trying to ground is a principle of one man one vote. Whitman's vision is of the United States as an organism—a living union—rather than as a means for establishing and sustaining rights of individuals, the purpose of government espoused, say, in the Declaration of Independence. In his essay *Democratic Vistas*, the synonymous designations "manly friendship," "fervid comradeship," and "adhesive love" are compared, in an extended metaphor, to the "threads" that make up a "half-hid warp" that undergirds and binds together the national fabric.[45] They are explicitly contrasted to "individualism, which isolates" but which Whitman admits is necessary "for very life's sake" and even takes as a "principle" that acts as "the compensating balance-wheel of the successful working machinery of aggregate America." Individualism has its uses, but the aggregate, caused in its deepest and effective forms by manly friendships, is where value lies for Whitman. In the poems themselves, the equality that emanates from the "intense and loving comradeship, the personal attachment of man to man," is also essentially conveyed by metaphors of multiplicity bound into permanent unity rather than of the establishment of autonomous individuals:

> The dependence of Liberty shall be lovers,
> The continuance of Equality shall be comrades.
>
> These shall tie and band stronger than hoops of iron,
> I, extatic, O partners! O lands! henceforth with the love of
>   lovers tie you.
>
> I will make the continent indissoluble,
> I will make the most splendid race the sun ever yet shown
>   upon,
> I will make divine magnetic lands.[46]

What is needed to ground democracy as majoritarian policy-making is not people eternally yoked of spirit, if not also body, into a single project: one can have tight unities of extreme unequals, as in traditional marriages and slave galleys. What is needed for democracy is a compelling sense of why we should take other people seriously to begin with—other than because some of them are fearsome.

Homosexual relations operating in a matrix of consent and filiation, cleaving between the purely libertarian and the purely communal, create and sustain just the right balance between self and other to provide the mutual respect needed to model democracy.

———

Another literary thinker, the late French philosopher and novelist Guy Hocquenghem, has offered still another comprehensive vision of gay male sexual relations as models for the good society. In his remarkable 1972 book *Homosexual Desire*, he writes (and I quote at length so you won't think I'm making things up):

> Homosexual desire is a group desire; it groups the anus by restoring its functions as a desiring bond, and by collectively reinvesting it against a society which has reduced it to the state of a shameful little secret. . . .
>
>   . . . Possibly, when the anus recovers its desiring function and the plugging in of organs takes place subject to no rule or law, the group can then take its pleasure in an immediate relation where the sacrosanct difference between public and private, between the individual and the social, will be out of place. We can find traces of this state of primary sexual communism in some of the institutions of the homosexual ghetto . . . in Turkish baths, for example, where homosexual desires are plugged in anonymously. . . . The grouping of the anus is not open to sublimation, it offers not the slightest crack for the guilty conscious to infiltrate.
>
>   The anus's group mode is an annular one, a circle which is open to an infinity of directions and possibilities for plugging in, with no set places. The group annular mode (one is tempted to spell it "anular") causes the "social" of the phallic hierarchy, the whole house of cards of the "imaginary", to collapse. . . .
>
>   Grouped homosexual desire transcends the confrontation. between the individual and the society by which the molar ensures its domination over the molecular. It is the slope towards trans-

sexuality through the disappearance of objects and subjects, a slide towards the discovery that in matters of sex everything is simply communication.[47]

Here, in the book's last paragraph, anonymous gay sex is viewed as a model for the Leftist dream of the collapse of oppressive social hierarchies, particularly patriarchal or phallic hierarchies, and for the disappearance of the allegedly invidious distinctions between private and public, self and others, individual and society. The vehicle of the dream's realization is the anus treated, not as a passive hole, but as an omnivorous agent indifferently taking on and in anything that can plug into it. The anus's annularity is both the symbol and the site for the realization.

There are at least two things wrong with this model. First, the dream's moral and metaphysical foundation, which Hocquenghem finds in the annularity of the anus, seems mislaid. Although round, amazingly round, the asshole is in fact not approached indifferently; gay ass fucking is like straight vaginal fucking in that it is done, differing orifice shapes notwithstanding, in only two positions—"missionary" and "doggie." This odd oversight by Hocquenghem means that he has really left the penis and its particularities out of his sexual model and so, simply by omission, overcomes the structural and functional differences that the penis and ass play in homosexual intercourse. To imagine the ass as a desiring subject (like the mouth, e.g.) hardly does away with the difference between doing and being done, action and passion, agent and patient—even if, as desiring "thing," the ass is no longer *merely* something done, used, dominated. But who with an experienced prostate gland would have thought that anyway? The model cannot get rid of hierarchies that it holds to be based on functional distinctions simply by overlooking the distinctions.

Anyway, in real-world cases, it does not appear that desiring orifices do the moral work that Hocquenghem supposes they do. Societies where vaginas are viewed not as merely passive receptors but as desiring appetitive agents, as Hocquenghem would have the anus be, are no less sexist, gender divided, and hierarchical for having this view. Men of the Mehinaku people, forest-dwelling Amazonian Indians, tell this story:

> In ancient times, all the women's vaginas used to wander about. . . . While Tukwi slept, her vagina would crawl about the floor of the house, thirsty and hungry, looking for manioc porridge and fish stew. Creeping about snail-like on the ground, it found the porridge pot and slid the top off. . . . As the vagina slurped up the porridge, a man awoke and took a brand from the fire . . . and scorched the vagina with his torch. Oh, it scurried back to its owner, slipping right back inside her. She cried and cried . . . she called all the women and lectured them: "All you women, don't let your genitals wander about. If they do, they may get burned as mine were!" And so today, women's genitals no longer go wandering about.[48]

Second, the price at which Hocquenghem would get rid of domination is too high; the price is the loss of human agency altogether—the very agency for the sake of which one supposes one wants to overcome domination in the first place. On Hocquenghem's model, the individual does not become equal with other individuals; rather, the individual simply disappears, disperses into a cloud-like existence of "communication," but communication in which, at least oddly, there are no hearers or speakers.

VI. Why Kundry Dies

We now should have a richer sense of why Kundry dies. Not for punishment. Not because exhausted. Not because she or someone else wills it. Not by accident. Not, in a way, because of anything. Her death is miraculous. It does not have a cause, but it does have an explanation. Her absence is required for the completion of the masculine world toward which the opera presses. Parsifal returns to Monsalvat as a first among equals having retrieved the phallic totem, the Spear, which once, under the old heterosexual order, killed by penetrating, but which now heals men by filling them, thereby transubstantiating, from the merely animal to the meaningful, the bodily fluids that it originally produced through killing. The phallic instrument of death, now sacralized through ritual, becomes the source of similarity and filiation among men, of renewal, healing, and peace.

Alluding silently to the AIDS crisis, San Francisco performance artist Keith Hennessy has produced a similar sacralizing ceremony of bodily fluids transubstantiated from death to healing, from fear to filiation, from waste to art. Echoing Wagner, he calls his works "radical holy male performance rituals." One titled *Saliva* (fig. 33) goes as follows:

> Without ceremony, Hennessy passes a clear glass bowl into the crowd and asks the audience to spit into it. The bowl moves from hand to hand. Some people don't spit; some refuse to touch the bowl at all. When the bowl returns to him, Hennessy mixes in black pigment, adds nonoxynol 9 (from his own bottle of lube), and begins to paint his naked body.
>
> In the audience, there is silence. A moment passes before everyone is breathing again. . . . At the center stands Hennessy with a crystal bowl and a question: "How much connection can you stand?"[49]

The only hierarchy in *Parsifal* is that of development into equality from boys to young men to knights, whose array images the sacred value of equal respect, the ritualistic affirmation of which is the opera's secular point.

One person on whom the opera's message of equality was not lost is Nietzsche. It was Nietzsche's receiving from Wagner an inscribed presentation copy of the text to *Parsifal* that precipitated the philosopher's break from the composer. At first read, Christianity appears to be what Nietzsche found particularly objectionable in the opera: "Incredible! Wagner had become pious."[50] "Richard Wagner, apparently most triumphant, but in truth a decaying and despairing decadent, suddenly

FIG. 33: Performance artist Keith Hennessy in *Saliva*, 1990. *(Copyright © Steve Savage.)*

sank down, helpless and broken, before the Christian cross."[51] But we might well ask, More pious than *Tannhäuser?* More Christian than *Lohengrin?* It is probably not Christianity per se but what for Nietzsche was some fraternal twin to it that repulsed him from *Parsifal* and its maker. What twin? Well, one concept that Nietzsche pairs with Christianity is "Woman."[52] But the pairing of Christian and Woman seems an unlikely branch from which the womanless *Parsifal* is to be hanged. More likely, it is Nietzsche's interpretation of Christianity as a generator of equality that grounds his specific hatred of *Parsifal:* "The poison doctrine of 'equal rights for all'—it was Christianity that spread it most fundamentally. Out of the most secret nooks of bad instincts, Christianity has waged war unto death against all sense of respect and feeling of distance between man and man."[53] As *Parsifal* telescopes the "distance between man and man" to less than zero, Nietzsche just could not stomach it.

The presence in *Parsifal* of boys, who will become the equal knights, is intentionally puzzling. In *Lohengrin's* final, revelatory scene, we learn from the title character that he is a Grail knight and the son of Parsifal, although we do not learn of whom, if anyone, he is born. Yet in *Parsifal* the Grail knights are all sworn to a priestly chastity. Given this intentional confusion on Wagner's part over the parenting Parsifal, we must ask whether there is not some secret that *Parsifal* is trying to give away. What does it hanker to state but pass over in silence? What, that is, does its ritualized masculine world look like if we take up, "sublate," its uncomfortable suggestive elements into a general unified form and then desublimate that form into concrete particulars? This double procedure, this recovery, opening up, teasing out, and clarification of the opera's possibilities, moves along several dimensions.

The amassing circle of equal knights, with which the opera ends, is in part a symbol of marriages of the masculine with the masculine; in *Parsifal*, although not Christianity, the knights-turned-priests are the guarantors of the sacred, not vice versa: "The Savior is saved." It is to each other, then, rather than like nuns to Christ, that they are married.

The amassing circle also marks the establishment of properly private masculine worlds. The knights-turned-priests occupy sacred space, not the public sphere, not the body politic, not the business world. Monsalvat is not Clubland, not a refuge, a retreat, a secret preserve for the hatching of conspiracies that are to be carried out against women in the public and political realms. Monsalvat is a promise that is realized and made good in the gatherings of the gay Radical Fairy movement that are called "fairy circles." Each gathering as a whole takes its name from a specific culminating ritual in which all the participants, communally caked in mud, form a cluster of vaguely concentric rings of men holding men, pressing together with the intention of producing "ecstasy for everyone."[54]

The amassed masculinity of Grail knights, adoring but not touching the flowing phallic totem, also sublates into the touching found in the vanishing functional differentiations of the tightly packed, thickly tangled swarm of struggling naked male flesh that is Michelangelo's 1492 sculpture *Battle of the Lapiths and Centaurs.* Here, the battlers, although nominally of different species, are indistinguishable from each other: "There were the men wrestling with horses as if they were in love. The men and horses were centaurs; they were struggling to be different."[55] And women, although nominally in the process of being saved in the midst of the battle, are wholly absent. But then, it seems the *Battle* is not really a battle either. It desublimates into the orgies of policemen, soldiers, even businessmen from Tom of Finland's fantasy drawings, some of which seem to be modeled after the Michelangelo sculpture. In these orgies, everyone by turns does everything to everyone; the differentiations of doer and done, top and bottom, dominant and submissive, remain as instrumentalities of sex acts but are stripped of moral or political hierarchy. The men are made similar through their sexual bonds, although the bonds are technically, mechanically diverse.

And what specifically of Lohengrin? Just as the Spear of the Crucifixion is obviously a symbol of the potent phallus, the Grail fluids that it produces are transubstantiated from matter to essence, from blood into sperm—of the color of the dove and light that descend over Parsifal—sperm that in its own transubstantiation is, like the divine, like the Paraclete, life giving. The asexual reproduction of the Good Friday Spell is taken up into the human sphere: Lohengrin is a product of parthenogenesis.

Only gay-dreading discourses that view vaginal birth as the only normatively acceptable, because natural, mode of reproduction take such fantasies of male asexual celibate or male homosexual reproduction as unhealthy attempts, in the words of Elaine Showalter, to "evade heterosexuality altogether" and to "reject natural paternity for fantastic versions of fatherhood" and so take the fantasies as insults to women because not only denatured but also denaturing avoidances of them. Showalter presses even further and views such fantasies of male self-creation as contagious diseases that spread "with a particular virulence in the 1880's." (*Parsifal* was penned in 1881.) She supposes that the fantasies represent an "envy of the feminine aspects of generation."[56] They could, however, simply be the result of gay men wanting to have children—no envy involved at all. The difference here between the fantastic and the actual is now simply technology, the magic of the modern.

And what of the boys and young men of *Parsifal?* I do not know whether—actually I doubt that—the gay eroticist Rex has ever heard of *Parsifal;* but one of his densest and, no doubt to some, most disturbing drawings, one of a tattooing scene (fig. 34), offers perhaps the best interpretation of the opera, which has puzzled into interpretative gridlock a century's worth of mainstream readings. The drawing shows how the developmental masculinist hierarchies of *Parsifal* would appear once they pass through the double motion of idealizing sublation and erotic desublimation. A whelp replaces Parsifal's dove, as a sign of the masculine world's harmony with the natural order when that order is respectfully adapted by man. The Grail boys who present Parsifal with a vessel full of male bodily fluids are replaced by a youth who ceremoniously holds, at frame's dead center, a full spent condom—the millennial chalice. The instrument of transubstantiation, the Spear of the Crucifixion, becomes a cock, which itself is undergoing transubstantiation, changing from a natural object into an artwork, into a tattoo, a matrix of dots, like the picture itself. The boy and the dog are our hero's

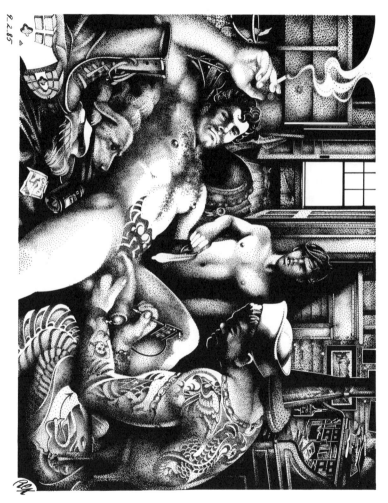

FIG. 34: Rex.

helpmates and colleagues, his future and his past. They are of ambiguous sexual standing, but wrapped in Parsifal's languorous embrace and surrounded by the trappings of the masculine—Budweiser, Camels, logger's boots, a saddle, a jockstrap—they and he together form a world of transformation without exploitation, a commodious, if cluttered, world, a sensuous and sensual world of pride, self-assurance, and self-presentation. As the smoke from his Camel literally frames the scene, our hero, limpidly robust as Michelangelo's *Bacchus*, looks with self-contentment and invitation toward the viewer. Woman is present only as a stock tattoo on the tattooist's forearm. She must be actually absent for the completion of this world of masculine development from hound to boy to man to, finally, a distinctly masculine art.

In 1859, the year Wagner completed *Tristan und Isolde*, the philosopher Arthur Schopenhauer at the age of seventy-one added an essay on the naturalness of pederasty to the third edition of his popular treatise *The World as Will and Representation*. The essay held that, as part of the natural perfection of the human species, "a tendency to pederasty gradually and almost imperceptibly makes its appearance" instinctively in all males beginning at about the age of fifty-four: with time "this tendency becomes more and more definite and decided."[57] Schopenhauer was the largest intellectual force operating in Wagner's work. Wagner was the perfect Schopenhauerite. Whether Wagner himself was conscious that he intended the boys in *Parsifal* to be sexy, or whether that truth "almost imperceptibly made its appearance" there, the appearance has not been lost on Western civilization. After the initial performances of *Parsifal* at Bayreuth in July and August 1882, Wagner—aged, tired, and ailing—traveled in September to Venice, where he died five months later. His death in Venice provided the prompt and title for the classic modern representation of pedophilic yearning—Thomas Mann's 1911 novella *Death in Venice*.

Eleven years later, T. S. Eliot acknowledged in *The Waste Land* that the boys of *Parsifal* were meant to be sexy, but maskingly buried his insight deep in obscure reference and foreign tongue. Just as the androgynous narrator of "The Fire Sermon" hears the horns of cars that will carry Sweeney to liaisons with Mrs. Porter, so too he hears the voices of boys singing in the cupola, voices that will, to complete the analogy, transport him to them: *"Et O ces voix d'enfants, chantant dans la coupole!"* Eliot appropriates the line from Verlaine's poem *Parsifal*, in which the adult male attraction to the singing boys is explicitly one of lust—true, a lust resisted, but nevertheless a desire that in the world of social identifications, if not laws, sufficiently and socially marks Parsifal as a pedophile. This is the only reference to a Parsifal in *The Waste Land*, although Eliot's "Notes on 'The Waste Land'" assure the reader that the very "plan" of the poem is based on the Grail legend.

Virginia Woolf of *The Waves* knew that Parsifal—her Percival—was the shadowy center of a world of male homosexual attractions. Others knew too: "Percy"—the diminutive of "Percival"—became and persisted through the 1950s as a regional equivalent for "sissy" or "fag." And Parsifal's parentage provided post-Freudian analysts the materials out of which they would conjure the purported causes of homosexuality: "A constructive, supportive, warmly related father precludes the possibility of a homosexual son; he acts as a neutralizing agent should the mother make seductive or close-binding attempts."[58] Born posthumously, Parsifal has the ultimately distant father, and his mother's smotherings of him are divinely, or at least bewitchingly, attended by Kundry.

This century has produced two valiant attempts to rescue *Parsifal* from its reception aqueering and to mobilize its ritual for heterosexuality. One is Hans Jürgen Syberberg's sumptuous 1982 staging of the opera on film.[59] The other is Richard Strauss's 1919 opera *Die Frau ohne Schatten*.

Syberberg's movie presents *Parsifal* note for note, but frequently departs from Wagner's stage directions. Virtually every departure attempts to turn the opera into a heterosexual rite that culminates in traditional marriages. Syberberg breaks up the purely masculine world of Wagner's *Parsifal* by tucking girls and young women in among the boys and young men. But rather than continuing this symmetry and introducing women as knights, he pulls a stunt that grabbed a great deal of media attention for the movie. Toward the end of act 2, Syberberg has a very effeminate male Parsifal change biological sex into a very feminine young woman. But just at the point where this textually unwarranted twist might at least be read as progressive gender-bending, it turns out that there really are two Parsifals, one solidly male and one silkenly female. They fall in love with each other. When at opera's end the libretto calls for the shrine to be opened and the Grail to be revealed, the film has the stage set, which consists of an enormous sectional death mask of Wagner, open up to create in Wagner's innermost brain a grotto where the two Parsifals, male and female, now in a nuptial embrace, are substituted as sacred objects for the male bodily fluids called for in the libretto. Heterosexual marriage is here sacralized.

Along the way, the Spear has been dephallicized. It becomes a crosier. At the report of liquids flowing from it, all in attendance are looking away from rather than toward it—and there are no liquids anyway. And Kundry, rather than sinking to the stage dead, is mysteriously crowned and lies down on a nuptial bed beside the healed Amfortas as his queen. So the filmed opera, rather than culminating in an all-male world of phallus worshipers, ends like a pastoral, or an Elizabethan comedy, with multiple heterosexual marriages clutched out of improbable circumstance. This ending would be funny if it were not presented—score soaring, religious symbols abounding—with an infectiously respectful seriousness that succeeds at taking its audience in and deploying the sacred dramatic festival's considerable power for insidious ends.

Richard Strauss knew that the whole opera *Parsifal* was queer and that, even with problems of Lohengrin's parentage aside, the opera's incarnation of angelic boys was skirting dangerously close to an affirmation of homosexual parthenogenesis and the supplanting of the heterosexual world order. He also knew that mere trickery of the sort Syberberg would eventually deploy would not solve the crisis. The opera had to be entirely rewritten, and who better to effect the salvation than he himself—he who had so much in need of proving.

Like glitter-rock bands of a later era, in his early operatic career Strauss had—whatever his actual sexual orientation—coyly flirted with the possibility of being assigned a homosexual identification. In 1903 Strauss set to music the closeted drama *Salomé* penned by the late convicted sodomite Oscar Wilde. Strauss had adopted Salome from Wagner's *Parsifal* musically. Moreover, Salome is the daughter of Kundry in her early life as Herodias. Sander Gilman has suggested that the Pharisees of Strauss's *Salome* are coded as stereotypical homosexuals. Gilman demurs from thinking that Salome herself is "the representation of homosexuality on stage." He admits, however, that the reason "Salome is perverted [is] because she serves as the audience's focus for a set of representations of difference, all of which are understood as perverted."[60] But only one further, suppressed, but culturally supplied, premise is required to convert Salome's necrophilia, incest, exhibitionism, hagiophilia, and other "differences" into codes for homosexuality. That premise is the cultural commonplace that "the historical task of being the idea of a sexual minority personified was performed under the label of 'homosexual.'"[61] All perversions, including Salome's, are weathervanes pointed into the storm of homosexuality. The treatments of multiple sex killings in Strauss's opera are like the liberal press accounts of the perversity of Jeffrey Dahmer's serial sex killings in Milwaukee during the summer of 1991. At the center of a festive orgy of "perversions"—miscegenation, sadism, incest, pedophilia, necrophilia, garroting-cum-buggery, cannibalism, and the like—homosexuality as a perversion was left a felt but unseeable black hole out of which the galaxy of other perversions is born and around which they spiral.[62]

In 1911, Strauss again flirted with possible homosexual identification in the inversions of gender, the play of appearances, and the dazzling effeteness of *Rosenkavalier*. And so, to recover a socially acceptable identity and to save Western civilization to boot, in 1919 Strauss recast the whole of *Parsifal* as a heterosexual pageant play and called it *Die Frau ohne Schatten*—the only major work of Western civilization (I think) *about* heterosexuality.

Frau has the form of a domestic problem play, although this problem play is drawn on a cosmic canvas. The problem that *Frau* introduces only so that it may be expelled at the play's resolution is a sensuality so self-indulgent that it arrests procreation. So great is the problem that it can take that which is so pervasive as to be incapable of attention—the heterosexual horizon of all social experience—and cast it center stage as a dramatic, indeed potentially cataclysmic presence. Charges of self-indulgence and of evading a purported duty to procreate are missiles so typically hurled at homosexuals that they here stand in for and dramatize the concept "homosexuality," even though the opera carefully manages to avoid having any homosexual characters. Order can be restored to the homosexually threatened cosmos only when the boys singing from on high in *Parsifal* become in *Frau* "The Unborn Children"—preborn boys *and* girls singing from a Mormon heavenly Pre-existence of their desire to be born into the world through the mechanics of heterosexuality. Indeed, by the final curtain, "rushing into life like starshine," they are so born:

> *(The light from the central dome grows brighter and brighter.)*
> VOICES OF UNBORN CHILDREN *(from above):*
> Listen: we want to say "Father!"
> Listen: we want to call "Mother!"
> Mount up!
> No, come down!
> All steps lead to us!
> . . . .
> Listen, we bid you:
> strive and suffer,
> that our day of life
> may dawn gloriously!
> What you have endured
> steadfastly in trial,
> for us is wrought
> into a glittering crown.
> . . . .
> Brothers! Friends!
> *(in the orchestra)*
> Father, nothing threatens you;
> see already trouble is vanishing,

Mother, the trouble
that perplexed you.
Would there ever be a feast,
if we were not, secretly,
at once the guests
and also the hosts!

Hosts? In this, the opera's last line, the now newly natal "Unborn" paradoxically announce themselves as hosts to their own parents. They seem to be asserting that having children is the ordering principle of human life: while they *receive* biological life and thereby are guests, they also *give* life, their parents' life, its meaning.

Although the libretto indicates an open landscape as the set for the opera's final lines, the Chicago Lyric Opera's production of the mid-1980s caught the heterosexual spirit of the opera just right and ended it insightfully, if incorrectly, at home: Mom and Dad, formerly childless, are joined at a groaning board by a swarm of hungry toddlers. One can imagine an even more inspirited production where the final set consists of scrims onto which are projected Lennart Nilsson's backlit photographs of fetuses floating whitely in clear, moon-like amniotic sacks, photographs that give the feeling that the fetuses are not merely human but also divine. Someone—Barbara Ehrenreich I think—has aptly noted that these photographs iconographically turn fetuses into "larval angels."[63]

It is heterosexuals who need the comfort of myth in their fantasies of reproduction—not homosexuals. Homosexuals just need technology. Under ideological stress, heterosexual mythology takes the risk of inverting the natural moral progression of child to adult, positing instead a hierarchy of child over adult. Children are the bearers of meaning, women *and men* their receptacle.

In July 1929, almost as a confirmation of this hierarchy, Hugo von Hofmannsthal—the librettist for *Frau* and for all Strauss's other major early operas—suddenly fell dead, seemingly without cause, following the suicide of one of his sons.[64] For Strauss, Hofmannsthal's unexpected death in middle age was as timely as the ritualized heterosexualist world of *Frau* was necessary. With his Jewish partner dead, and with his ideology purified of homosexual suggestion, the way was open for Strauss to become the Nazis' court composer.

Plato thought that the problem with heterosexuals—different sexers, baby makers, whatever—was their lack of eternity.[65] My view is that their problem is lack of equality. Derrida says that the problem with democracy is that it is too homosexual.[66] I say that its problem is that it is not homosexual enough.

Identity

What's wrong with theory?
Altaira Morbius, in *Forbidden Planet*
(1956)

CHAPTER 7

The Thing of It Is:
Some Problems with Models for the Social Construction of Homosexuality

Language is strong, but not that strong; people are weak, but not that weak.

As reality rejects the Left, the Left needs must reject reality.

Nominalism in the history of ideas is like henbit in the rockery: once it is there, you can never get rid of it for good—no matter how good the help. The reason for this is that there will always be some people who are so weak that they are only capable of talk and so come to believe that they can simply chat their way to freedom—by seizing not the day but the discourse.
Chad Rrohmir

I. Introduction

Within the emerging academic discipline of lesbian and gay studies, there is nearly universal agreement among scholars that social factors are in some sense determinant in homosexuality, that homosexuality is culturally constituted or produced.[1] Indeed, especially as espoused by Michel Foucault, this variant of cultural determinism—the social construction of homosexuality—has achieved hagiographical status within lesbian and gay studies, where it is almost always an object for witness rather than of analysis.[2]

This chapter is a dissent from the way in which lesbian and gay studies is now uncritically proceeding. It raises doubts about the leading academic understanding of who lesbians and gay men are and of what a minority is. It does not advance a positive account of what constitutes gayness and minority standing—that account will be the project of the following chapter.

I think the claim that homosexuality is a social construction has no core content; it does not constitute an intellectual paradigm with a content clear enough to be evaluated. Rather, the thesis is ambiguous, with senses that are often uncritically lumped together and between which its advocates skid, unaware that they have shifted ground.[3] I will try to disentangle and organize the various senses of what the thesis of the social construction of homosexuality might reasonably mean and then show that there is something wrong with the thesis in each sense, leaving the general thesis a genus bereft of species.

There are two basic types of social constructionism, each (we will eventually see) with two subspecies. I will call one basic model "antirealist," the other "antiessentialist." Realism, in this debate, I take to be a claim about the *causes* of a person's sexual orientation; realism on homosexuality here is a claim that there are sufficient causes in or from nature to explain the sexual desires of a person for members of his or her own biological or genital sex—where nature stands in opposition to culture. The antirealist stripe of social construction, then, holds that no one could be considered of some sexual orientation without taking into account causal forces from society or culture, forces that vary from culture to culture and within the same culture over time. Both the realist and the antirealist *in this sense* hold views that are *in theory* subject to analysis by the tools of traditional, progressive empirical science, which seeks out causal explanations of events and behaviors.

Essentialism, on the other hand, is here a theory, not of causes, but of *definitions* of sexual orientations. The essentialist claims that homosexuality can be intelligibly defined in such a way that all the definition's component concepts are capable of culturally neutral interpretation and that the definition's correct application to individuals is objective, that is, can be determined from a God's-eye point of view. The antiessentialist claims there is no such definition: that if the term "homosexuality" is used across cultures, it must be being used equivocally.[4]

II. Antirealist Social Construction

What I call antirealist social construction has its clearest form in labeling theory. Labeling theory holds that, once a person is socially assigned a label (usually a label suggesting deviance), not only do those who relate to the person do so as if the individual possessed the constellation of characteristics associated with the label, but also the person herself so labeled comes to view herself as of the type labeled and assumes behaviors congruent with the label. Here we have a causal theory that, by appeal to social rather than natural factors, explains why people are the type of people they are. The British sociologist Mary McIntosh first put forward this view for homosexuality in 1968.[5] Although it is usually overlooked, such labeling theory is part of Foucault's thought on social construction. It has its clearest, generalizable expression in the famous Panopticon passage of his *Discipline and Punish*, where prisoners are held to internalize the gaze, the view, of the (unseen) watchtower guardians and so become and act out the criminal type.[6] For Foucault, the function of prisons is not to punish criminals but to create them. By the end of *Discipline and Punish*, Foucault has generalized the Panopticon labeling model to virtually all organized areas of human life, including schools, factories, the military, indeed, any institutional setting—what he calls the carceral system.

Quite generally, Foucault thinks that individuals' bodies are blank slates on which society writes a script, which the individual then reads off to find out who he is—what type of person he is.[7] Foucault applies this model of the gaze's inscriptions and inductions specifically to sexuality in *The History of Sexuality:* "[Pleasures] were fixed by a gaze, isolated and animated by the attention they received. Power operated as a mechanism of attraction; it drew out those peculiarities over which it kept watch."[8]

Now, stereotypes should provide a good test case of labeling theory and of this brand of construction. For stereotypes are paradigmatically social constructions—social ideas having their source not in fact but in society's conception of itself, its ideology, ideas that are pinned label-like on various people by society. Indeed, at the start of *The Use of Pleasure*, Foucault, if parenthetically and with bets hedged, accepts stereotypes into his social analysis of homosexual construction: "In the nineteenth-century texts there is a stereotypical portrait of the homosexual or invert [—basically an image of male effeminacy]. . . . One could doubtless trace the long history of this image (to which actual behaviors may have corresponded, through a complex play of inductions and attitudes of defiance)."[9] Foucault does not elaborate, but defiance here apparently simply gets one more stuck, like a fish wiggling on a barbed hook.

On this analysis, the labeling process becomes a self-fulfilling prophesy: if you don't fit the label when it is first applied to you, soon enough you do come to fit it. This feature of the process means that labeling theory is a testable hypothesis: for one can check and see whether those who are labeled do indeed behave in accordance with the label's dictates. But this causal type of social constructionism fares very poorly on empirical examination. However well labeling theory applies in general or in such specialized settings as hospitals or prisons, it appears not to hold true of homosexual men. At least three of the chief stereotypes of gay men simply do not fit the facts as they should if stereotypes cause people to act in accordance with them. Empirical studies have shown that gay men are not crazy, are not effeminate—women's souls trapped in men's bodies—and are not child molesters.[10] Importantly, these characteristics that do not apply to gay men include the very property that Foucault uses to formulate the homosexual construction—the "inverting [of] the masculine and feminine in oneself."[11] Not only "accidental" stereotypes but also the very labels by which Foucault, at least, wants to define the homosexual fail to apply to homosexual males. The alleged results of labeling simply do not hold.

Further, Foucault fails more generally to give a convincing account of the method of labeling—or "inscription," as he and his followers prefer to call it.[12] Foucault speaks as though the site of the inscription process, the process of homosexuality's "perverse implantation" (as he calls it), occurs on the psychiatrist's couch.[13] The psychiatrist makes the blank slate of a person into a homosexual, paradoxically as Foucault would have it, even as the psychiatrist is trying to cure his patient of homosexuality. There are several things wrong with this theory. First, the theory fails to explain the homosexuality of all those millions of people who are homosexual but who have never laid so much as a hip pocket on a psychiatrist's couch. To counter by saying that it is sufficient that the medical or psychiatric conception of homosexuality is simply out there "circulating" in the air or discourse will not do as a causal explanation. For this variant fails to explain why some people do and others do not come to fall under the conception. In any case, the conception does not come to be thus "perversely implanted" (even in the theory's own terms) if in fact, as is the case, most people actively seeking homosexual sex are coded and scripted by society at large as nonhomosexual. The psychiatric account also fails to note that many people are sent to the couch *because* they already are actively seeking out homosexual outlets—already are, that is, homosexual, have homosexual desires. Finally, the theory fails to account for why, of those people who do indeed end up on the couch, some do and others do not come off the couch as homosexual—other than by the whim of the psychiatric people maker. I do not want to suggest that a psychiatrist could *never* help make up a person as a homosexual, only that appeal to psychiatric people making is lousy as a general theory of the causation of homosexuals.[14]

So as a general theory of social causation for people being the type of people they are, this brand of social construction—labeling theory— fails. Gay men and lesbians as a minority have been more creative than labeling theory and social constructionism allows. They can evade the stereotypes that society imposes on them. History has provided examples of people in same-sex relations who have been able to adapt, revise, and live and work "across the grain" of society's expectations for such relations.[15] It is not surprising, then, that "stereotype" is not, in general, part of social constructionists' lingo—(I would say) tellingly so.[16]

Causal antirealist social construction seems an odd theory to have tried to apply to homosexuals of modern times. For even people who regularly have same-sex sex relations are usually (as noted) labeled as nonhomosexual. By labeling theory's lights, again, one would have thought that this would mean that these people would start behaving straight—not just "acting" straight. But this is not so.

The closet is perhaps the mechanism that has tripped up labeling theory as applied to gays, by insulating them from the direct gaze of society.[17] And so, not surprisingly, Foucault and his followers are at pains to deny the closet. They wish to claim that all secrets are open secrets; homosexuality is supposed to be, like being fat, "a secret that always gives itself away,"[18] so that nothing really can hide, or elude the social, the penetrations of the social gaze and its attendant inductions and inducements. But this claim about secrets is simply false. Not all closets are glass closets; not all secrets are, like the emperor's false beliefs about his new clothes, open secrets, known to everyone but the secret's self-deceived object. On the one hand, people's comings out are frequently met with expressions of utterly sincere surprise—by spouses, parents, and children, for example. On the other hand, frequently the slightly embarrassed claims of acknowledgment running to the effect, "Well, we thought you might be," are simply lies told as an attempt to sweep the whole issue under the carpet: "Now that you know that we know, there's nothing really to discuss, is there?" Such a preemptory claim to epistemological superiority turns a closet opened to knowledge into a closet locked to understanding. Still, that people—endlessly labeled straight—nevertheless do come out at all, even into conditions of intense adversity, is a sign of the indomitability of the individual human spirit, an individualism that social constructionists are so set to deny but that current gay experience resoundingly affirms.

Now, stereotypes are not the only conceptualizations that reveal a misfit between social construction and reality. Sexual thinking is rife with disjunctures between conceptualizations that are social constructions and conceptualizations that track reality. Consider the social construction of cum. If one were to take as one's guide the discursive genres pillow talk and pornographic script, one would firmly believe that male ejaculates are gradually stored up in the testicles, which, like wineskins, can become distended by their contents, which in turn are released explosively from the testicles at orgasm: "I asked him if he was horny and he just gave a big grin and said 'Fuckin' yeah, man! I got nuts so swollen up with cum I can hardly walk! Want to drain my oil for me, don't you?' . . . Within minutes he was panting and grunting out his second load. A thick, warm load of cream exploded from his balls, gagging me with his flood."[19] But this common hydraulic portraiture—a social construction to be sure—is entirely false. Only an imperceptibly small amount of male ejaculates ever have their source in the testicles, whose production is, in any case, continuous and which (as anyone who pays attention to them knows) do not distend. As Yogi Berra says, you can observe a lot just by watching.

One response to the problems that stereotypes and other demonstrably false sexual conceptualizings pose for social construction is for the constructionist simply to deny the very validity of science. Foucault—inconsistently to my mind—launches just such a preemptive strike in *The History of Sexuality*, claiming that "between techniques of knowledge and strategies of power there is no exteriority."[20] This claim that all science is bogus—that there is no such thing as disinterested science, no knowledge independent of social power, no ability of science to self-correct—ought simply to lead to universal skepticism, the view that there can be no justified true beliefs about anything. Yet social construction is interesting only if it applies in some *distinctive* way to sexuality and not to all other things. Or, as Ed Stein puts it: "Social constructionism is an interesting position *about sexual orientation* only if the relativism involved in it is limited. Extreme social constructionism just collapses into metaphysical relativism, a position which may be interesting for metaphysics but which has nothing particular to say about sexual orientation; using metaphysical relativism as an argument for social constructionism is like using an atomic bomb to kill a fly."[21]

The price of skeptical defenses of constructionism is high in another way: the claim that science is bogus denies most of what we know and indeed denies most of what is common sense and everyday presumption, worked up from guessing and checking and from trial and error—the very elements and procedures of progressive science.[22]

III. The Social as a Necessary Part of Homosexuality

Even if the social concepts of what homosexuality is do not sufficiently explain the existence of homosexuals, still perhaps they are necessary conditions for their existence. In his dazzling Foucauldianly inspired paper "Making Up People," Ian Hacking offers a subtle argument for such an understanding of the social construction of homosexuality.[23] Hacking claims that a minimum requirement of all intentional actions is that the intending agent performs an act "under a description." That is, I take it, the agent must have, prior to a deliberate action, a description in mind of what is intended in or from the action. If homosexual activity is intentional activity, so it is claimed, then the homosexual must have a description of the homosexual in mind in order to perform homosexual acts. This view, if true, would entail that finding homosexuals in the past cannot be analogized to the using of the exclusively twentieth-century description of DNA to find DNA in past peoples, say, fifth-century Athenians, who did not know that they had DNA in them and did not have any description of DNA, even though they did indeed have DNA in them. Having DNA or, say, color blindness or spirochetes is not an intentional activity—no concept of the property is needed to have it. But if homosexual behavior is intentional (so it goes), having a description of it is necessary to being one who performs it. And so too, if the description of the homosexual is a social construction limited to the twentieth century, then the homosexual is also.

There are two responses to this view. First, homosexual behavior may not be intentional behavior. The more homosexual behavior is like eating and drinking as a need fulfillment, the less it will appear to be intentional.[24] Homosexual behavior may be genetically driven like the drive to eat or sleep in their aspects as biological needs, which have nonintentional roots (if you will) that are merely animal behavior—mechanical, that is, in the great scheme of things. The intentional aspects of these activities ("I'm going to roll over now and go to sleep, honey"; "We're having pesto for dinner"; "I think I'll try out the gloryhole shop tonight") are, as it were, layered over the nonintentional. Sex drive appears to be relevantly like such biological needs as eating and sleep, in that it recurs independently of one's acts and intentions. And it seems unlikely that this recurrence is the result of addiction or unconscious habit since many people have such drives who have never acted on them. Sex drive then too, at heart, may be a nonintentional "action" that is modified, shaded, given various importance, but not overturned or voided by intentional acts. I say "at heart" because some intentional actions may well even be necessary for sexual performance. In higher mammals, it appears that there is no sexual behavior without sexual learning. Gorillas raised in zoos cannot reproduce unless they are shown blue movies. When they are left to their own devices, it is clear that they want to do something but don't know what to do. What is learned are the techniques by which nonintentional desires are realized. Learning and intention do not create sexual desire; they provide the instruments of its fulfillment.

Early social constructionist Robert Padgug has tried to distance "human sexuality" from what he calls "animal sexuality," as though humans were not animals. He claims that "biology as a set of potentialities and insuperable necessities provides the material of social interpretation and extensions; it does not *cause* human behavior, but conditions and limits it."[25] But, if sexual object choice and sexual drive are limits that biology imposes on people, then biology will in fact determine what people do when they act sexually—whether one wants to call this determination a "cause" or not, and whether one wants to call this doing "human behavior" or not.

Second, we need here to distinguish between words and concepts. What one needs for intention is a description understood as a concept or string of concepts, not a description understood as a word or string of words. And while the macaronic word "homosexual" is an invention of the last one hundred years, there is nothing, so it would appear, that necessarily tethers the concept to the same period—the concept "desire to have sex with members of one's own biological sex."

There is an enormous slippage between language and concepts in sexual matters, as in other matters, a slippage that largely goes unremarked by social constructionists, who, following Foucault, generally limit the object of their inquiry to language and texts.[26] Noretta Koertge observes of this slippage:

> Lexical change often parallels conceptual or cultural change, but there is no simple one-to-one mapping between them. For example, there *may* be more difference between "friends" as understood in 1890 and "friends" as understood in 1990 than there is between the 19th c. concept of *invert* and the classical description of the *pathicus* in the Pseudo-Aristotelian *Problemata*.
>
> Terminology must be used as a clue, not as a touchstone. (Remember that although Eskimos have twenty-seven words for *snow*, there is no indigenous German word for *efficiency*.) Some social constructionists act as if language were the only clue to communal beliefs and social practices. (They may claim to be nominalists but they sure do reify language!)[27]

And in this slippage between word and idea, one can clearly have in mind the concepts "heterosexual" and "homosexual" without also having the corresponding words. Many of the black males taking the gay issues courses that I offered in the early 1980s, when coming into the courses, did not know (to the racist amusement of the white students) what the term "heterosexual" meant, although they had a clear understanding of the concept "heterosexual" and generally fell under it. Rather, they expressed the wordless concept with the phrase "just a regular guy, man." Conversely, in the movie *Teenage Mutant Ninja*

Turtles, the turtles pick up along the adventure's way, as a safely non-miscegenous love interest for the movie's human heroine, a "white-trash" human male sidekick. When first they take him into the sewers, he expresses discomfort. A turtle says, "I know what you are. You're claustrophobic." The sidekick snaps back, "I've never even looked at a guy."[28] Here, the sidekick clearly has the concept "homosexual desire," even though he does not know the word for the concept. Or again, frequently, in recountings of the coming-out process, one hears that the person coming out had at some point thought that she was the only "one." One what? Well, one homosexual—even when the person didn't know the word. Social constructionists are prone to overlook the difference, the slippage, between words and concepts because they choose to call the subject of their inquiries "discourse"—or the bastardized plural "discourses"[29]—words that, in their vagueness, simply fudge, blur, or erase the very distinction between language and ideas.

A stunning example of the confusion of the term "homosexual" with the concept "homosexual" is provided by classicist and committed constructionist David Halperin, who claims that "the invention of homosexuality [was effected] by Charles Gilbert Chaddock." How did one man accomplish this stupendous feat? By his "having introduced 'homo-sexuality' into the English language in 1892. . . . Before 1892 there was no homosexuality. . . ."[30] For Halperin, what needs answering is, "In what *terms* was sexual experience constructed?" "The real issue . . . is . . . how to recover the *terms* in which the experiences of individuals of past societies were actually constituted." If it is merely *terms* or *language* that are doing the construction in social construction, then the social constructionist's point is obviously true: there are no transhistorical categories because there is no transhistorical vocabulary. But once attention is drawn to the issue, I do not think that anyone believes that mere vocabulary constructs whatever gets constructed in society. It is my hope that, just because culture, gay and otherwise, currently has no term for the relation that my lover and I have, some future, benighted constructionist won't look back from a time in the next century when the term finally has been coined and claim that the relation, for want of a word, did not exist, ye verily, could not have existed, as indeed it has existed, in the 1970s, 1980s, and 1990s.

Now, if one acknowledges, as one should, that the absence of a specific word does not mean that a society fails to have the corresponding concept, and if one has as a minimal definition of the concept "homosexual" "a person with desires for sex acts with partners of the same biological sex," then this concept is not hard to find even in cultures that the social constructionists have most often claimed for themselves as proofs of their position.

No one disputes that some Attic Greek males performed sex acts with other males, but—tellingly for the issue at hand—some of these males knew of themselves and it was socially acknowledged that they predominately or exclusively desired other males as sex objects, although this information usually gets buried and acknowledged only in the footnotes of such social constructionists as David Halperin and the late Jack Winkler.[31] The general social importance and typical personal form that these self- and socially acknowledged desires took vary greatly from the importance and form they take today, but this acknowledgment does mean that, even if there is not a word for it, the concept did exist in ancient Greece.

Among the "Sambia" of Papua New Guinea, whose male initiation rites involve compelled fellation between males, each taking in time both insertee and insertor roles, it is acknowledged that there are three types of males. First, some small percentage of males shun the socially coerced postinitiation transition to sexual relations only with females and continue seeking out sexual relations with other males. Second, some other males stop having sex with other males immediately at the point when they are no longer compelled to have such relations because they simply do not like having such sexual relations. Third, still others, the majority of males, in the initiation rites come to like having same-sex relations but give them up in favor of different-sex relations when socially called on to do so.[32] This socially acknowledged arrangement—although without the *words* "homosexual," "heterosexual," and "bisexual"—looks for all the world to incorporate the same *conceptual arrangement* we find now in the modern West and in the ancient Greek lyric that John Boswell is fond of quoting: "Zeus came as an eagle to god-like Ganymede, as a swan came he to the fair-haired mother of Helen. So there is no comparison between the two things: one person likes one, another likes the other; I like both."[33] Now, again, the form and salience of each conceptualized sexual mode may vary from culture to culture. Indeed, it would be surprising if it did not.[34] But the concept "homosexual" is there in each case even though the word is not. And so again, intentional homosexual behavior is possible in various cultures even on Hacking's account.

Despite social constructionists' general ideological allegiance to *différence*, they spend too much time looking at core cases, normal cases, the expected in each society that they study, and not enough time examining the fringes of societies to see if the concept—"desire for sex with a person of the same biological sex"—and behavior in accordance with it are to be found there lurking in the unusual. Recently, (re)discovered Attic Greek vase paintings have been found that portray, against the social norm of the active adult male trying to dominate and manipulate male youths into sexual passivity, adult males seeking out for themselves insertee sex roles with other adult males and youths. This clearly shows that the concept of same-sex desire was present in Attic Greece and in specific forms not too distant from the highly ramified version of the concept in our own culture.[35]

Conversely, if one rummages around modern culture enough, one can find contemporary conceptual counterparts to many terms and classificatory schemes that constructionists have thought to mark out concepts distinctively ancient. Take the Latin verb *irrumo*, which means "to offer the penis for sucking," usually with the connotation that the act degrades the fellator.[36] Americans do not have a single-word counterpart for the concept conveyed by the Latin word. But we do have the concept. It is conveyed in the following passage of a jerk-off story from *Jocks*, a soft-core gay men's porn magazine:

I opened my mouth wider and sucked on the giant cock.
He abruptly pulled his prick out of my mouth.
"You're biting me, punk."

"I'm sorry, really."

"Continue," he said.

I put my tongue and lips over my teeth as best I could while I proceeded to suck him off.[37]

Or consider the daunting, indeed definitional, importance that the Greeks gave to the idea of penetration: the physical male body must be impenetrable if it is to be the normative male body. The one unthinkable thing for a real man to be is a *kinaidos*—a genitally male person who actively seeks to be sexually penetrated. Shameful is it even to speak the word.[38] It seems that the male body presented as penetrable also provided the silencing anxiety that in Cincinnati drove the obscenity charges laid against the display of five Robert Mapplethorpe photographs of adult nude males. The *New York Times* described the photographs as depicting "homosexual acts" or "sadomasochistic acts."[39] But a majority of these photographs were of *solitary* individuals. Rather, what the photographs have in common and what distinguishes them from the subjects of the other eight male nude photos that make up Mapplethorpe's controversial sex-charged *X Portfolio* is that the photos show some object (variously, a finger, a hand, a leathern dildo, a whip handle, and urine) entering into the desiring male body (variously, its mouth, penis, and anus). It is telling that the only *X Portfolio* photo that suggests sexual violence was not thought obscene by Cincinnati officials. In this photo of genitorture, a cock and balls pass through a hole in a small board on their fellow's tummy and then are trussed and pinioned to the board and splattered with who knows what.[40] The cock here—whatever else is going on, and even though it is limp—is formally doing what it is supposed to be doing: penetrating. Much that makes the past and the foreign seem different and remote to the social constructionists is simply their own ignorance of the present and domestic.

Indeed, most social history is simply irrelevant to the question whether there is an innate biological drive in some people to have erotic encounters with members of their biological sex. Simply showing that different cultures give a different importance to same-sex relations (in some cultures held sacred, in others profane) or showing that same-sex relations manifest themselves differently, are differently structured between cultures (in some cultures men fuck boys, in others boys fuck men), is completely compatible with the naturalistic claim that there are root biological drives and that they are shaped this way and that by cultural forces and given this and that social importance, just as is done with biological drives to eat or sleep or drink.[41]

A boy who wants to be with males, likes the way they look and smell, wants to touch and rub up against them, and is excited by physical contacts with them will find his developing sexual attraction to men realized through various channeling influences laid out by social norms, especially as these are embedded in the beliefs and actions of the men whom the boy finds exciting and in the techniques and instrumentalities through which the boy learns to fulfill his desires. The norms will tend to determine whether, for instance, the desire is actualized in an active or a passive sexual role or is realized with someone of one age but not another. The norms may well even require, as they did in Greek citizen culture and do in contemporary hustler culture, that the boy deny that he finds the pleasurable contacts pleasurable.

Claims that same-sex relations are embedded in varying forms of social life cut not a whit against the realist. Even claims that in some societies, either past or foreign, there is no homosexual behavior—should such claims indeed turn out on careful examination to be true[42]—would not be dispositive on the issue. For there are various bodily conditions—for example, eye color and various diseases (like sickle-cell anemia among blacks and cystic fibrosis among whites)—that are not universal to all cultures and yet are naturalisticly, biologically caused.[43]

IV. Antiessentialist Approaches to Social Construction

I now shift from forms of social construction that attempt to give causal accounts of homosexuality to those that give conceptual or definitional accounts. I call the latter "antiessentialist," or "no-essence" theories.[44]

235

Frequently, the same author will uncritically combine elements from the two basic forms of constructionism or unwittingly vacillate between the two.

The antiessentialists hold that the very nature of the concept "homosexuality" or of the definition—or definitions—of "homosexuality" prevents its univocal application to different societies, tethering it just to modern European-based culture. This mode of social constructionism divides into two kinds.

One approach I will call "no-content nominalism," an account on which homosexuality as a concept simply evaporates altogether as something one might study historically or sociologically. For it becomes an entirely nondenoting concept; it cannot pick out anything in the world. Take social historian Jonathan Katz's much-quoted formulation of social construction. Katz claims that "all homosexuality is situational, influenced and given *meaning* and character by its location in time and social space."[45] Robert Padgug has given a similar formulation of "sexuality" more generally: "The content of human sexuality is ultimately provided by human social relations, human productive activities, and human consciousness. The history of sexuality is therefore the history of a subject whose *meaning* and contents are in continual process of change."[46] Katz and Padgug claim that the very "meaning," the very definition, of sexuality or homosexuality—that is, the conceptual makeup of homosexuality that at once distinguishes it from all other concepts and captures everything that is in fact homosexual—has no fixed content.

But if this claim is true, I suggest that the subject—the possibly denoted subject—homosexuality simply vanishes. For the sentence "All homosexuality is situational" is logically equivalent to the sentence "All widgets are indeterminate." Suppose that we do not know what a widget is and so we look to the definition for an understanding of what a widget is, by learning the complex of concepts that describe all things that are widgets and no other things; but when we turn to the definition, we find that there is no such complex—all widgets are indeterminate. Nothing can be essentially indeterminate and still be definable,

yet this is what Katz seems to be claiming of the concept "homosexual"—not that it can be manifested in instantiations that have various
and sundry diverse and nonrepeating accidental attributes, but that the
essential parts neither require nor exclude anything. But homosexuality,
if so conceived, could apply, like wholly indeterminate widgets, to
anything and nothing. Assertions of the existence of homosexuality on
this account are nonsense in the sense of being contentless claims. The
definition is ill formed. There is no subject for anyone to investigate
on such an account.

The other conceptual, definitional approach to social construction I
call "fine-textured nominalism." This approach defines homosexuality,
to be sure, but defines it in such a way, typically with such a specificity,
that it can apply *only* to one era or place. On such an account, homosexuality is so fine textured of definition, so ramified or particular in its
content, that it is incapable of application to more than one culture.
On this account, it becomes question-beggingly true that homosexuality occurs only in the modern era.

For examples of the basic structure of this approach to social construction, take the terms "yuppie," "hippie," and "opera queen." The
terms, the phrases, to be sure are unique to the very modern era. But
what about the concepts? Well, their range of applicability depends on
how one defines them. If one defines "yuppie" in such a way that in the
very definition there is an essential reference to Volvos or VCRs or
"thirtysomething," then necessarily the term can apply only to the
modern era. On this account, it is question-beggingly true that yuppies
did not exist in Attic Greece. If, however, one defines yuppies as
middle-aged, effete, money-grubbing conspicuous consumers, then we
have something that at least in theory could apply to other eras and
places; it has at least the possibility of being instantiated in different
cultures because definitionally it is culturally neutral. It is a concept
that could be instantiated in, say, the oligarchs of Plato's *Republic* 8.
Now, it looks like "yuppie" is not in fact transcultural—not, that is,
occurring in all cultures. For there are no middle-aged, effete, money-
grubbing conspicuous consumers in hunting-and-gathering tribes. Still,

"yuppie" so defined is at least a *candidate* for being transcultural, for it is defined in such a way that we can look in other cultures to see whether it picks anything out there, whether it is there denoting.

Or again take "hippie." If one tethers its definition to beat-up Volkswagens, one, by necessity, is not going to find hippies in the Roman Empire. But if you define "hippie" in a culturally neutral way so that the thesis that hippies did not exist in the past has bite, then it is at least possible, conceivable, thinkable, that there were hippies in the Roman Empire; and if one specifically defined "hippie" in culturally neutral terms such that hippies are communally living, socially detached spiritualists, then it is at least arguable that we should consider the early Christians as hippies.

Or again, if we say that "opera queens" did not exist before Jacopo Peri wrote the first opera *Dafne* in 1598, we have said nothing of interest whatsoever; we have made a historical claim that is simply vacuously, question-beggingly true.

A lot of formulations of social construction beg questions in exactly this way. The most famous case is the bit from Foucault on homosexuality so frequently used as boilerplate for academic witnessings and pledge takings.[47] Foucault says that there is a "nineteenth century homosexual," by which, in his approach that divides history into epochs, he means "a nineteenth *and* twentieth century homosexual." In elided form, the famous passage reads: "The nineteenth century homosexual became a personage, a past, a case history, a childhood, . . . a morphology, [a] physiology. . . . It [i.e., homosexuality] was consubstantial with him, less a habitual sin than as a singular nature."[48] Now, the question to be asked here is, Are there homosexuals other than the nineteenth- and twentieth-century homosexual?—as Foucault's first formulation "the nineteenth century homosexual" would suggest. If not, the qualification "nineteenth century" is gratuitous; indeed, by paragraph's end, the qualification has disappeared, and we have unqualifiedly the expression "homosexuality appeared as one of the forms of sexuality" in the nineteenth century.

If the nineteenth-century homosexual is just one sort of homosexual, then we must suppose that Foucault has a definition of "homosexual"

that he does not give us but with which he presumes we are operating
and that is defined in socially and culturally neutral fashion so that the
qualification "nineteenth century" adds something, is significant. We
could use this definition (whatever it is) to look elsewhere to see
whether in fact homosexuals existed there. This approach would at least
be intellectually respectable, but it does not seem to be what Foucault
has in mind. Rather, by the end of the passage, we have the homosexual
defined in terms of characteristics that could be found only in the very
modern era: a homosexual is a person who is *thought of* by a certain
segment of the *modern* medical profession as having some set of properties.[49] But by proceeding in this way, Foucault has made the claim
that there are no homosexuals before the nineteenth century question-
beggingly true in exactly the same way that the statement "there were
no opera queens before 1598" is true. To the extent that Foucault's
project in the passage is definitional (rather than giving a causal account
of homosexuality), he has performed an intellectual sleight of hand.
Foucault has said no more than that the nineteenth-century homosexual is the nineteenth-century homosexual, that the modern homosexual
is the modern homosexual. He has made a stunningly uninteresting
claim, vacuous as a historical and sociological thesis.

The philosopher Arnold Davidson takes a similar approach. Following Foucault, he wishes to claim that "'sexuality' is the product of a
system of psychiatric knowledge that has its own very particular style
of reasoning and argumentation."[50] But since psychiatry is a recent
development, by definition sexuality can occur only in the modern era.
No neutral criteria are advanced by which it would even be possible to
ask intelligibly whether homosexuals existed earlier.[51] What for Davidson ties the definition of "homosexuality" to the modern era appears to
be the very complexity of the conceptual matrices that make up
(homo)sexuality's definition:

> We should examine the word "sexuality" in the sites in which it
> issued, that is, we must look at the sentences in which "sexuality"
> appears, and see what is done with these sentences by the various
> people who use them. Typically at least when we are dealing with

an epistemological break, we find that the concept under investigation enters into systematic relation with other very specific concepts.[52]

Sexuality, he wants to claim, is as tethered to the specificity of psychiatric discourse as the term "pain" is attached distinctively to certain English prepositions and to the particular metaphors with which we try to describe it.[53] The use, in different cultures, of other metaphors and prepositions of and with "pain" would mean (so it is claimed) that we were not talking of the same thing as they. But this requirement of specificity again simply question-beggingly ties the concept of pain, and of sexuality, to the present since no other culture could in practice replicate all the filaments of the definitions.

I do not want to deny that there are now cultural accretions—connotations—surrounding the word "homosexual" (even beyond the medical and clinical) that would not translate without loss or misplaced residue into other cultures' thinking about what is denoted by the concept "homosexual." Take, for instance, Fran Lebowitz's witticism: "If you removed all of the homosexuals and homosexual influence from what is generally regarded as American culture, you would be pretty much left with *Let's Make a Deal.*"[54] There is much fine grained here that will not translate into non-American culture even as the witticism claims to be made externally about American culture. If these fine senses could not be conceptually disengaged from the term "homosexual"—that is, if "homosexual" *only* has this sense—then, even without appeals to medical workings on the concept "homosexuality," social constructionists would have successfully tethered the term exclusively to the modern era, indeed, to just one country of the era. But the point is that we can and typically do disambiguate senses of a term even when its multiple senses are applied correctly to the same object. At a barbecue with an inattentive chef, a steak that is "rare" in the sense of being lightly cooked will also be "rare" in the sense of unusual, and no one is confused about this state of affairs. So too we can disambiguate the Lebowitzian sense of "homosexual" from its possible minimal or core sense, "the desire for sexual relations with members of one's own biological sex," and use the core sense in perfectly respectable, culturally neutral ways.

David Halperin's main constructionist thesis—that "nothing resembling [homosexuality and heterosexuality] can be found in ancient antiquity"—too seems to be a variant, after Foucault, of fine-textured nominalism.[55] *Homo*sexuality (he supposes) had to await sexuality plain and simple, before it could be a subdivision of it. And while Halperin allows that the Greeks had "sexual contacts with other persons" and "sexual attitudes" and even a "sexual system," he denies them the referent of the paronymous abstract noun "sexuality." Why? Because sexuality is given a Pickwickian definition appealing to scientific cant and "definitions" that first appear only in the eighteenth and nineteenth centuries.

At one point, Halperin hints at a definition of sexuality that might be culturally neutral: sexuality describes "a characterological seat within the individual . . . from which all sexual expression proceeds," permeating the whole "human personality." But it would appear that Plato's doctrine of the tripartite soul from the *Republic* and other dialogues, a doctrine that Halperin nowhere discusses, fits this definition of sexuality: sexual drives are paradigmatic of the desiderative or appetitive part of the soul, and, if not checked, uprooted, or tamed, their natural tendency to dominate and disrupt the other two parts of the soul (the honor-loving part and the part that thinks) will be actualized; thus these sexual drives come to control the individuals' actions, attitudes, and even politics.[56] The sexual drives even have a specific physiological seat and a specific biological mechanism and economy—which Halperin seems to require of "sexuality."[57] In light of Plato's psychology, which provides the model for so much in Freud's tripartite psyche, it is puzzling how Halperin can claim that, in the ancient world, "'sexuality' obviously did not hold the key to the secrets of the human personality." But he does leave himself an out: "human personality" itself is a social construction present only in the modern era, so the Greeks could not have thought that *anything* held its secret. Thus, after a brush with offering culturally neutral definitions, Halperin retreats again to fine-textured nominalism to avoid general failure of the constructionist model.[58]

The price of Davidson's and Halperin's Foucauldian strategy, taken at full strength, is quite high. If Foucault's strategy is a sign of a general theory of meaning for anything touched with the social,[59] and if the sense of terms or concepts is determined by their proliferating, rami-fied, filament-like attachments to specific historical periods and social customs, then Foucault and friends ought simply to be skeptical about our ability to understand other cultures and times. For in these episte-mological circumstances, our conceptual equipment simply will not go over into theirs. But not only does this seem simply to be false—we are moved by Greek dramas, we understand Oedipus's pain, Philoctetes' pain, we do not view the plays as nonsense, blathering, noise, or find them ineluctable—but there is also something terrifically arrogant about such social constructionism. While it bumptiously holds that all science's claims to objectivity and cultural neutrality are rendered bogus by the social forces and ideologies in which the practices of science are located, it claims of and for itself (its theory of the social relativity of meanings notwithstanding) a God's-eye perspective, a view unwarped by ideology, a crystal clear understanding of the past and of social change.[60] When paired with this posture of omniscience, the belief in relativity is the height of intellectual hypocrisy.[61]

CHAPTER 8

Gay Studies as
Moral Vision

In American Sign Language, the infinitive "to fuck" is indicated, not surprisingly, by the repeated passing of the index finger of one hand in and out of a hoop formed by the index finger and thumb of the other. One prepares to indicate a male orgasm by pursing and drawing palmward the fingertips of the right hand; then, one signs the infinitive "to cum" by poking the index finger of the left hand to the heel of the right, triggering its finger tips to thrust sharply away and somewhat apart. Another sign for a male climax is a blend of the signs for "gravy (drippings)" and "spread."[1]

The signs for sexual activities in ASL are not mere abstract symbols, in the way, say, stars and stripes are symbols of America. Rather, they are pictographs, moving hieroglyphs. Unlike stars and stripes, which have reference by mere convention, the ASL expressions image and resemble the very things for which they serve as signs—vividly. In ASL, the signs for the following sexual or genital *acts* are also pictographs: "masturbation," "gay mutual masturbation," "vaginal masturbation," "cunnilingus," "fellatio," "gay male mutual oral sex," "anal intercourse," "group sex," and "rape."[2] In its single concession to the existence of sexual discourse in ASL, the *American Sign Language Dictionary*, gives the same sign for the actions "copulate," "fornicate," and "sexual intercourse." It too is a pictograph: "(The motions of the legs during the sexual act.) The upturned left 'V' hand remains motionless, while the downturned right 'V' hand comes down repeatedly on the left."[3]

However, the derogatory ASL expressions for gay men are not pictographs. Slang in ASL tends to be regional, but the most widespread sign for "faggot" is the pinched tips of the index finger and thumb touched a couple of times to the chin. Another sign for "faggot" is the flitting of finger tips near the forward temple and corner of the eye, as though one were trying to cut and fluff the air there. A recent innovation for "faggot" is twice tugging an earlobe. Still another sign is the touching of the tip of the middle finger to the nose and then sweeping it up and over the crown of the head. An older sign is dry licking a fingertip with which one then quickly strokes the hairs of the corresponding eyebrow, as though one were painting them. ASL has shown considerably less "imagination" with lesbians. "Lesbian"—in all its connotations—is signed simply by holding the letter "L" to the chin.

These expressions do not image actions. In particular, they do not image the acts that it might be argued place a person in the class of gay men. The signs simply presuppose that gay men as a class are worthy of derision independent of the acts that define an individual as a member of the class, and they contribute to the derision by enhancing stereotypes—of flightiness, misplaced femininity, and exaggeration. The gestural conventions of ASL clearly suggest that gay men are despised in virtue of some perceived group status that gays have rather than in virtue of the acts they perform.

The creation of slang is a nonreflective activity, and here, in ASL, slang unconsciously captures and conveys a basic truth about social attitudes toward gay men. Those who have reflected on the position of gays in modern social structures have shown a marked tendency to misunderstand this truth. In his seminal work of the early 1960s *Stigma*, Erving Goffman advances the following cosmology of the dispossessed:

> Three grossly different types of stigma may be mentioned. First there are abominations of the body—the various physical deformities. Next there are blemishes of individual character perceived as weak will, domineering or unnatural passions, treacherous and

rigid beliefs, and dishonesty, these being *inferred from a known record of,* for example, mental disorder, imprisonment, addiction, alcoholism, *homosexuality,* unemployment, suicidal attempts, and radical political behavior. Finally there are the tribal stigmas of race, nation and religion, these being stigmas that can be transmitted through lineages and equally contaminate all members of the family.[4]

This cosmology, which categorizes homosexuals by what they do, or allegedly do, has proved amazingly persistent in liberal American thought. It is even imaged in the American Civil Liberties Union's current basic brochure *Guardian of Freedom:* "ACLU programs . . . have most often been on behalf of people with the special vulnerability of the powerless: members of racial and ethnic minorities; women; children; those subjected to the arbitrary discipline of closed institutions such as mental patients, prisoners and servicemen; the poor; non-conformists of every kind, from splinter radical parties to gays to anti-war protesters."[5]

These quotes presume that *in society's eyes* gays are essentially performers of radical acts akin to those of political activists. This presumption could not be farther from the truth. The record of those social forms in which stigma and derision are most clearly advanced against groups—slang, jokes, stereotypes, violence, symbolic legislation, and judicial abuse—shows what ASL shows, namely, that society does not treat gays as of a piece with radical politicians, social misfits, alcoholics, suicides, and the like, who are grouped by acts that they perform. Neither is homosexuality chiefly viewed as a flaw of individual character (like being nasty or rude). And it certainly is not viewed as a character inferred from a known record of behavior. It is not by their behavior that gays are judged and classified. Rather, the evidence in lopsided preponderance shows that society ranks homosexuals with racial groups and the physically deformed. Stigmas against gays are a blend of Goffman's abominations of the flesh and tribal stigmas. Gays are viewed first and foremost simply as morally lesser beings, like animals, children, or dirt, *not* as failed full moral agents. Objections of some religions and conservatives to the contrary, it is against the sinner, not the sin, that society deploys the armaments of anti-gay oppression. Such acts as gays are thought to perform—whether sexual, gestural, or social—are viewed socially as the expected or even necessary efflorescence of gays' lesser moral state, of their status as lesser beings, rather than as the distinguishing marks by which they are defined as a group. Such purported acts—the stuff of stereotypes—provide the materials for a retrospectively constructed ideology concocted to justify the group's despised status, in the way, for instance, that the social belief that Jews, Germans, Japanese, or Native Americans poison wells is concocted, as socially "needed," to justify society's hatred of these groups. Here, hatred's fixing of status is primitive and behavior an ideologically inspired afterthought.

I cannot even begin to summarize here all the data that exist for this understanding of the social record, but, as we saw in chapter 4, such moral classification of gays by status rather than action is at work in major legal forms—immigration policy, marital law, the military, the Supreme Court, and lesser courts. In the mid-1980s, two other major institutions weighed in to this classificatory model—religion and medicine. In 1986, the Catholic church, in a major ideological shift, branded as "an objective moral disorder" the mere status of being a homosexual, even when congenitally fixed and unaccompanied by any homosexual behavior.[6] Previously, such status had been held morally neutral, and only homosexual acts were morally censured. This retooled racism, although new in the church's treatment of gays, simply codifies what society has believed all along anyway; here, the church's barbarism is simply trying to catch up with the times.

On April 15, 1985, in Atlanta during her keynote address for the First International Conference on AIDS, President Reagan's cabinet secretary of health and human services, Margaret Heckler, in a burst of good intentions gone painfully awry, held: "We must conquer AIDS before it affects the heterosexual population . . . the general population. We have a very strong public interest in stopping AIDS before it spreads outside the risk groups, before it becomes an overwhelming problem."[7] The determinate prospect of a million or so dead gay men was not seen to be a problem for the Reagan administration. Now, in

America, we do not normally distinguish the worth of individual lives with respect to the means by which people come to have diseases. We do not, for instance, think that the life of a CEO who suffers a heart attack from years of gluttony is worth less than a person who suffers a heart attack under torture. Even if one drew a moral distinction between the AIDS-conveying sex acts of heterosexuals and those of homosexuals, this would still not ground a further distinction between lives to be saved and lives to be junked. So it is not the moral assessment of actions that grounds Heckler's distinction; rather, she holds heterosexual status as more worthy of care and concern than gay status. Gays, here, are lesser beings.

The social understanding of homosexuality as essentially a degenerate status rather than a form of behavior has important consequences for understanding gay men and lesbians as a minority and for understanding the objects and objectives of lesbian and gay studies. In its most central, frequent, and important usage, "minority" is a normative rather than a descriptive term. Its use in its descriptive, statistical meaning—"less than 50 percent"—is rare (one example can be found in the sentence "Ontario's Progressive Conservatives after forty years of continuous rule are now a minority party in the Ontario parliament"). The more common, normative rather than statistical sense of the term was clearly evinced in media discussions over where AIDS was going in the late 1980s. Once it appeared that Margaret Heckler's prediction was incorrect, that white heterosexual males were not coming down with AIDS in great numbers, the media needed to find some other place on which to settle its concern for the disease and settled on "minorities."[8] But not once in this media blitz were gay men named a "minority." Indeed, the term was regularly used in ways that necessarily implied that gays were not a "minority" affected by AIDS, even though a constitutional majority of AIDS cases were falling on that but 5 or so percent of the population that is gay and male.

Now, "minority," as we saw of "privacy" in chapter 1, is a concept that is both norm dependent and norm invoking: that is, on the one hand, for the correct application of "minority," certain normative conditions must be fulfilled, and in turn, on the other hand, once correctly applied, "minority" prescribes certain norms, calls for certain actions. Perhaps surprisingly, in its norm-dependent dimension, "minority" seems not to entail any nonmoral facts. At least it does not entail the term's descriptive or statistical sense. The expression now found in job advertisements encouraging "women and other minorities to apply" shows that the statistical sense of "minority" is not a necessary condition for the correct application of the term taken in its normative sense.[9] To the chagrin of some black leaders, minority set-aside programs for federal contracts count the statistical majority *women* as a minority.[10]

On what, then, does "being a minority" turn? I think American Sign Language, the Catholic church, and Margaret Heckler provide sufficient clues. A minority is a group treated unjustly because of some status that the group is socially perceived to possess independently of the behavior of the group's members. This definition captures the scope and normative force of the term. On it, women, although statistically a majority, are a minority, but the statistical minority people-with-blue-eyes is not. Not surprisingly, there are no minority set-aside programs in federal contracts for people with blue eyes. Yet, given this definition, current discussions of gays as a minority have been largely misguided because irrelevant.

Almost all the popular debate about gays—and a fair amount of the academic—has turned on whether being gay is an immutable characteristic. If it is, gays would be, so it is claimed, relevantly like blacks—like in that one's group characteristic is not of one's own doing, with the result that in a group-based discrimination one is treated unjustly because treated without regard to what one oneself has done. But even if it were conclusively proved that being gay is not a matter of choice, such a biology-based or psychology-based strategy gets morality on the cheap, indeed too cheaply.[11]

Sometimes, drawing moral distinctions with respect to nonchosen properties is morally acceptable, even morally to be expected. For example, "grandfather provisions" are not, on their own, considered unjust. A law with a grandfather provision blocks future access to a privilege but allows those currently with the privilege to maintain it (say, a vendor's license or a past land use in the face of newly restrictive zoning). If grandfather exceptions do not front for some illegitimate goal (e.g., perpetuating racial oppression in the post-Reconstruction era), then they are not felt to be substantially unjust, even though they create closed classes of people with privileges to which others, sometimes as a matter of when they were born, can have no access no matter what they do.[12] Or again, a law that lowers the inheritance tax rate will disadvantage a person whose parents have already died compared to people whose parents have not yet died. Still, this disadvantage is not an injustice to him even though its falling on him is not a consequence of anything that he has done.

When taken as a moral principle, the claim that one is not to be discriminated against with respect to some property over which one has no control has all the usefulness but roughness of a rule of thumb—immutable characteristics *usually* will be morally irrelevant. Yet if we suppose that good reasons ought to stand behind all claims of morality and immorality, then the principle does not produce even a presumption, let alone trumping judgment, of immorality for exceptions to it since the exceptions themselves will have good reasons standing behind them. A more accurate principle is the broader, if blander, one that a person is not to be treated in ways that are irrelevant to the person's immutable properties or that a person's immutable properties are not to be given a moral weight that they do not warrant. And the relevant principle of social equality, then, is not the clean, clear one holding that distinctions may not be drawn with respect to people's immutable characteristics, but the more sinuous principle holding that people may not be held in lesser moral regard irrespective of what they have done. Distinctions may be drawn without reference to individuals' moral responsibility, but when such distinctions are drawn, they must not degrade those individuals. For instance, if it were established that exclusive homosexuality is an immutable characteristic, that finding would not instantly make baby bonuses a violation of rights to equal protection because of the favorable disparate impact and economies of scale that such bonuses would have for heterosexual households. Whether they were to be barred would depend on whether the policy enhanced social structures that degraded gays. And to determine that would require looking at social customs. Sometimes, fixed physical characteristics are morally relevant.

Yet immutable characteristics are not necessary conditions for moral minority status. Among star cases of minorities that have properly invoked civil and constitutional protections are religious minorities and the physically challenged—and the physically challenged even when the challenge in question is the result of personal responsibility as in a negligently caused car accident or a botched suicide. Those who take skin color as the exclusive paradigm for minority status, then, are simply ignorant of actual social circumstance and current justified law. Minority standing that is based on biological or psychological determinism lets in both too much and too little.

Determinists miss the moral dimension of minority status in another major way as well. The sources of injustice against groups lie chiefly in the nature of society's treatment of the group rather than in the selection of any objective characteristics of the group on which the treatment focuses. Injustice against minorities lies chiefly in the *manner* or *mode* of social operations rather than in the operations being directed at the wrong *objects*. Consider slavery. Slavery is not a social treatment the remedy for which might be found in a shift in its focus, say, from blacks to blonds. Or again, slavery would not become an acceptable way to treat blacks if some alchemist's alembic produced an inexpensive pill that could convert to white both primary and secondary Negroid features, such that being black became a mutable characteristic.

No, the injustice of slavery is not that it has the wrong objects. Nor is the source of its injustice that it causes unwarranted unhappiness, nor even that, like a tax too high, it unjustifiably restricts independence. Rather the injustice of slavery in virtue of which its direction at blacks established blacks as a normative minority is that it views blacks as lesser moral beings. Whatever may be said of the Supreme Court's subsequent race cases, it correctly understood the moral dynamics of slavery when in 1857 it held that blacks could not be considered U.S. citizens by the founding fathers because, as the Court wrote, "that unfortunate race . . . [was correctly] regarded as being of an inferior order, and altogether unfit to associate with the white race, either in social or political relations; and so far inferior, that they had no rights which the white man was bound to respect; and that the negro might justly and lawfully be reduced to slavery for his own benefit."[13]

An alarming number of current-day racist jokes continue this same moral vision—that blacks are not moral agents but lesser beings that exist (or even perish) for the sake of use in the projects of "fully" human beings: "How many blacks does it take to shingle a roof? Just two if you slice them thin enough."[14] It is only as signaling lesser moral standing rather than failed moral agency that race is relevant here. Any treatment of other groups that puts them in the same moral orbit, that of lesser moral status rather than failed moral agency, would equally justify the application to them of the moral sense of "minority" and in turn invoke the civil and constitutional norms we think appropriate for minority status. Society's treatment of gays—as shown in its treatment of them in slang and invective, derogatory group-based jokes, stereotypes, group-directed violence, symbolic legislation, and, as we have seen, Catholic theology, health policy, and constitutional law—does exactly this: presuppose and reinforce the moral vision that gays are lesser moral beings. Whether gays are or are not in fact objectively like a highly distinctive ethnic group, that is how society views and treats them—as a despised ethnic minority and not as a pack of criminals. It is this, rather than because sexual orientation is or is viewed as some immutable characteristic or social statistic, that makes gays a minority.

To summarize, even if the biological determinists are right about their facts, they are, in the main, irrelevant in establishing gays as a minority.

Now, my thesis that society treats gays *as though* they constitute an ethnic minority does not entail and should not be confused with a somewhat different claim about the relation between nature, culture, and sexuality. I am not claiming that, either in its general arrangements or in its specific treatment of gays, society constitutes or constructs homosexuality (whether behavioral, gestural, or social) *as a sexual category*. The social constructionist claims that social forces do not simply shape the direction or expression of homosexuality, understood as a

251

presocietal natural kind, but enter into its very definition, such that social structures, especially structures of discourse, rather than natural properties, establish gays as a sexual minority. For them, "gayness"—and note the shift to the abstract noun—is now understood intentionally, not extensionally, that is, is understood as a "meaning" or classificatory matrix of concepts rather than as—and independently of—any actual designatable group of persons in the world.[15] Here, "minority" is understood as a small category—small simply because but one of various and sundry such categories. The social constructionists' position, even if true, is as irrelevant to the normative sense of minorities as is the view of their opponents, the biological determinists. Their irrelevance intriguingly mirrors the materialists'. They can offer explanations, but not justifications; they can offer facts, but not values. Indeed, their relativism—"one person says one thing, another another; one culture says one thing, another another"—ought to make them skeptical that any critical morality is possible.

The role of nonmoral facts in morality is that they set the limit of the morally possible. Perhaps this fact about facts explains paradoxically why the early great works that one is most tempted to call gay studies, works chiefly of history and anthropology, have *appeared* to have such a strong moral component.[16] Their great virtue has not been explanation but revelation. Who would have thought that such stuff was out there—in past Christianity, in New Guinea, among Native American peoples? Who would have thought that there were so many possibilities? The limits of the possible have been dilated hugely, while that which previously appeared good because seemingly necessary and natural is now seen to be just one more damn thing. But we must not read positive moral claims into these findings. To change the horizon is not to set a course. What might be done does not tell us what ought to be done.

My model of gay studies, then, views gay studies as the study of a minority but offers an understanding of "minority" that is a tertium quid. Minority status is a moral vision, and gay studies, as the study of a minority, should be viewed chiefly as a normative inquiry rather than as either an empirical study of the world or a nonempirical study of discourses. The normative object of any minority study—and the chief reason that one is properly motivated to bother with the study in the first place—is the social treatment of a group that is socially defined independently of the behavior of its members. The form and end of gay studies is the evaluation of the treatment of gays so viewed and, in turn, the prescription of social forms in light of that moral evaluation. The architectonic of gay studies is not knowledge in the sense of the accumulation and systematizing of empirical facts and the hypothesizing of causal relations among them those facts. On the one hand, then, gay studies is not paramountly concerned with the biological or psychological features of the group's members. On the other hand, the relevant social treatment of the group—its moral treatment—is not to be confused with the alleged social construction of the minority as a category into which individuals might fall through either social forces or self-definition. Gay studies ought not to devolve into either biology or social history, as it currently seems to be doing. We have been playing things safe, perhaps too safe. History, anthropology, sociology, and literary studies make gays appear acceptable and nonthreatening because muted and transmuted by tales of the past, the exotics of distance, the abstractions of statistics, or the irrelevance of theory's jargon.[17] We need to be a bit braver and say that gay studies matters because gay people matter—here, now, and breathing.

Lest this all appear hopelessly flat-footed, thin, or abstract, or all three, allow me to give an example of how my program for gay studies would work, in particular with respect to other conceptions of gay studies and to the traditional academic disciplines. I will sketch briefly how gay studies might articulate itself in one area of the study of minorities: the study of stereotypes. The study of stereotypes is central to an understanding of the study of gays, for the existence of anti-gay stereotypes is a sufficient mark that gays are a minority in both the norm-dependent and the norm-invoking dimensions of that notion.

Stereotypes variously preempt and trip up the normal and adequate ways by which social knowledge is gained and social evaluations made. Stereotypes are bad faith writ large.

Society holds chiefly two groups of anti-gay stereotypes; they are an oddly contradictory lot. One revolves around alleged mistakes in an individual's gender identity, mismatches between a person's self-perceived gender and his or her biological sex. Lesbians are women who want to be, or at least look and act like, men—bulldykes, diesel dykes. Conversely, gay men are those who want to be, or at least look and act like, women—queens, fairies, limp wrists, nellies. These stereotypes of gender inversion and the jokes based on them, although derisive, basically view gay men and lesbians as ridiculous.

Another set of stereotypes revolves around the perception of gays, especially gay men, as a pervasive, sinister, conspiratorial threat. The core stereotype here is the gay man as child molester and, more generally, as sex-crazed maniac. This stereotype carries with it fears of the very destruction of family and civilization itself. Now, that which is essentially ridiculous, frivolous, and clownish can hardly have such a staggering effect.

Something must be afoot in this incoherent amalgam of stereotypes. Sense can be made of it if the nature of stereotypes is clarified. Stereotypes are not simply false generalizations from a skewed sample of cases examined. False generalizations *help maintain* stereotypes; they do not, by themselves, *form* them. Stereotypes have a life beyond facts. Their origin lies in a culture's ideology—the general system of beliefs by which it lives—and they are sustained across generations by diverse cultural transmissions, hardly any of which, including slang and jokes, even purport to have a scientific basis. Stereotypes, then, are not simply the products of bad science or of prescientific or ascientific generalizing from observation but are social constructions that perform central functions in maintaining society's conception of itself.

The stereotypes surrounding gender inversion function to shape and reinforce still powerful gender roles in society. If, as this stereotype presumes and condemns, one is free to choose one's social roles independently of one's biological sex, say, men choosing the roles traditionally assigned to women, then many guiding social divisions—domestic, commercial, political, military, and religious—might be threatened. The socially gender-linked distinctions would blur between breadwinner and homemaker, protector and protected, boss and secretary, doctor and nurse, priest and nun, hero and whore, saint and siren, lord and helpmate, mind and matter, God and earth.

The stereotype of gay men as child molesters, sex-crazed maniacs, and civilization destroyers has two social functions. First, it serves to give the family unit a false sheen of absolute innocence. It keeps the unit from being examined too closely for incest, child abuse, wife battering, and the terrorism of constant threats. Second, the stereotype functions socially to keep individuals' sexuality contained. This stereotype makes it appear as though the problem of how to address one's considerable sexual drives can and should be answered with repression, for it gives the impression that the cyclone of dangerous psychic forces is *out there* where the fags are, not within one's own breast. The stereotype of gays as child molesters is the complex product of a social need to protect the appearance of the family as innocent and sex as simple, manageable, and useful rather than awesome, ecstatic, and risky. Not surprisingly, the two protected appearances overlap in the ideal that sex is only for reproduction.

One could not rebut the cultural presumptions made in these stereotypes without changing culture itself. The modes of social knowledge represented by slang, jokes, stereotypes, and the mass media mutually reinforce and ramify each other—all in nearly complete ignorance of actual lesbians and gay men. No facts could disrupt the resulting web of received opinions, none of which rely in their origin or import on generalizations from experience.

Because "the facts" largely do not matter when it comes to the generation and maintenance of stereotypes, the effects of scientific and academic research and of enlightenment generally will be, at best, slight and gradual in the changing fortunes of gay men and lesbians. But it is important to note what form such study should take. The proper or core study of gay stereotypes does not fall to empirical social science or to the social history of the alleged social construction of sexuality. Science's role here is at best that of debunker, but neither does it have a handle on the social significance of stereotypes, nor, given the nature of stereotypes, does it much aid in solving the problems that stereotypes raise. Science's role will be that of underlaborer.

Neither, however, is the proper study of gay men and lesbians the study of the social construction of sexuality. Although stereotypes themselves are social constructions, they are not the categories into which actual gays have been lured or have fallen. Like traditional social science, then, social constructionism will have a subordinate role to play in gay studies. It will help keep track of what social concepts are in need of moral examination, but its own moral relativism will prevent it from being the engine of the needed moral critique.

Stereotypes, as norm-laden ideology, cannot be adequately understood by science or social constructionism. Ideology must be confronted by morality, and stereotypes can be addressed (to the degree they can be addressed at all) only by the study of ethics. Anti-gay stereotypes reveal society as profoundly immoral in its treatment of gays. The problem is not that society's usual procedural standards in coming to judgments of social policy have been misapplied to gays and require for justice only a correction of honestly made mistakes. Stereotypes are not simply textbook social science gone awry. Rather, standards of evaluation themselves, ones that all people would presume operate in their own evaluations of others and would insist on in evaluations of themselves, have not been applied at all when it comes to gays. They have simply been ruled out of court or disregarded in favor of mechanisms, like jokes and received opinions, that at best are simply dismissive of gays and that usually encourage unexamined fear and hatred of them, while the mechanisms themselves reinforce willful ignorance of gays' actual attributes and experience. When it comes to gays, the social inquisitor does not even ask questions before his judgments are made. When it comes to gays, the social negotiator has no thought of taking them into the bargaining, into the social contract. Stereotypes are bad faith raised to a social form.

As my model of gays as a minority predicts, this lack of appropriately equal social care and concern for gays is the product of social attitudes toward gays that bear no relation to what gays do: if they did bear a relation to what gays do, the normal mechanisms of procedural justice are all that would be needed to give gays their desert.

The existence of anti-gay stereotypes, then, establishes gays as fulfilling the norm-dependent criteria for minority status. Anti-gay stereotypes also generate and prescribe norms in relation to gays as a group, thus fulfilling the norm-invoking promise of minority status. That gays are subject to stereotypes means, for example, that they ought to have enhanced equal protection rights. For stereotypes corrupt both the substance and the procedures of a constitutionally restrained democracy. The existence of such stereotypes shows that the concerns of gays severally are not *substantively* given equal care and concern with the concerns of members of the dominant culture. Rather, gays as subjected to degradation in and through stereotypes are simply useful in society's maintenance of its view of itself. Stereotypes stand to the spirit of a nation as slavery stands to economics—and for that reason gays need protection from majoritarian decision making. Further, by short-circuiting the standard *procedures* for intelligent public policy-making, stereotypes undercut the very reasons for supposing that representational democracy is warranted as a form of government to begin with.[18] For reasons of the coherence of democratic theory, gays ought also to be given enhanced equal protections against majoritarian policy-making.

In the legislative sphere, the existence of severe anti-gay stereotypes ought to engage all three standard adequate justifications for affirmative action programs. First, since stereotypes have affected all gays disadvantageously (e.g., by maintaining bars to their marrying each other), affirmative action programs as compensation for *past harms* are warranted.[19] Second, such programs are warranted as necessary counterweights to balance the effects of present (frequently unconscious but empirically verified) prejudices so that *current procedures* (say, hiring practices) affecting gays are fair.[20] Third, such programs are warranted on grounds of *future social utility* by providing, among other things, models and fostering conditions that will help break the social forms that perpetuate invidious stereotypes and their baleful consequences.[21] So stereotypes establish gays as a minority in both dimensions of its moral sense, that of depending on norms and that of invoking or prescribing them—the very dimensions along which it matters, in the first instance, to worry about the study of minorities.

There is, then, a sense in which gay studies is not simply the study of gays by historians, anthropologists, biologists, sociologists, or literary critics or by any of the other established special disciplines. Lesbian and gay studies is the study of gays as a minority—the normative study of the social circumstances and treatment of lesbians and gay men. Although in the first instance the study affects the fortunes of gay men and lesbians, it is by no means limited in its inquiry to an isolatable segment of the population. For the social treatment of lesbians and gay men, in particular the social concepts under which society tries to classify lesbians and gay men, affects the way many dimensions of society are socially understood and normatively configured.

What is universally applicable in gay studies is not the possibility that everyone might secretly be bisexual, queer, or whatever, that gay sex acts are a live possibility for everyone—whether that is so is a question for the hard sciences to answer. What is universal about gay studies is that homosexuality and heterosexuality are definitional parts of, definitionally precede, or provide the core cultural paradigms for other distinctions that radiate throughout society, chief among them gender.[22] Much current work in gay studies by social constructionists is of great use in getting at these broader understandings.

The most interesting projects in gay studies now are not those of a new historicist stripe that, brain numbed by the mantra "the historically and culturally specific," look for this twist and that turn in the history of how homosexuality—or whatever it is—was represented in this text or that custom in different times and places. That project is gay studies at its cottage-industry worst. Rather, the most interesting works of lesbian and gay studies are those that show just how embedded, indeed fundamental, in our culture the categories of sexuality are, particularly the marked sexuality—homosexuality. Eve Sedgwick programmatically holds that "an understanding of virtually any aspect of modern Western

culture must be, not merely incomplete, but damaged in its central
substance to the degree that it does not incorporate a critical analysis
of modern homo/heterosexual definition." And she holds that homosexual definition "ineffacably marks" the understanding of at least
the following clustering categories: "secrecy/disclosure, knowledge/
ignorance, private/public, masculine/feminine, majority/minority,
innocence/initiation, natural/artificial, new/old, discipline/terrorism,
canonic/noncanonic, wholeness/decadence, urbane/provincial, domes-
tic/foreign, health/illness, same/different, active/passive, in/out, cogni-
tion/paranoia, art/kitsch, utopia/apocalypse, sincerity/sentimentality,
and voluntarity/addiction."[23]

There is something very right about this. Discipline/terrorism, uto-
pia/apocalypse: In 1989, the military thought that it had found a per-
suasively clear way to justify and resolidify its challenged and stressed
world vision by inventing a homosexual suicide on whom to peg the
fiery mass death of scores of sailors on the USS *Iowa*. On the Navy's
(later retracted) account of the gun turret explosion, a dejected, shadowy homosexual, Clayton Hartwig, despondent at the heterosexual
marriage of his naval buddy and spurned sexually by a shipmate, on
thus finding himself unable to corrupt the Navy, decides to wreak
revenge on it; he sets into action the instability and treachery inherent
in the homosexual's true pathological nature by sabotaging a cannon,
so that when it is test-fired the next day, he and forty-six other sailors
are blown to charred smithers.[24] In the Navy's view, which the gunnery
inferno was to undergird and rededicate, homosexuality is *the* lurking,
internal threat to society's very existence. Indeed, this threat is as
insidious as AIDS: just as AIDS kills by attacking the very thing by
which the body defends itself from invasion—the immune system—so
too (the Navy reasoned) homosexuality attacks the very thing by which
the body politic protects itself from invasion, the military. The
military's fantasy completes itself in a ritual of purification. Although at
great sacrifice to the Navy itself, the problem has, at the closet drama's
end, exited the scene. Hartwig is dead, the Navy is queer free, civilization is rescued.

Cognition/paranoia, private/public: On the very day that the chair-

man of the Journalism Department at the University of Illinois declined to cosponsor a major gay studies lecture on the ground that it
could not possibly have anything to do with journalism, Houston's
major daily fired a columnist on his trying to mention his own gayness
in a column on a local fatal queer bashing; the firing was tendered on
the ground that, in being openly gay, he could be neither objective nor
trusted. He was eventually rehired when he agreed to have his column
run, not in the news section of the paper as before, but only on the
opinions-and-editorials page. Journalism's self-touted claims to objectivity are always suspect, as are those of anyone who poses reality for a
price. Journalistic truth and reality may, in journalism's thinking, be
surveyed and purveyed by the closeted homosexual and may even
require that unseen ultimate manipulator of appearances to maintain
the props and ruses of the real. But the public, disguiseless homosexual
can be counted on only to present mere subjective, isolated opinion—
or, as the *Houston Post* put it, "the personal agenda of an individual."[25]
Here the secret homosexual is the worker for and the bearer of truth,
while the public homosexual is the social marker for the privately
selfish and the socially distorting.

One could extend and ring changes on the list: sanity/insanity, com-
munity/loneliness, partnership/alienation, home/ruin, seriousness/plea-
sure, purpose/fun, industry/sloth, authentic/inauthentic, trust/doubt,
objective/subjective, agent/patient, doer/done, domination/submission,
freedom/slavery, quest/destiny, human/animal, person/thing, real-
ity/appearance, being/becoming, eternity/generation, revelation/his-
tory, God/world, life/death.

These distinctions are not mere intellectual niceties. All are heavily
freighted with norms. They cut to our core as moral beings. The larger,
expanded gay studies project will remain centrally a normative one.
Virtually everything remains to be done in the program, but how it
turns out will affect how everyone lives.

NOTES

INTRODUCTION

1. Harris Wofford, *Of Kennedys and Kings: Making Sense of the Sixties* (New York: Farrar, Straus, & Giroux, 1980), p. 110.

2. *The Advocate*, #543, January 30, 1990, p. 22. (All references to *The Advocate* are to the nationally available gay news magazine published in Los Angeles.)

3. *New York Times*, November 7, 1991, p. 11. (All references to the *New York Times* are to its national edition unless otherwise noted.)

4. *New York Times*, December 17, 1989, p. 25; January 29, 1990, p. A13; February 12, 1990, p. A16; February 2, 1991, p. 10. *The Advocate*, #546, March 13, 1990, pp. 8–10; #547, March 27, 1990, pp. 12–14. The bishop, John Shelby Spong, "outs" Saint Paul in his book *Rescuing the Bible from Fundamentalism: A Bishop Rethinks the Meaning of Scripture* (New York: HarperCollins, 1991), pp. 116–26.

5. Walter Benjamin, "Theses on the Philosophy of History" (1940), in *Illuminations*, ed. Hannah Arendt, trans. Harry Zohn (1955; New York: Harcourt, Brace & World, 1968), pp. 256, 265.

6. Richard Mohr, *Gays/Justice—A Study of Ethics, Society, and Law* (New York: Columbia University Press, 1988).

CHAPTER 1. OUTING

1. *New York Times*, March 30, 1991, p. 8.

2. *New York Times*, March 27, 1990, p. A11; April 12, 1990, p. A11; *The Advocate*, #549, April 24, 1990, p. 37; #555, July 17, 1990, p. 9; #576, May 7, 1991, p. 50; Jane Rule, "Closet-Burning," from *Outlander* ([Tallahassee, Fla.:] Naiad, 1981), pp. 201–2.

3. *OutWeek* (New York), March 18, 1990, p. 4; *The Advocate*, #554, July 3, 1990, p. 63.

4. Here I am following Sissela Bok, *Secrets: On the Ethics of Concealment and Revelation* (New York: Pantheon, 1982), pp. 5–14.

5. For more detail, see Richard Mohr, *Gays/Justice—A Study of Ethics, Society, and Law* (New York: Columbia University Press, 1988), pp. 96–97.

6. Bok, *Secrets*, p. 11.

7. *New York Times*, March 13, 1991, p. A16.

8. *Oliver W. Sipple v. The Chronicle Publishing Co.*, 201 Cal. Rprt. 665 (Cal. App. 1984); Sipple's obituary, *New York Times*, February 5, 1989, p. 23.

9. Some critics have claimed that gay bars should be considered private spaces and that therefore to report publicly on what is seen only there would be an invasion of privacy of the bar-goer. But if bars, or even just gay bars, were indeed private spaces, they should be, like marriages, exempt from antidiscrimination laws and so could legitimately discriminate on the basis of, say, race—which seems pretty objectionable. In any case, both at common and statutory law, inns and taverns are paradigmatic cases of public accommodation. "Pub," remember, is just an abbreviation for "public house." So claims based on alleged privacy at bars will not aid those opposed to outing.

10. For details, see Mohr, *Gays/Justice*, pp. 100–105.

11. Vito Russo, letter, *Village Voice*, April 24, 1990, p. 4.

12. For elaborations and defenses of some of the claims about privacy in this paragraph, see Mohr, *Gays/Justice*, pp. 95–114.

13. It was this sense of privacy, e.g., that was held to protect abortion as a privacy right (*Roe v. Wade*, 410 U.S. 113, 152–53 [1973]).

14. *Bowers v. Hardwick*, 478 U.S. 186 (1986).

15. *The Advocate*, #590, November 19, 1991, p. 56.

16. See Charles Fried, *Medical Experimentation: Personal Integrity and Social Policy* (Amsterdam: North-Holland, 1974), pp. 95–96.

17. It seems unlikely that under the federal Constitution one could use state law to sue someone successfully for the public disclosure of truthful claims about oneself. See *Florida Star v. D.J.F.*, 109 S. Ct. 2603 (1989), which held that a newspaper cannot be held criminally liable under a state victims' rights law for printing the name of a rape victim gleaned from a legally obtained police report giving the victim's name. See also *Cox Broadcasting Corp. v. Cohn*, 420 U.S. 469 (1975), which held that the state may not, consistently with the first amendment, impose sanctions on the accurate publication of a rape victim's name obtained from judicial records that are maintained in connection with a public prosecution and that themselves are open to public record. But see *People v. Heinrich*, 470 N.E.2d 966, 970 (1984), in which the Illinois Supreme Court astonishingly held that in a

criminal defamation case truth is a defense only "when communicated with good motives and for justifiable ends."

18. Quoted in *Sipple*, 201 Cal. Rptr. at 667–670.

19. This argument also holds against those who view normative privacy as covering only information, not substantive actions (like abortion and sex). They hold that what is properly considered private is personal information. Personal information is that which most people do not want reported about themselves. But this sense of privacy could never legitimately have the status of a right since what is private on this account is simply a matter of popular opinion. For a defense of privacy as mere control over information, see William A. Parent, "Privacy, Morality, and the Law," *Philosophy and Public Affairs* 12 (1983): 269–88. Parent also counts as personal information *anything* a person strongly objects to having reported. But if that is so, and if privacy is a right, a person can insulate himself from every possible inquiry. This tactic makes privacy too broad.

Further, if privacy is just information control, it will conflict with the value that is knowledge and so have to be a very weak, easily overridden right. For trenchant criticisms of Parent and the view that privacy should be limited to the control of certain information, see Judith DeCew, "The Scope of Privacy in Law and Ethics," *Law and Philosophy* 5 (1986): 145–73.

20. Gabriel Rotello, "Tactical Considerations," *OutWeek*, May 16, 1990, p. 52.

21. See, e.g., Michael Bronski's otherwise excellent "Outing," *Gay Community News* (Boston), June 3, 1990, centerspread.

22. Benjamin Schatz, "Should We Rethink the Right to Privacy?" *The Advocate*, #571, February 26, 1991, p. 90.

23. These critics include Tom Stoddard, past director of the Lambda Legal Defense Fund, and gay arch-assimilationist Hunter Madsen (*New York Times*, March 27, 1990, p. A11; Madsen, "Tattle Tale Traps," *OutWeek*, May 16, 1990, p. 43).

24. Frank's views can be found in the *Boston Globe*, June 7, 1989, p. 1; June 16, 1990, p. 29; *Boston Sunday Herald*, June 17, 1990, p. 4.

25. This position is taken by the philosopher Jerry McCarthy in his unpublished 1991 paper "The Closet and the Ethics of Outing" (further information about this paper is available from Richard Mohr).

26. Ferdinand Schoeman, "Privacy and Intimate Information," in *Philosophical Dimensions of Privacy: An Anthology*, ed. Ferdinand Schoeman (Cambridge: Cambridge University Press, 1984), p. 409.

27. See Judith Shklar's "Let Us Not Be Hypocritical," in *Ordinary Vices* (Cambridge, Mass.: Harvard University Press, 1984), esp. pp. 69–70. Indeed, Shklar has argued that in liberal democracies, which alone among types of

governments allow moral and ideological testing of leaders, the greater the leader the greater the likelihood that the leader is charged with hypocrisy: "Antihypocrisy is a splendid weapon of psychic warfare, but not a principle of government. . . . The best politicians are those who can both reinforce the ideology upon which their authority is based and devise adequate policies. But very few are equally adept at both. Even those who are are peculiarly subject to charges of hypocrisy and debunking. Such was the fate of both Lincoln and Franklin D. Roosevelt. Each one was able to use rhetoric and showmanship to give new vigor to flagging political principles and loyalties. With that, they also raised the level of moral and political expectations. They failed to fulfill the standards they themselves revived."

28. "Employees could be fired for homosexuality while Bakker himself engaged in sex with men" (Charles E. Shepard, *Forgiven: The Rise and Fall of Jim Bakker and the PTL Ministry* [New York: Atlantic Monthly Press, 1989], p. 560; see also pp. 174–76, 187–89, 224–25, 244, 323–24, 441, 529, 537).

29. For example, Fran Lebowitz, interview, *The Advocate*, #554, July 3, 1990, p. 63; Andrew Sullivan, *New Republic*, September 9, 1991, p. 43.

30. Sarah Schulman, letter, *Village Voice*, April 24, 1990, p. 4.

31. Russo, letter, p. 4.

32. Indeed, these structures of coercion cover the case of the closet as "open secret"—where what is closeted is not knowledge of gayness but an acknowledgment of that knowledge. The subject of the open secret is like a fart: everyone knows that it happened and who did it, but no one, including the farter, acknowledges it.

33. E. J. Graff, op-ed, *Gay Community News*, July 29, 1990, p. 5 (emphasis added).

34. See *Texas v. Johnson*, 491 U.S. 397 (1989), which held that flag burning is first amendment protected.

35. Lebowitz, interview, p. 63; Graff, op-ed, p. 5.

36. "Abjection is the feeling of loathing and disgust the subject has in encountering certain matter, images, and fantasies—the horrible, to which it can only respond with aversion, with nausea and distraction. The abject is at the same time fascinating: it draws the subject in order to repel it. The abject is meaningless, repulsive in an irrational, unrepresentable way. . . . Abjection is expressed in reactions of disgust to body excretions—matter expelled from the body's insides: blood, pus, sweat, excrement, urine, vomit, menstrual fluid, and the smells associated with each of these. The process of life itself consists in the expulsion outward of what is in me, in order to sustain and protect my life. I react to the expelled with disgust because the border of myself must be kept in place. The abject must not touch me, for I fear that it will ooze through, obliterating the border between inside and

outside necessary for my life, which arises in the process of expulsion. If by accident or force I come to touch the abject matter, I react again with the reflex of expelling what is inside me: nausea. . . . The abject, as distinct from the object, does not stand opposed to the subject, at a distance, definable. The abject is other than the subject, but is only just the other side of the border. So the abject is not opposed to and facing the subject, but next to it, too close for comfort. . . . Homophobia is the paradigm of such border anxiety" (Iris Young, *Justice and the Politics of Difference* [Princeton, N.J.: Princeton University Press, 1990], pp. 143–44, 146).

37. *New York Times*, March 31, 1982, p. 24.
38. Schoeman, "Privacy," p. 406.
39. *Gay Community News*, January 21, 1991, p. 2.
40. *The Advocate*, #562, October 23, 1990, p. 56.
41. For an example of the latter, see *The Advocate*, #526, June 6, 1989, p. 40.
42. For example, Lebowitz, interview, p. 63.
43. Thus C. Carr, "Why Outing Must Stop," *Village Voice*, March 19, 1991, p. 37.
44. In "The Closet and the Ethics of Outing," McCarthy gives an extended account of the relevance to gay life of Vaclav Havel's vision of "living in the truth."
45. Russo, letter, p. 4.
46. Steve Berry, "Liz Smith Mon Amour," *OutWeek*, May 16, 1990, p. 44.
47. The editorial policy of *OutWeek* originally defended its outing of celebrities on the theory that such outing provided to gays, especially young ones, positive role models (*OutWeek*, #38, March 18, 1990, p. 4). Editor Michelangelo Signorile later gave a different, more interesting argument, one that moves in the spirit of John Stuart Mill's belief that the lives of alcoholics, drug addicts, and others who have made a botch of their lives, even in their botches, advance social utility—by showing others how *not* to live. In this new mode, Signorile asserts: "I agree that [those filled with shame and dragged out of the closet] are not going to be a good role model. But . . . they'll be a bad role model, which is very important too. The message will be 'Don't let this happen to you'" (*New York*, May 14, 1990, p. 94). If utilitarian arguments are called for, this is a pretty good one, although it should be remembered that increasing social utility is not enough to override a right. So the argument will not succeed if there is a right to the closet.
48. *Frontiero v. Richardson*, 411 U.S. 677, 686 (1973).
49. "Many readers would quickly agree that snitching on other hapless nobodies is mean, pointless and bad for the gay community in the long run" (Madsen, "Tattle," p. 42).

50. Ibid., p. 42.

51. Still the best account of gay self-oppression is Andrew Hodges and David Hutter's pamphlet *With Downcast Gays: Aspects of Homosexual Self-Oppression* (1974; Toronto: Pink Triangle, 1979).

52. Madsen, "Tattle," p. 42. Misleading are Madsen's pejorative terms for the truth-telling which is outing: "tattling," "snitching," "finking." For outing's report is not dirty and its aim is neither the punishment of its object nor the perverse delight of its subject.

53. Hannah Arendt, *Men in Dark Times* (New York: Harcourt, Brace & World, 1968), p. 186.

54. Madsen, "Tattle," p. 42.

55. Ibid., p. 41. It is puzzling that, in light of these high claims for openness, Madsen can then go on to defend the closet by claiming that outers should "keep in mind, after all, that coming out isn't *everything*" (p. 42).

56. *The Advocate*, #377, September 29, 1983, p. 21.

57. *The Advocate*, #376, September 15, 1983, p. 15.

58. *The Advocate*, #570, March 12, 1991, p. 72.

59. For example, see *The Advocate*, #555, July 17, 1990, p. 9.

60. Randy Shilts, op-ed, *New York Times*, April 12, 1990, p. A11; Bronski, "Outing," p. 11.

61. Schatz, "Privacy?" p. 90.

62. Russo, letter, p. 4.

63. *New York Times*, March 5, 1991, p. A1.

64. Gunnar Myrdal, *An American Dilemma: The Negro Problem and Modern Democracy* (1944; New York: Harper & Row, 1962), pp. 683, 687–88, quoting Charles S. Johnson, *Growing Up in the Black Belt* (Washington, D.C.: American Council on Education, 1941), p. 301.

65. Myrdal, *American Dilemma*, p. 686.

66. "Passing had become a non-issue by the time black power consciousness came into being. At least it didn't emerge significantly in [its] political discourse" (Alycee J. Lane, correspondence with the author, April 20, 1991).

67. Myrdal, *American Dilemma*, p. 687.

68. On secrets ended, see Rotello, "Tactical Considerations," p. 53.

CHAPTER 2. ON SOME WORDS FROM ACT UP

1. Then vice-president George Bush speaking in early 1988 (*Windy City Times* [Chicago], March 17, 1988, p. 4).

2. *The Advocate*, #580, July 2, 1991, p. 63.

3. Vito Russo, speech delivered on 7 May 1988 to an ACT UP rally in Albany, N.Y., reprinted in *Windy City Times*, July 28, 1988, p. 10.

4. Larry Kramer, *Reports from the Holocaust: The Making of an AIDS Activist* (New York: St. Martin's, 1989), pp. 246, 263.

5. The Equal Rights Amendment, which was passed by Congress in March 1972, but which failed to be approved by a sufficient number of states by its ratification deadline (extended in 1979 to) June 1982, read: "Equality of rights under the law shall not be denied or abridged by the United States or by any State on account of sex." If ratified, it would have given women the same constitutional immunity rights against governmental discrimination as blacks have under the equal protection clause of the fourteenth amendment.

6. See *New York Times Magazine*, October 6, 1991, p. 28.

7. *American Booksellers Association, Inc. v. Hudnut*, 598 F. Supp. 1316 (D. Ind. 1984), aff'd, 771 F.2d 323 (7th Cir. 1985), aff'd, 475 U.S. 1001 (1986).

8. *New York Times*, October 7, 1990, p. 19; September 18, 1991, p. B1; September 20, 1991, p. B2.

9. Robert Chesley, *Jerker, or the Helping Hand: A Pornographic Elegy with Redeeming Social Value and a Hymn to the Queer Men of San Francisco in Twenty Telephone Calls, Many of Them Dirty* (1986), in *Out Front: Contemporary Gay and Lesbian Plays*, ed. Don Shewey (New York: Grove, 1988).

10. *The Advocate*, #564, November 20, 1990, p. 65; #573, March 26, 1991, p. 64.

11. *Gay Community News* (Boston), September 1, 1991, p. 3; *New York Times*, September 13, 1991, p. B9.

12. For an example of how welfare "rights" end up destroying privacy rights, see Richard Mohr, *Gays/Justice* (New York: Columbia University Press), pp. 152, 222.

CHAPTER 3. BLACK LAW AND GAY LAW

This chapter covers federal and state court cases reported through December 1991.

1. *Manual Enterprises v. Day*, 370 U.S. 478, 490 (1962).

2. *Boutillier v. Immigration and Naturalization Service*, 387 U.S. 118 (1967).

3. *Bowers v. Hardwick*, 478 U.S. 186, 188 n.2 (1986) ("homosexual sodomy").

4. *San Francisco Arts and Athletics, Inc. v. United States Olympic Committee*, 483 U.S. 522 (1987).

5. For an account of how black cases served as a major vehicle for the expansion of first amendment rights, see the classic *The Negro and the First Amendment* by Harry Kalven, Jr. (Chicago: University of Chicago Press, 1966).

6. *Palmore v. Sidoti*, 466 U.S. 429 (1984). Further references in this section are to pp. 430–31, 432, and 433 (where emphasis is added).

7. Beginning in the late 1930s, the Court has developed a three-tiered equal protection analytic. At the highest tier, laws that discriminate against certain groups (to date, racial groups, ethnic groups, and legal aliens) are held to be "suspect" classifications and, in order to be constitutional, are required to be drawn as narrowly as possible to achieve governmental objectives that are themselves compelling. This requirement is the highest degree of protection provided by any constitutional right, and virtually no laws that engage this test pass it. At the middle tier, laws that discriminate against certain other groups (to date, women, illegitimate children, and illegal immigrant children) are held to be "quasi-suspect" classifications and, to pass constitutional muster, must be found to be substantially related to an important state interest. At the lowest tier—unenhanced or "weak" equal protection—*all* laws must be found to be rationally related to some legitimate state interest in order to be constitutional. In practice, this last standard has proved toothless. Virtually all laws have been upheld under it.

8. For example, *Globe Newspaper Co. v. Superior Court*, 457 U.S. 596, 607 (1982).

9. *City of Cleburne v. Cleburne Living Center, Inc.*, 473 U.S. 433, 448 (1985). And on suspectness, see n. 7 above.

10. *Bowers*, 478 U.S. at 196.

11. *Bowers*, 478 U.S. at 212 (Blackmun dissenting).

12. *U.S. Department of Agriculture v. Moreno*, 413 U.S. 528, 534–35 (1973) (quoting lower court case).

13. *O'Connor v. Donaldson*, 422 U.S. 563, 575 (1974), which held, on vague due process grounds, that a state cannot confine a nondangerous individual, declared by the state "mentally ill," who is capable of surviving safely in freedom by himself or with the help of willing and responsible family members or friends.

14. *Lyng v. International Union, UAW*, 108 S. Ct. 1184 (1988).

15. Department of Defense Directive 1332.14, 46(19) Fed. Reg. 9571–78 (January 29, 1981). Subsequently, a seventh reason for barring gays from the military—that they allegedly are security risks—has been dropped by the government. This shift occurred even before the secretary of defense in August 1991 called the rationale "a bit of an old chestnut" (*New York Times*, September 1, 1991, sec. 4, p. 10). See Rhonda Rivera, "Queer Law: Sexual Orientation Law in the Mid-Eighties," pt. 2, *University of Dayton Law Review* 11 (1986): 313.

16. *Padula v. Webster*, 822 F.2d 97 (D.C. Cir. 1987); *Ben-Shalom v. Marsh*, 881 F.2d 454 (7th Cir. 1989), cert. denied, 110 S. Ct. 1296 (1990); *Woodward v. United States*, 871 F.2d 1068 (Fed. Cir. 1989), cert. denied, 110 S. Ct. 1295 (1990); *High Tech Gays v. Defense Industrial Security Clearance Office*, 895 F.2d

563 (9th Cir. 1990). In all four of these cases, gays were held to have no enhanced equal protection rights comparable to those of blacks or women.

Gays have also been held to have no enhanced equal protection rights in the Fifth and Sixth Circuits: *Rowland v. Mad River Local School District, Montgomery County*, 730 F.2d 444 (6th Cir. 1984), cert. denied, 470 U.S. 1009 (1985); *Baker v. Wade*, 769 F.2d 289 (5th Cir. *en banc* 1985), cert. denied, 478 U.S. 1022 (1986). But see *Jantz v. Muci*, 759 F. Supp. 1543 (D. Kan. 1991), a federal district court case that held that gays *do* have the same high level of equal protection rights as blacks and insightfully criticized the various circuit court cases denying gays such rights.

17. *S.N.E. v. R.L.B.*, 699 P.2d 875, 879 (Alaska 1985).
18. The case that tries to apply *Palmore* to gay soldiers is *Pruitt v. Cheney*, 57 E.P.D. para. 40940 (9th Cir. 1991). The case that denied gays enhanced equal protection rights is *High Tech Gays v. Defense Industrial Security Clearance Office* (1990).
19. For example, *Dronenburg v. Zech*, 741 F.2d 1388, 1398 (D.C. Cir. 1984), which rejected the existence of the right to privacy and upheld military rationales for discrimination against gays as "common sense"; *Padula*, 822 F.2d at 104, which rejected equal protection challenges to FBI discrimination against gays.
20. *The Advocate*, #579, June 18, 1991, p. 24.
21. Both the fifth and the fourteenth amendment have due process clauses. The former applies to the actions of the federal government; the latter applies to the actions of state governments and reads: "Nor shall any State deprive any person of life, liberty, or property, without due process of law." Although the clauses speak only of required legal *procedures* and not about what *substantively* the law is barred from prohibiting, traditionally the Court has felt that some actions are so important (in one way or another) that barring them could not be carried out by any just procedures; these actions are protected then by *substantive* due process. For example, and significantly, it is through this elusive substantive dimension of the due process clause that most of the provisions of the Bill of Rights have come to be incorporated into the fourteenth amendment and so have come to apply against the *states*, even though in their own terms they just apply against the *federal* government. Freedom of speech, e.g., is held to be a fundamental right and so is applied, from the first amendment through the fourteenth amendment's due process clause, to the states: "Congress shall make no law . . ." becomes "No governmental agency—federal, state or municipal— shall make laws. . . ." Prior to 1937, substantive due process was frequently used by conservative Justices to strike down business regulations.
22. *Bowers*, 478 U.S. at 190, 190–92, 192.

23. Compare *Roe v. Wade*, 410 U.S. 113 (1973), which under the right to privacy voided virtually all bars to abortion, with *Webster v. Reproductive Health Services*, 109 S. Ct. 3040 (1989), which held that any abortion regulation that is rationally related to a legitimate state interest is constitutional; specifically, *Webster* upheld a statutory ban on the performance of nontherapeutic abortions either by public employees or at public facilities.

24. *Roe v. Wade*, 410 U.S. at 140 n.37 and at 174–75 (Rehnquist dissenting).

25. *Griswold v. Connecticut*, 381 U.S. 479 (1965), which declared unconstitutional under the right to privacy bars to marital use of contraceptives. On the history of contraception in America, see John D'Emilio and Estelle Freedman, *Intimate Matters: A History of Sexuality in America* (New York: Harper & Row, 1988), pp. 60–61, 160–61, 242–55.

26. *Stanley v. Georgia*, 394 U.S. 557, 564–65 (1969).

27. *Eisenstadt v. Baird*, 405 U.S. 438, 453 (1972); *Roe v. Wade*, 410 U.S. at 152 (1973).

28. *Paris Adult Theatre I v. Slaton*, 413 U.S. 49, 66 (1973), which held that the exhibition of obscene materials in places of public accommodation, like a movie theater, is not protected by any constitutional right of privacy or free speech.

29. *Osborne v. Ohio*, 110 S. Ct. 1691, 1695 n.3 (1990).

30. *Osborne*, 110 S. Ct. at 1711 n.12 (Brennan dissenting) (citations to lower courts omitted).

31. *New York Times*, November 5, 1990, p. A9.

32. *Palko v. Connecticut*, 302 U.S. 319, 325, 326 (1937).

33. *Moore v. City of East Cleveland*, 431 U.S. 494, 503 (1977).

34. *International Shoe Co. v. Washington*, 326 U.S. 310, 316 (1945).

35. *Bowers*, 478 U.S. at 191–92.

36. See generally Ronald Dworkin, *A Matter of Principle* (Cambridge, Mass.: Harvard University Press, 1985), chap. 2.

37. *Burnham v. Superior Court of California*, 110 S. Ct. 2105 (1990) (plurality opinion) (jurisdictional authority); *Michael H. v. Gerald D.*, 109 S. Ct. 2333 (1989) (plurality opinion) (parent-child relations); *Cruzan v. Director, Missouri Department of Health*, 110 S. Ct. 2841 (1990) (right to die).

38. *Burnham*, 110 S. Ct. at 2105 (plurality opinion); at 2119 (Justice White); at 2120 (Brennan); at 2126 (Stevens).

39. *Bowers*, 478 U.S. at 192, 194.

40. *Michael H.*, 109 S. Ct. at 2344 n.6.

41. *Michael H.*, 109 S. Ct. at 2360 (White dissenting). Justice Brennan gives an overview of the chaos at 2349.

42. *Michael H.*, 109 S. Ct. at 2340, 2344 n.6, 2345 & n.7; at 2352–53 (Brennan dissenting).

43. *Meyer v. Nebraska*, 262 U.S. 390 (1923); *Pierce v. Society of Sisters*, 268 U.S. 510 (1925); *Bowers*, 478 U.S. at 190–91; *Griswold v. Connecticut*, 381 U.S. 479 (1965).

44. All the *Cruzan* references in this paragraph are to 110 S. Ct. at 2851 (1990).

45. *Skinner v. Railway Labor Executives' Association*, 489 U.S. 602 (1989) (railway workers); *Treasury Employees v. Van Raab*, 489 U.S. 656 (1989) (customs officials).

46. *Treasury Employees*, 489 U.S. at 666–67, 668–72.

47. *Rutan v. Republican Party of Illinois*, 110 S. Ct. 2729, 2752 (1990) (citing *Bowers*, 478 U.S. at 192–94) (Scalia dissenting). By a five to four vote, *Rutan* held that patronage hiring practices violate first amendment protections of political association.

48. *Barnes v. Glen Theatre, Inc.*, 111 S. Ct. 2456 (1991).

49. *Barnes*, 111 S. Ct. at 2462 (1991) (quoting *Bowers*), and at 2474, 2476 (White dissenting).

50. *City of Richmond v. J. A. Croson Co.*, 109 S. Ct. 706 (1989).

51. Although civil rights suits usually drag on for years and years, the response to *City of Richmond* was swift. As early as July 1990, the *New York Times* could report: "In the wake of the January 1989 decision ruling that a Richmond, Virginia, ordinance was unconstitutional, lower courts have struck down [minority set-aside] programs in San Francisco, Atlanta, Philadelphia, Birmingham, Alabama, Jacksonville, Florida, and Dayton, Ohio, and at the state level in Michigan" (*New York Times*, July 16, 1990, p. A1).

The year after *City of Richmond*, the Supreme Court upheld (to my mind correctly but in contradiction to that case) even noncompensatory, forward-looking *federal* affirmative action programs, as though what equality rights one has vary depending on what government agency would intrude on them: whites have more rights against the states than against the federal government, but blacks have the same rights against both (*Metro Broadcasting v. Federal Communications Commission*, 110 S. Ct. 2997 [1990]).

52. *United States v. Carolene Products, Co.*, 304 U.S. 144, 152 n.4 (1938). For more on this case, see sec. IX below.

53. *Brown v. Board of Education*, 347 U.S. 483 (1954).

54. *City of Cleburne v. Cleburne Living Center, Inc.*, 473 U.S. 433 (1985).

55. *New York Times*, June 18, 1990, p. A1.

56. *New York Times*, November 7, 1991, p. A12.

57. *City of Richmond*, 109 S. Ct. at 721 (1989).

58. *Patterson v. McClean Credit Union*, 109 S. Ct. 2363 (1989); *Lorance v. AT&T*, 109 S. Ct. 2261 (1989); *Martin v. Wilks*, 109 S. Ct. 2180 (1989); *Wards Cove Packing Company Inc. v. Antonio*, 109 S. Ct. 2115 (1989); *Price Waterhouse v.*

Hopkins, 109 S. Ct. 1775 (1989); *Jett v. Dallas Independent School District*, 109 S. Ct. 2702 (1989); *Will v. Michigan*, 109 S. Ct. 2304 (1989).

59. *Board of Education of Oklahoma City v. Dowell*, 111 S. Ct. 630 (1991).

60. *Palmore*, 466 U.S. at 433 (1984) (emphasis added).

61. *Brown*, 347 U.S. at 495 (1954).

62. *San Francisco Arts and Athletics v. U.S. Olympic Committee*, 483 U.S. 522 (1987). The case cut back on both first and fifth amendment rights. I will discuss only its first amendment consequences.

63. References in this section to *San Francisco Arts and Athletics* are to 483 U.S. at 535, 536–37, and 569 (Brennan dissenting).

64. *State University of New York v. Fox*, 109 S. Ct. 3028, 3033 (1989), which upheld against first amendment challenge a state university's ban on corporations conducting product demonstrations in campus dormitory rooms.

65. *Texas v. Johnson*, 109 S. Ct. 2533, 2552 (1989) (Rehnquist dissenting).

66. *Dronenburg v. Zech*, 746 F.2d 1579 (1984).

67. *Webster v. Doe*, 496 U.S. 592 (1988).

68. *Webster*, 486 U.S. at 592 (1988) (Scalia dissenting).

69. *Society for Individual Rights v. Hampton*, 528 F.2d 905 (1975) (federal employment); *Singer v. U.S. Civil Service Commission*, 530 F.2d 247 (1976), which upheld the firing of a man for being openly gay, and so, it was claimed, for holding the government up to shame; *Beller v. Middendorf*, 632 F.2d 788 (1980), which, in an opinion written by Kennedy, upheld the ban on gays in the armed forces and indeed provided the wording for the government's current exclusion; and *Sullivan v. Immigration and Naturalization Service*, 772 F.2d 905 (1985), in which Kennedy's opinion upheld the deportation of a gay man, by claiming that the consequent likely destruction of his decade-long marital-like relation with his life-partner would not count as an "extreme hardship," a condition that, by statute, would have barred the deportation.

70. *Opinion of the Justices*, 530 A.2d 21 (N.H. 1987).

71. *The Family: Preserving America's Future: A Report to the President from the White House Working Group on the Family* (Washington, D.C.: U.S. Department of Education, Office of the Under Secretary, December 2, 1986), pp. 12, 51.

72. Clarence Thomas, "The Higher Law Background of the Privileges and Immunities Clause of the Fourteenth Amendment," *Harvard Journal of Law and Public Policy* 12, no. 1 (1989): 64 n. 4; Harry Jaffa, "Judge Bork's Mistake," *National Review*, March 4, 1988, pp. 38–39.

73. For cases, see n. 16 above.

74. *Lesbian and Gay Student Association v. Gohn*, 850 F.2d 361 (8th Cir. 1988).

75. In 1987, the District of Columbia Court of Appeals—which would be a

state supreme court if the District of Columbia were a state—held tangentially in a first amendment case that gays have enhanced equal protection rights (*Gay Rights Coalition v. Georgetown University*, 536 A.2d 1, 36 [D.C. App. *en banc* 1987]).

76. *New York Times*, September 30, 1991, p. A11.

77. *Braschi v. Stahl Associates Co.*, 544 N.Y.S.2d 784 (Ct. App. 1989).

78. *Alison D. v. Virginia M.*, 569 N.Y.S.2d 586, 587 (Ct. App. 1991).

79. *Buchanan v. Warley*, 245 U.S. 60 (1917).

80. *In the Matter of Emanuel S.*, 78 N.Y.2d 178 (1991).

81. *Curran v. Mt. Diablo Council of the Boy Scouts of America*, No. C 365529 (Cal. Super., L.A. Co.) (May 21, 1991).

82. *Dignity Twin Cities v. The Newman Center*, 472 N.W.2d 355 (Minn. App. 1991).

83. *West Coast Hotel v. Parrish*, 300 U.S. 379 (1937), which upheld Washington State's minimum wage legislation and reversed a 1923 case barring federal minimum wage laws for women and children.

84. *United States v. Carolene Products Co.*, 304 U.S. 144, 152 n.4 (1938).

85. *Payne v. Tennessee*, 111 S. Ct. 2597, 2610 (1991). This case reversed *Booth v. Maryland*, 482 U.S. 496 (1987), and *South Carolina v. Gathers*, 490 U.S. 805 (1989), cases barring victim impact statements in capital sentencing hearings.

86. *Gay Community News* (Boston), October 6, 1991, p. 2.

87. See also the Court's 1991 decision expanding constitutional property rights under the due process clause, *Connecticut v. Doehr*, 111 S. Ct. 2105 (1991), which held that states must provide a hearing before permitting a plaintiff in a private lawsuit to place a lien on the other side's property and thus found a due process violation in a procedure that does not actually amount to a "physical seizure" of assets.

88. *Coleman v. Thompson*, 111 S. Ct. 2546 (1991), which restricted *habeas corpus* appeals; *Gregory v. Ashcroft*, 111 S. Ct. 2395 (1991), which reduced the rights of the elderly; *Riverside v. McLaughlin*, 111 S. Ct. 1661 (1991), which held that arrestees may be jailed for up to forty-eight hours without a probable cause hearing.

89. In November 1991, Argentina's Supreme Court upheld a government ban on the country's principal gay rights organization's maintaining a bank account and receiving donations, reasoning as follows: "The defense of homosexuality offends the nature and dignity of the human person. The constitutional right of freedom of expression is limited by the need and duty to preserve public morals for the common good" (*The Advocate*, #593, December 31, 1991, p. 25).

CHAPTER 4. SOCIAL LENSES, SOCIAL PROGRESS
This chapter is a stump speech written in the "we" of manifesto.

1. *Black's Law Dictionary* (1891; St. Paul, Minn.: West, 1990), s.v. "Marriage"; *Singer v. Hara*, 11 Wash. App. 247 (1974).

2. *New York Times*, February 2, 1990, p. A1. Immigration Reform Act of 1990, Pub. L. No. 101-649, § 601(a)(1)(A)(ii), 104 Stat. 4978, 5067. Department of Defense Directive 1332.14, Fed. Reg., January 29, 1981, 46(19), pp. 9571-78. Approximately fifteen hundred gay men and lesbians are thrown out of the armed forces each year. For a splendid, usefully documented, comparative analysis of discrimination against blacks, women, and gays in the armed forces, see Kenneth L. Karst, "The Pursuit of Manhood and the Desegregation of the Armed Forces," *UCLA Law Review* 38, no. 3 (1991): 499-581.

3. *Bowers v. Hardwick*, 478 U.S. 186, 188 n.2 (1986).

4. Indeed, since *Bowers*, heterosexuals have fared well in sodomy cases. In October 1986, soon after its *Bowers* decision, the Supreme Court let stand without review an Oklahoma appellate court ruling that had declared heterosexual sodomy constitutionally protected by privacy rights (*Post v. State of Oklahoma*, 715 P.2d 1105 [Okla. Ct. Crim. App. 1986]). In order to finesse the constitutional issue, Maryland's highest court, by statutory interpretation, has held the state's sodomy law, despite its verbal neutrality with respect to sexual orientation, as in fact not applying to heterosexuals (*Schochet v. State*, 580 A.2d 176 [Md. 1990]). Even the Air Force Court of Military Review has held that heterosexual sodomy is constitutionally protected by privacy rights (*United States v. Fagg*, CM 29129 [A.F.C.M.R. August 6, 1991]).

5. *New York Times*, October 22, 1990, p. A4; March 18, 1990, p. 14.

6. *Adams v. Howerton*, 486 F. Supp. 1119 (D.C. Cal. 1980).

7. *The Advocate*, #579, June 18, 1991, p. 19.

8. *Palmer v. Thompson*, 403 U.S. 217, 219-21, 226 (1971).

9. *New York Times*, December 2, 1991, p. A8. On states passing mandatory testing laws, see *Gay Community News* (Boston), October 13, 1991, p. 1; *New York Times*, July 20, 1991, p. 7.

10. "A Message from NGLTF Co-Chairs," *1989 Annual Report of the National Gay and Lesbian Task Force* (Washington, D.C., [Summer 1990]), p. 1A.

11. Guy Hocquenghem, interview, *Christopher Street* 4, no. 8 (April 1980): 40. James Baldwin has written with similar pessimism: "White People were, and are, astounded by the holocaust in Germany. They did not know that they could act that way. But I very much doubt whether black people were astounded—at least, in the same way. For my part, the fate of the Jews, and

the world's indifference to it, frightened me very much. I could not but feel, in those sorrowful years, that this human indifference, concerning which I knew so much already, would be my portion on the day that the United States decided to murder its Negroes systematically instead of little by little and catch-as-catch-can. I was, of course, authoritatively assured that what had happened to the Jews in Germany could not happen to the Negroes in America, but I thought, bleakly, that the German Jews had probably believed similar counsellors" (*The Fire Next Time* [1963; New York: Dell, 1988], pp. 74–75).

12. *The Advocate*, #593, December 31, 1991, p. 82.

13. *New York Times*, July 14, 1990, p. 7.

14. *The Advocate*, #486, November 24, 1987, p. 15.

15. During the 1988 presidential campaign, Michael Dukakis signed into law what had previously been an administrative policy of his creation establishing a hierarchy of preferred homes for foster and adoptive children in which gays—who could only ever count as "singles"—came out on the very bottom, virtually assuring that no gay man or lesbian would ever be able to foster or adopt. Massachusetts courts found that the policy, although not specifically mentioning gays, was adopted with the intent to discriminate against gays (*The Advocate*, #507, September 13, 1988, p. 13).

16. Harvey Milk, "The Hope Speech," tape transcript in Randy Shilts's *The Mayor of Castro Street: The Life and Times of Harvey Milk* (New York: St. Martin's, 1982), p. 362.

17. Catharine R. Stimpson, *Where the Meanings Are* (New York: Methuen, 1988), pp. 11–37.

18. *Rust v. Sullivan*, 111 S. Ct. 1759, 1767–69 (1991).

19. Even as in November 1991 President Bush signed a compromise bill reversing some of the Supreme Court's 1989 decisions narrowing civil rights, the meaning of many of the bill's major provisions was in dispute among the bill's major players (*New York Times*, November 23, 1991, p. 8).

20. *New York Times*, December 30, 1989, p. 11.

21. Gay civil disobedience is finding quite a variety of forums: "6 Arrested Protesting Gay Housing Policy [at the University of California, Irvine]" (*New York Times*, October 12, 1990, p. B4); "Connecticut Activists Stage Civil Disobedience at State Capitol: A Mostly Lesbian Group Disrupts the Governor's Speech" (*Gay Community News*, February 18, 1990, p. 3). Civil disobedience is also one of the main strategies of ACT UP and Queer Nation.

Of the ACT UP demonstrations of which I am aware, only three have been morally objectionable: (1) a disruption at the Museum of Modern Art of the showing of Nicholas Nixon's photographs of people with AIDS, (2) a disruption of Sunday Mass at Saint Patrick's Cathedral on December 10, 1989, and the companion disruption of the ordination of eleven Roman Catholic priests by Boston cardinal Law on June 16, 1990, and (3) the complete drowning out of Department of Health and Human Services secretary Louis Sullivan's address to the Sixth International AIDS Conference in June 1990. All three actions passed beyond legitimate (indeed, I would say, protected) political heckling; they would all be gross violations of first amendment rights if carried out by the state. I view them as acts of terrorism, where a terrorist act is understood as an act that not even the state could legitimately carry out in deploying its monopoly of justified coercion.

For a history of ACT UP with an emphasis on its graphics and reasoning, see Douglas Crimp, *AIDS/DEMO/GRAPHICS* (Seattle: Bay Press, 1990). Crimp tries to justify the disruption of the Mass as nonviolent civil disobedience—in the very same breath that he condemns Operation Rescue's blocking of women's access to reproductive rights at abortion clinics as "terrorism" (p. 133). Crimp passes over in silence the photography show's disruption, perhaps raked in by images fresh in the mind of the arrests of Robert Mapplethorpe's photographs in Cincinnati.

More recently, ACT UP (admirably to my mind) disrupted the Senate confirmation hearings for Justice David Souter. The twelve arrested ACT UP members, among other things, called for there to be an openly gay male or lesbian member of the Supreme Court.

On the Saint Patrick's protest, see *The Advocate*, #542, January 16, 1990, pp. 6–10; *New York Times*, December 11, 1989, p. 16. On the ordination disruption, see *The Advocate*, #556, July 31, 1990, p. 18. On the obliteration of Sullivan's speech, see *New York Times*, June 25, 1990, p. A8. On Souter's confirmation, see *New York Times*, September 14, 1990, p. A13.

22. Bernard Boxill, *Blacks and Social Justice* (Totowa, N.J.: Rowman & Allanheld, 1984), p. 215.

23. Two examples of betrayals of gays by black politicians:

In May 1986, Washington, D.C., council member John Ray spearheaded the passage of legislation barring the insurance industry from using HIV screening. Socially, the issue was treated as a gay one: the *Washington Post* editorialized against the measure as "special treatment" for the "gay community" (May 9, 1986, p. A18). Yet, when speaking before a gay group as part of an unsuccessful 1990 mayoral bid, Ray held that he "believes in" the heterosexual life-style and that heterosexuality "is the best way" for the black community, as though gays were somehow a threat to the black community (*Gay Community News*, May 13, 1990, p. 2).

U.S. Representative Gus Savage, although a sponsor of federal gay civil rights bills, resorted to the crassest gay baiting when investigated by the House Ethics Committee for alleged sexual harassment of a female federal employee. At two press conferences on the investigation, he called reporters from the gay press "faggots," "fag-boys" and "cross-dressers and transvestites" and called homosexuality "unnatural." At the same time, Savage took to gay baiting openly gay congressman Barney Frank (*Outlines* [Chicago], August 1989, p. 4; *New York Times*, February 2, 1990, p. A11).

24. *Gay Community News*, October 6, 1991, p. 2.

25. *The Daily Illini* (Champaign, Ill.), October 24, 1991, p. 1.

26. *The Advocate*, #582, July 30, 1991, p. 54.

27. The Utah "branch of the American Civil Liberties Union has petitioned its parent organization to make legal recognition of polygamy a national cause like gay and lesbian rights" (*New York Times*, April 9, 1991, p. A8).

CHAPTER 5. TEXT(ILE)

1. Thucydides, *History of the Peloponnesian War* 2.47, 53–54 (quotations from the translation by Rex Warner [Harmondsworth: Penguin, 1986], pp. 152, 155–56).

2. Cindy Ruskin, *The Quilt: Stories from The NAMES Project* (New York: Pocket Books, 1988), p. 9.

3. A useful account of Powers's life and the social context of her quilts is given as an epilogue to Gladys-Marie Fry's *Stitched from the Soul: Slave Quilts from the Ante-Bellum South* (New York: Dutton Studio Books, 1990).

4. Ibid., p. 90.

5. *My Life* by, variously, Mohammed Ali, Marc Chagall, Anton Chekhov, Isadora Duncan, Henry Havelock Ellis, Oskar Kokoschka, Golda Meir, Leon Trotsky, and Richard Wagner.

6. E. G. Crichton, "Is The NAMES Quilt Art?" *OUT/LOOK* 1, no. 2 (Summer 1988): 7–8.

7. Ibid., p. 9.

8. Sigmund Freud, "Mourning and Melancholia" (1915), in *The Standard Edition of the Complete Psychological Works of Sigmund Freud*, ed. and trans. James Strachey (London: Hogarth, 1957), 14: 245, 252, 255, 257.

9. Emily Post, *Emily Post's Etiquette: The Blue Book of Social Usage* (1922), 11th rev. ed., rev. Elizabeth L. Post (New York: Funk & Wagnalls, 1965), pp. 335–36. A similar view of mourning is advanced by Douglas Crimp, who thinks that we should mourn so we can get back to the serious business of life—not the business of having parties, but the business of having demonstrations ("Mourning and Militancy," *October*, #51 [Winter 1989]: 3–18).

10. Ruskin, *The Quilt*, p. 44 and passim.

11. Aristotle, *Nicomachean Ethics* 1.10.

12. Although the march was covered by the *New York Times* and the *Washington Post*, it was not covered by either *Time* or *Newsweek* (*Washington Post*, October 12, 1987, p. 1).

13. *Washington Post*, October 11, 1987, p. B1.

14. *Washington Post*, October 14, 1987, p. 1.

15. *School Board of Nassau County, Fla. v. Arline*, 480 U.S. 273 (1987), which held that infectious diseases, including AIDS, are covered by the civil rights protections of the 1973 Rehabilitation Act.

16. *Lesbian and Gay Studies Newsletter* (Duke University), 18, no. 3 (November 1991): 7.

17. *The Advocate*, #576, May 7, 1991, p. 94.

CHAPTER 6. "KNIGHTS, YOUNG MEN, BOYS"

1. We are told that angels have brought the Grail and Spear from heaven and entrusted them to mankind's safekeeping because of unnamed troubles in and threats to heaven (Gurnemanz, *Parsifal*, act 1, scene 1). Translations of Wagner's libretto are made with an eye to Frank Freudenthal's translation for Philips's recording of the opera's 1961 Bayreuth Festival performances. The opera's final chorus is: "Höchsten Heiles Wunder! / Erlösung dem Erlöser!"

2. Anton Webern, *Das Augenlicht* (1935), Cantata no. 1 (1939), and Cantata no. 2 (1943).

3. The critic is Donal Henahan, the *New York Times*'s chief music critic ("*Parsifal* Still Awaits Its Einstein," March 31, 1991, sec. 2, p. 19).

4. Some social constructionists claim that even biological sex is the product of social forces and understandings. See, for a chief example, Judith Butler's *Gender Trouble: Feminism and the Subversion of Identity* (New York: Routledge, 1990), pp. 134–41.

5. I am thinking especially of Michel Foucault in *History of Sexuality*, vol. 1, *An Introduction*, trans. Robert Hurley (1976; New York: Vintage, 1980), p. 157; and "Sex and the Politics of Identity: An Interview with Michel Foucault," reprinted from *The Advocate*, #400, August 7, 1984, in Mark Thompson's *Gay Spirit: Myth and Meaning* (New York: St. Martin's, 1987), pp. 25–35. I am also thinking of Foucault's disciples Ed Cohen ("Foucauldian Necrologies: 'Gay' Politics? Politically Gay?" *Textual Practice* 2 [1988]: 87–101) and Diana Fuss (*Essentially Speaking: Feminism, Nature and Difference* [New York: Routledge, 1989], pp. 102–12).

6. Sir Kenneth Dover recounts one of the world's great stories of the political consequences of individual goodness: "Harmodios and Aristogeiton killed

Hipparkhos, the brother of the tyrant Hippias, in 514 B.C., and were regarded in popular tradition as having freed Athens from tyranny, though Hippias was not in fact expelled until 510. Both Harmodios and Aristogeiton perished in consequence of their act; Harmodios was the eromenos [in a sexually loving male pair, the junior partner] of Aristogeiton, and Hipparkhos's unsuccessful attempt to seduce him was the start of the quarrel which had such a spectacular political outcome" (K. J. Dover, *Greek Homosexuality* [1978; Cambridge, Mass.: Harvard University Press, 1989], p. 41).

7. Paraphrase of Roger Brown, *Social Psychology: The Second Edition* (1965; New York: Free Press, 1986), pp. 313–14.

8. So correctly, Judith Butler: "In a sense for Foucault, as for Nietzsche, cultural values emerge as the result of an inscription on the body, understood as a medium, indeed a blank slate." Butler herself presses further. She claims that the body is *even less* than a blank slate and that Foucault is wrong in "maintaining a body prior to its cultural inscription" (*Gender Trouble*, p. 130).

9. *Newsweek*, April 2, 1990, p. 12.

10. Judith Butler thinks that drag is liberating because, when set against the background of sex, the foreground of gender shows the whole system of sex and gender to be a social artifice rather than a thing constrained by nature (*Gender Trouble*, pp. 123, 138–39, 148–49). But this schema misunderstands the relation of grounds to artifice. That a painting or a dream has a foreground and a background does not establish it as any more of an artifice than, say, an abstract painting that does not have them. Rather, it is the relation between a picture or a dream and the nonpictorial or nondream world that establishes it as an artifice. There is no artifice without reference to reality. But given this entailment, things go awry for Butler. For she holds that there is no real world over and above or behind the socially confected one, the world of artifice. Indeed, she claims that all talk of ontology is a Right-wing plot. But then, with no real world in sight, we are not able to know whether the sex-and-gender complex is indeed artificial. It is no surprise, then, that Butler ends up talking of gender as an imitation that has no original. But an imitation *just means* to be "of an original," so it is hard to know quite what in the end she does mean.

11. The quatrefoil picture can be found in Janet Kardon, *Robert Mapplethorpe: The Perfect Moment* (Philadelphia: Institute of Contemporary Art, University of Pennsylvania, 1988), p. 111.

12. Louis H. Sullivan, *Kindergarten Chats and Other Writings* (1918; New York: Dover, 1979), chat no. 6, "An Oasis," pp. 29–30. On this passage, and for

a cautiously argued attribution of homosexuality to Sullivan, see Robert Twombly, *Louis Sullivan: His Life and Work* (New York: Viking, 1986), pp. 399–402.

13. *New York Times,* July 19, 1990, p. A1; May 9, 1991, p. A16.

14. Both photographs are photographs of women. Figure 11 is Edgar Degas's 1896 bromide print *After the Bath* (courtesy of the J. Paul Getty Museum, Malibu, Calif.). Figure 12 is a 1980 Mapplethorpe photograph of the bodybuilder Lisa Lyon (courtesy of the Robert Mapplethorpe Foundation).

15. Lawrence Barns, ed., *The Male Nude in Photography* (Waitsfield, Vt.: Vermont Crossroads, 1980), photograph p. 39, *Times* quoted p. 94.

16. The photograph can be found in Peter Weiermair's *The Hidden Image* (Cambridge, Mass.: MIT Press, 1988), p. 174.

17. Allan Bloom, *The Closing of the American Mind* (New York: Simon & Schuster, 1988), p. 131; later citations are to pp. 110, 112, and 115.

18. William H. Masters and Virginia E. Johnson, *Homosexuality in Perspective* (Boston: Little, Brown, 1979), pp. 71, 72.

19. Muriel Beadle, *The Cat* (New York: Simon & Schuster, 1977), pp. 45–47.

20. For the separation of reproduction and sexuality, see Claudia Card, "Intimacy and Responsibility: What Lesbians Do," in *At the Boundaries of the Law: Feminism and Legal Theory,* ed. Martha Fineman and Nancy Thomadsen (New York: Routledge, 1991), pp. 77–94.

21. A longer, better version of this chapter would include a discussion of whether there are masculine virtues, in the way that some feminists have claimed that there are specifically feminine virtues, even specifically feminine ethical systems, which have as their motors such concepts as caring, sympathy, attentiveness, and nurture. For telling criticisms of such views, see Sarah Lucia Hoagland's *Lesbian Ethics: Towards New Value* (Palo Alto: Institute of Lesbian Studies, 1988), chap. 2; and Claudia Card's "Gender and Moral Luck," in *Identity, Character, and Morality: Essays in Moral Psychology,* ed. Owen Flanagan and Amelie Rorty (Cambridge, Mass.: MIT Press, 1990), pp. 199–218.

22. James D. Steakley, *The Homosexual Emancipation Movement in Germany* (New York: Arno, 1975), p. 54; on the Community of the Special, founded in 1902, see pp. 42–54.

23. For photographs, see Robert Mapplethorpe, *Black Males* (Amsterdam: Galerie Jurka, 1980), pp. 20, 26, 32, 33; Richard Marshall, *Robert Mapplethorpe* (Boston: Little, Brown, 1988), pp. 65, 96–99, 202; George Dureau, *New Orleans: 50 Photographs* (London: GMP [Gay Men's Press], 1985), pp. 35–53, 57–77, 109.

For diverse opinion on this issue, see Edmund White's introduction to

Mapplethorpe's *Black Males;* and Jackie Goldsby's "What It Means to Be Colored Me," *OUT/LOOK,* #9 (Summer 1990): 8–17. Carrie Mae Weems claims: "Mapplethorpe's aesthetization of Black men for the gaze of white men leaves Black male sexuality tamed, docile, and cooperative" (*Gay Community News,* September 30, 1990, p. 8). For an elaborate argument that history-destroying formalism renders racist most of Mapplethorpe's photos of black men, see Thomas Yingling, "How the Eye Is Caste: Robert Mapplethorpe and the Limits of Controversy," *Discourse: Theoretical Studies in Media and Culture,* 12, no. 2 (1990): 3–28. But see Jill Dolan's "Practicing Cultural Disruptions: Gay and Lesbian Representation and Sexuality," in *Critical Theory and Performance,* ed. Janelle Reinhelt and Joseph Roach (Ann Arbor: University of Michigan Press, 1992). Dolan writes: "By offering homosexual and cross-racial visual pleasure in flesh, [the Mapplethorpe photographs of sexy black males] visually flaunt a rejection of compulsory heterosexual practice. Exhibited in galleries and museums, the photographs take public representational space to image eroticized organs that simply by virtue of being seen contest dominant cultural regimes of knowledge and power about sexuality and race. The possibility for transgression in such representations lies in the hint of sexual practice and seduction they envision, not in the gay lifestyle to which they refer." See generally Judith Butler, "The Force of Fantasy: Feminism, Mapplethorpe, and Discursive Excess," *differences,* 2, no. 2 (1990): 105–25.

24. Pace Elaine Showalter, *Sexual Anarchy: Gender and Culture at the Fin de Siècle* (New York: Viking, 1990), chap. 5.

25. Rex and the late Tom of Finland stand to gay male life of the 1970s and 1980s as Grandma Moses stands to rural American life of the 1940s and 1950s. All used the forms of high art to produce intense but cartoonish works of folk art, works that at once captured, valorized, and yet prepared for nostalgia a spirit of an era always on the verge of vanishing. Partly through the efforts of the Tom of Finland Foundation, Tom's work has been receiving the attention of museums, including purchases by the Whitney Museum of American Art. Rex's work has been shown in art galleries, but the reclusive artist has largely shunned the channels of high art, selling his work directly to his fans through advertisements in the gay press.

Tom of Finland (1920–1991) was indeed from Finland. "Tom's earliest sexual experiences were with German soldiers during the [Nazi] occupation of Helsinki. . . . His first drawings were attempts to recreate those experiences and fantasies" (interview in *Christopher Street,* 4, no. 8 [April 1980]: 16–21). Tom's pencil drawings are most accessible through the 1988 coffee-table collection of his work *Tom of Finland: Retrospective* (Tom of Finland

Foundation, P.O. Box 26658, Los Angeles, Calif. 90026). Many of his drawings are multiple-frame stories without words published as free standing outsized pamphlets. By 1980, he had stopped allowing his early drawings of Nazis to be circulated.

In biography, Rex is obscure—and that by his own choice. His work is most accessible through a beautifully produced, although, he claims, censored, 1986 coffee-table collection of his work covering the years 1975–85, *Rexwerk: 50 Dessins par Rex* (Les Pirates Associes, B.P. 332, 75962 Paris Cedex 20 France; or "Designs by Rex," P.O. Box 347, San Francisco, Calif. 94101). Rex's "drawings" are pointalistic, made up of tiny ink dots in the manner of tattooing—an activity that is the subject of many of his works.

Both draftsmen's work has been disseminated chiefly in the gay male world through its use either in advertisements for gay products and services (like poppers and telephone sex) or as graphics accompanying, but not illustrating, jerk-off stories.

26. "The extremes [of gay male life] were outre, such as fist fucking, or marathon ejaculatory frenzies performed through holes bored in a barroom wall; but milder modes, too, employed the excretory orifice in a manner that mammals had all but stopped using seventy to a hundred million years ago and that tore lesions in the rectal lining through which the strange, savage virus entered. Writers in numbers witnessed all this, but forbore to comment for fear of becoming unpopular" (Edward Hoagland, "Shhh! Our Writers Are Sleeping," *Esquire*, July 1990, p. 62).

27. Hoagland, *Lesbian Ethics*, pp. 54ff.

28. James Baldwin, *The Fire Next Time* (1963; New York: Dell, 1988), pp. 110–11.

29. *Tom of Finland: Retrospective*, [p. 25].

30. Arthur Tress, *Facing Up* (New York: St. Martin's, 1980), p. 16.

31. The drawings can be found in Douglas Blair Turnbaugh, *Duncan Grant and the Bloomsbury Group* (Secaucus, N.J.: Lyle Stuart, 1987), pl. 42.

32. A National Institute of Mental Health researcher found that one-third of campus gang rapes were committed by student athletes: "My gut feeling about gang rape is that it takes place in front of guys who know each other; they live together, have a way that they become bonded together." Another researcher found that "most [campus gang rapes] involved fraternities or athletic team members, football or basketball. It usually occurs in a group of young men with a team spirit and usually living together. I think they end up relating to each other so intensely even their sexual experiences become shared" (*New York Times*, June 3, 1990, sec. 8, p. 4 [New York City ed.]).

33. *New York Times*, August 29, 1989, p. 21.

34. Boyd McDonald, ed., *Juice: True Homosexual Experiences from S.T.H. [Straight to Hell] Writers*, vol. 5 (San Francisco: Gay Sunshine, 1984), p. 84.

35. In her book *Fraternity Gang Rape: Sex, Brotherhood and Privilege on Campus* (New York: New York University Press, 1990), Peggy Reeves Sanday holds that fraternity members use gang rape to shore up their uncertainties about sexuality and that their bonding is based largely on hostility to women. Sanday is oblivious to the homoerotic dimensions of gang rape.

36. "Mr. Salaam admitted to taking part in the attack on the woman, striking her twice with a pipe and grabbing her breasts. . . . The detective said: 'How could you possibly do something like this?' 'It was just something to do, it was fun'" (*New York Times*, July 24, 1990, p. A12). Compare Gary Comstock, *Violence against Lesbians and Gay Men* (New York: Columbia University Press, 1990), p. 76: "Social disapproval of homosexuality was less the [queer bashers'] reason and more the permission for attacking their victims. It mitigated the responsibility for the damage and injury they might have caused. Apparently, they did not attack gay men because they hated and, therefore, wanted to punish or hurt them, as much as they attacked a socially vulnerable people to alleviate their own boredom."

37. The copy print used here was made from the now-damaged negative at the Robert Mapplethorpe Foundation.

38. By "democracy," I mean the political *procedures* whereby policy-making is held accountable to an electorate in which each person counts for one. I do *not* mean by "democracy" some set of substantive political *ideals*, as when people loosely speak of constitutional rights as a key part of democracy, where in fact constitutional rights void the results of democratic procedures. Nor do I mean by "democracy" what some Leftists call "democratic socialism" or "participatory democracy," wherein what gets rightfully engaged in policy-making procedures is not individuals (each counting as one) but certain diverse groups of people (Lapps, gays, women, Native Americans, workers) or diverse types of interests (the environment, jobs, health care, the arts).

39. Hoagland, *Lesbian Ethics*, pp. 247–65.

40. For a world roundup of "homosexually" shamanistic societies, see Walter Williams, *The Spirit and the Flesh: Sexual Diversity in American Indian Culture* (Boston: Beacon, 1986), chap. 12.

41. The essay was originally published in the November 15, 1969, issue of the Leftist antiwar magazine *WIN* and has been reprinted in *Nature Heals: The Psychological Essays of Paul Goodman*, ed. Taylor Stoehr (New York: Free Life Editions, 1977), pp. 216–25; quotations below are from pp. 219, 220, 221.

42. Armistead Maupin, *Sure of You* (New York: Harper & Row, 1989), p. 68.

43. Masters and Johnson, *Homosexuality in Perspective*, pp. 212–13; cf. p. 72. The subsequent reference is to pp. 180–83.

44. Walt Whitman, *Leaves of Grass: Comprehensive Reader's Edition*, ed. Harold W. Blodgett and Sculley Bradley (New York: Norton, 1965), p. 753.

45. Walt Whitman, *Democratic Vistas*, in *Complete Prose* (Boston: George H. Ellis, 1898), p. 240n. Subsequent quotations are from pp. 213 and 221.

46. Walt Whitman, *Leaves of Grass* (Boston: Thayer & Eldridge, 1860), p. 351.

47. Guy Hocquenghem, *Homosexual Desire*, trans. Daniella Dangoor (1972; London: Allison & Busby, 1978), pp. 97, 136.

48. Esther Newton, "Yams, Grinders, and Gays: The Anthropology of Homosexuality," *OUT/LOOK* 1, no. 1 (Spring 1988): 31 (quoting Thomas Gregor, *Anxious Pleasures*, p. 72).

49. *The Advocate*, #559, September 11, 1990, pp. 64–66.

50. *Ecce Homo*, in *The Basic Writings of Nietzsche*, ed. Walter Kaufmann (New York: Random House, 1968), p. 744.

51. *Nietzsche Contra Wagner*, in *The Portable Nietzsche*, ed. Walter Kaufmann (New York: Viking, 1954), p. 676.

52. For example: "The progress of [truth]: it becomes more subtle, insidious, incomprehensible—*it becomes female*, it becomes Christian" (*Twilight of the Idols*, in *The Portable Nietzsche*, p. 485). Nietzsche's contempt for women is well known. See esp. *Beyond Good and Evil*, secs. 231–39.

53. *The Antichrist*, in *The Portable Nietzsche*, p. 619.

54. A photograph of the ritual as performed at the first fairy circle in 1978 can be found in Thompson, ed., *Gay Spirit*.

55. Nicholas Mosley, *Impossible Object* (1968; Elmwood Park, Ill.: Dalkey Archive Press, 1985), p. 163.

56. Showalter, *Sexual Anarchy*, pp. 78, 82.

57. The essay is "An Addendum" to the chapter of the second edition titled "The Metaphysics of Sexual Love" (chap. 44) (Arthur Schopenhauer, *The World as Will and Representation*, trans. E. F. J. Payne [New York: Dover, 1966], 2: 560–67). The quotes are from p. 564. Like recent sociobiological accounts of homosexuality, Schopenhauer's teleological explanation of "pederasty" appeals to the indirect beneficial effects of homosexuality for procreation. Men beyond the prime years for begetting healthy offspring and men younger than these years will (so it goes) be normally and naturally attracted to each other for sex, so that their sperm—inferior for purposes of reproduction—will in fact not be deployed reproductively: "The result of this discussion is that, whereas the vice we are considering appears to work directly against the aims and ends of nature, . . . it must in fact serve these very aims, although only indirectly, as a means for

preventing greater evils" (p. 566). Pederasty here is sexual theodicy—an explanation of evil's existence in a world ably designed for the best.

58. The quote is from the late doyen of anti-gay psychiatry Irving Bieber in his 1962 anthology *Homosexuality: A Psychoanalytical Study of Male Homosexuality*, quoted in his obituary (*New York Times*, August 28, 1991, p. B9).

59. Hans Jürgen Syberberg, *Parsifal* (Triumph Films, distributed by Corinth Films, 1982).

60. Sander L. Gilman, *Disease and Representation: Images of Illness from Madness to AIDS* (Ithaca, N.Y.: Cornell University Press, 1988), pp. 168–176.

61. Guy Hocquenghem, interview, *Christopher Street* 4, no. 8 (April 1980): 40–41. Hocquenghem correctly rejects Foucault's belief that sexual perversions and sexual minorities based on them are indeterminately various and arise independently of each other.

62. "'All these crimes have a sexual basis' [said the forensic expert]. 'And the more they practice bizarre sexual perversions, the more bizarre they get.' Even so, in the making of a serial killer [the expert said], 'the main thing is not the sexual preferences but the dynamics of personality'" (*New York Times*, August 7, 1991, p. A8). The *New York Times* ran lengthy articles on Dahmer daily from July 24 to August 4, 1991, and intermittently for months after, bearing titles like "Slaying Suspect: Loner with a Dark Side," "Hunting for Clues in the Life of Accused Mass Killer," and "Child's Love of Cruelty May Hint at the Future Killer: The Dark Nurturing Ground of the Serial Killer."

63. Lennart Nilsson's photographs were first widely circulated in the April 30, 1965, issue of *Life*. They are most accessible in his book *A Child Is Born* (1965; New York: Delacorte, 1978).

64. H. A. Hammelmann, *Hugo von Hofmannsthal* (New Haven, Conn.: Yale University Press, 1957), p. 62.

65. Plato, *Symposium* 206c, 206e–207a, 208e.

66. Jacques Derrida, "The Politics of Friendship," *Journal of Philosophy* 85, no. 11 (1988): 632–44, esp. 642. For a discussion of Derrida's strained relation to homosexuality, see Fuss, *Essentially Speaking*, p. 111.

CHAPTER 7. THE THING OF IT IS

1. The dissents from social construction are so few that they can be listed without burden: John Boswell, "Revolutions, Universals, and Sexual Categories," *Salmagundi* 58–59 (1982–83): 89–113, "Gay History," *The Atlantic*, February 1989, pp. 74–78, "Concepts, Experience, and Sexuality," *differences* 2, no. 1 (1990): 67–87, and interview, *Christopher Street* 13, no. 6 (1990): 23–40, reprinted from Lawrence Mass, *Homosexuality as Behavior and Identity: Dialogues of the Sexual Revolution*, vol. 2 (New York: Haworth,

1990); Michael Ruse, *Homosexuality: A Philosophical Inquiry* (Oxford: Basil Blackwell, 1988); Edward Stein, "The Essentials of Constructionism and the Construction of Essentialism," in *Forms of Desire: Sexual Orientation and the Social Constructionist Controversy*, ed. Edward Stein (New York: Garland, 1990), pp. 325–53; Wayne R. Dynes, "Wrestling with the Social Boa Constructor," in *Forms of Desire*, pp. 209–38. Most of the important theoretical papers in the debate on the social construction of homosexuality have been reprinted in Stein's *Forms of Desire*. Noretta Koertge has an intriguing, unpublished paper ("Constructing Concepts of Sexuality"); see also her published variant of the same paper in *Homosexuality/Heterosexuality: Concepts of Sexual Orientation*, ed. David P. McWhirter, et al. (New York: Oxford University Press, 1990), pp. 387–97.

Any sampler of books preponderantly committed to social constructionism on homosexuality would probably include most prominently Michel Foucault's *The History of Sexuality*, vol. 1, *An Introduction* (1976; New York: Vintage, 1980) (hereafter cited as *History I*); and also Jeffrey Weeks, *Coming Out: Homosexual Politics in Britain, from the Nineteenth Century to the Present* (London: Quartet, 1977); Kenneth Plummer, ed., *The Making of the Modern Homosexual* (London: Hutchinson, 1981); John D'Emilio, *Sexual Politics, Sexual Communities: The Making of a Homosexual Minority in the United States, 1940–1970* (Chicago: University of Chicago Press, 1983); Jonathan N. Katz, *Gay/Lesbian Almanac* (New York: Harper & Row, 1983); Jeffrey Weeks, *Sexuality and Its Discontents: Meanings, Myth and Modern Sexuality* (London: Routledge & Kegan Paul, 1985); Eve Kosofsky Sedgwick, *Between Men: English Literature and Male Homosocial Desire* (New York: Columbia University Press, 1985); Simon Watney, *Policing Desire: Pornography, AIDS and the Media* (Minneapolis: University of Minnesota Press, 1987); Barry D. Adam, *The Rise of a Gay and Lesbian Movement* (Boston: Twayne, 1987); Celia Kitzinger, *The Social Construction of Lesbianism* (London: Sage, 1987); David F. Greenberg, *The Construction of Homosexuality* (Chicago: University of Chicago Press, 1988); virtually all the contributions to Martin Bauml Duberman, Martha Vicinus, and George Chauncey, Jr., eds., *Hidden from History: Reclaiming the Gay and Lesbian Past* (New York: New American Library, 1989); Diana Fuss, *Essentially Speaking: Feminism, Nature and Difference* (New York: Routledge, 1989); Shane Phelan, *Identity Politics: Lesbian Feminism and the Limits of Community* (Philadelphia: Temple University Press, 1989); Judith Butler, *Gender Trouble: Feminism and the Subversion of Identity* (New York: Routledge, 1990); David M. Halperin, *One Hundred Years of Homosexuality and Other Essays on Greek Love* (New York: Routledge, 1990); John J. Winkler, *The Constraints of Desire: The Anthropology of Sex and Gender in Ancient Greece* (New York: Routledge, 1990); Allan Bérubé, *Com-*

ing Out under Fire: The History of Gay Men and Women in World War Two (New York: Free Press, 1990); Thomas E. Yingling, *Hart Crane and the Homosexual Text: New Thresholds, New Antinomies* (Chicago: University of Chicago Press, 1990); Eve Kosofsky Sedgwick, *The Epistemology of the Closet* (Berkeley and Los Angeles: University of California Press, 1990); Lillian Faderman, *Odd Girls and Twilight Lovers: A History of Lesbian Life in Twentieth-Century America* (New York: Columbia University Press, 1991); Michael Moon, *Disseminating Whitman: Revision and Corporeality in* Leaves of Grass (Cambridge, Mass.: Harvard University Press, 1991); Jeffrey Weeks, *Against Nature: Essays on History, Sexuality and Identity* (London: Rivers Oram, 1991).

For an especially useful overview of the history and theories of social construction written by a cautious partisan, see Carole S. Vance, "Social Construction Theory: Problems in the History of Sexuality," in *Homosexuality, Which Homosexuality?* ed. Anja van Kooten and Theo van der Meer (London: GMP [Gay Men's Press], 1989), pp. 13–34.

2. For generic worship of Saint Foucault, see, e.g., Halperin's *One Hundred Years*, where Foucault is described as a philosopher and historian who took up "theoretical questions" of sexuality "with characteristic brilliance and matchless penetration" (pp. 5–6). For uncritical acceptance of Foucault, see Sedgwick's *Epistemology of the Closet*, where the "results" of "Foucault's demonstration[s]" are "take[n] to be axiomatic" for her whole project (p. 3).

3. To my knowledge, only Ed Stein ("The Essentials of Construction") and Carole Vance ("Social Construction Theory") have shown any awareness that "social construction" can mean quite a variety of things. Vance usefully points out: "A close reading of constructionist texts shows that social construction spans a theoretical field of what might be constructed, ranging from sexual acts, sexual identities, sexual communities, the direction of sexual desire (object choice) to sexual impulse or sexuality itself" (p. 18).

4. Claudia Card is developing a nonessentialist theory of lesbianism in which the concept "lesbian" is not baldly equivocal across times and cultures but rather is a "family resemblance" notion in Wittgenstein's sense—one that has diverse senses that, although having no one feature common to all, have features that crisscross and overlap, just as some, but not all, Churchills will have a Churchillian nose, some, but not all, will have similar eyes, ears, and so on, yet all, in the end, are properly discernible as Churchills (see Claudia Card, "Lesbian Ethics," in *The Encyclopedia of Ethics*, ed. Lawrence C. Becker [New York: Garland, 1992], pp. 693–94).

For two developments of "dialectical" approaches to understanding lesbians and gay men as minorities, approaches that both draw on and criticize as incomplete a number of competing earlier models, see Ann Ferguson's

"Is There a Lesbian Culture?" in *Lesbian Philosophies and Cultures*, ed. Jeffner Allen (Albany, N.Y.: State University of New York Press, 1990), pp. 63–88; and Steven Epstein's "Gay Politics, Ethnic Identity: The Limits of Social Construction," in *Forms of Desire*, pp. 239–93, esp. 274–93.

5. Mary McIntosh, "The Homosexual Role," *Social Problems* 16, no. 2 (Fall 1968), reprinted in *Forms of Desire*, pp. 25–42. For an extensive bibliography of labeling theory, see Halperin, *One Hundred Years*, p. 157, n. 10.

6. Michel Foucault, *Discipline and Punish: The Birth of the Prison* (1975; New York: Vintage, 1979), pp. 195–228.

7. Foucault writes: "The body is the inscribed surface of events (traced by language and dissolved by ideas), the locus of a dissociated Self (adopting the illusion of a substantial unity), and a volume in perpetual disintegration. Genealogy, as an analysis of descent, is thus situated within the articulation of the body and history. Its task is to expose a body totally imprinted by history and the process of history's destruction of the body" ("Nietzsche, Genealogy, History," in *Language, Counter-Memory, Practice: Selected Essays and Interviews*, ed. Donald F. Bouchard (Ithaca, N.Y.: Cornell University Press, 1977), p. 148 (the essays are by and the interviews with Foucault). For discussion, see Butler, *Gender Trouble*, pp. 129–30.

8. Foucault, *History I*, p. 45.

9. Michel Foucault, *The Use of Pleasure: The History of Sexuality*, vol. 2 (1984; New York: Vintage, 1986), p. 18.

10. On the alleged craziness of gay men, see Evelyn Hooker's debunking study "The Adjustment of the Male Overt Homosexual," *Journal of Projective Techniques* 12 (1957): 18–21, reprinted in *The Problem of Homosexuality*, ed. Hendrik M. Ruitenbeek (New York: Dutton, 1963), pp. 141–61.

It is hotly debated in social science circles whether boys who become gay men are more effeminate and think of themselves as more effeminate than those who do not, but, as applying to adults, the stereotype of mismatched gender identities is wildly off the mark. There is no empirical support for the stereotype of effeminate gay men and masculine lesbians (see Kirk Stokes et al., "Sexual Orientation and Sex Role Conformity," *Archives of Sexual Behavior* 12 [1983]: 427–33).

For an empirical study confirming that a perceived mismatch between biological sex and gender-role expectations is a major constituent in the general public's definition of homosexuals, and for a useful discussion of stereotypes more generally, see Alan Taylor, "Conceptions of Masculinity and Femininity as a Basis for Stereotypes of Male and Female Homosexuals," *Journal of Homosexuality* 9 (1983): 37–53.

For studies showing that gay men are no more likely—indeed, are less likely—than heterosexual men to be child molesters and that the most widespread and persistent sexual abusers of children are the children's fathers, stepfathers, or mothers' boyfriends, see Vincent De Francis, *Protecting the Child Victim of Sex Crimes Committed by Adults* (Denver: American Humane Assoc. 1969), pp. vii, 38, 69–70; A. Nicholas Groth, "Adult Sexual Orientation and the Attraction to Under Age Persons," *Archives of Sexual Behavior* 7 (1978): 175–81; Mary J. Spencer, "Sexual Abuse of Boys," *Pediatrics* 78, no. 1 (July 1986): 133–38.

For an empirical study that refutes the general theory of labeling as applied to homosexuality, see Martin S. Weinberg and Colin J. Williams, *Male Homosexuals: Their Problems and Adaptations* (New York: Oxford University Press, 1974).

11. Foucault, *History I*, p. 43.

12. Foucault's "inscription" metaphor is wholly bogus in this context, for the ideological uses to which it is put do not hold even of its literal sense as applied to bodies. I am thinking of tattoos—which literally are inscriptions on the body, yet which do not cause the inscribed, on reading one of them off himself, to become the thing the inscription names or represents, say, Mom, a ship, Shirley, or chrysanthemums and dragons.

13. Foucault, *History I*, p. 45.

14. The philosopher and committed constructionist Ian Hacking gives a stunning, quite convincing example of a psychiatrist making up a patient as a person with a multiple personality disorder ("Making Up People," in *Reconstructing Individualism: Autonomy, Individuality, and the Self in Western Thought*, ed. Thomas C. Heller et al. [Stanford, Calif.: Stanford University Press, 1986], pp. 224–25).

David Halperin believes that social processes construct sexual desires at the level of the individual. But other than giving nodding approval to labeling theory, he offers no account of how this construction works (*One Hundred Years*, p. 40). To give an account of a society's sexual categories, as Halperin does for the Greeks (pp. 29–38), goes not one step toward establishing a causal connection between the conceptual categories and things in the world. Halperin seemingly tries to evade this problem by using, in his most careful formulations of the constructionist thesis, "experience" as his term of choice to describe what gets constructed in social construction (esp. pp. 2, 7, 9, 29). Halperin, however, has to drain "experience" of its usual senses of sensation, perception, and feeling since he rightly admits that these are not socially constructed (pp. 32n, 36n). But this admission then leaves "experience" meaning little more than "having the thoughts and conceptual schemas that the average person is likely to have"—in which

case the social construction thesis becomes vacuous: the going sexual concepts of the times are going to be the thoughts that the typical person holds
about matters sexual.

15. For a fascinating account of such creativity, see Paul Gordon Schalow,
"Male Love in Early Modern Japan: A Literary Depiction of the 'Youth,'"
in *Hidden From History*, pp. 118–28.

Walt Whitman's free adaptation of the phrenological term "adhesiveness"
as early as 1856 for what would come to be termed "homosexuality" in 1892
is an example, on the linguistic plane, of creativity by an individual living
and thinking across the grain of social expectations and socially constructed
concepts. Robert K. Martin writes: "Although it has been argued that
homosexuality is a creation of medical science as part of a process of social
control, the experience of Whitman would seem to indicate that homosexuals themselves sought an identity and a name, that they conceived of
themselves as differing in specific ways from heterosexuals. Whitman's
search for a word to identify his sexuality would seem to argue against the
assumptions of critics like Michel Foucault and Guy Hocquenghem, although they are right to say that homosexuality *as illness* is a creation of
nineteenth-century science" (*The Homosexual Tradition in American Poetry*
[Austin: University of Texas Press, 1979], p. 226, n. 50). On the phrenological background of Whitman's term, see Michael Lynch, "'Here Is
Adhesiveness': From Friendship to Homosexuality," *Victorian Studies* 29,
no. 1 (Autumn 1985): 67–96.

16. Ian Hacking is aware that individuals and groups are capable of living
across the grain of the social expectations that are laid on them. To save
labeling theory from this embarrassment, Hacking limits the scope of
labeling theory. He holds that the theory works only for the initial instil-
lation of an identity in an individual: after the laying on of the label, its
acceptance by the labeled, and the labeled's initial actions in accordance
with the label's dictates, the individual can change, adapt, and "become
autonomous of the labeling" ("Making Up People," p. 233). But surely this
is an odd saving move. For why would one be more free to reject a label
once operating under its spell than before it was pinned to one in the first
place? This move would appear to be a variant of the belief that shackles
make one free.

17. On this point, and on gays and labeling theory more generally, see Frederick Suppe, "Curing Homosexuality," in *Philosophy and Sex*, ed. Robert
Baker and Frederick Elliston, 2d ed. (Buffalo: Prometheus, 1984), pp. 408–
10.

18. Foucault, *History I*, p. 43—right in the middle of his main discussion of
homosexuality. For accord, see D. A. Miller, "Secret Subjects, Open Se-

crets," in his *The Novel and the Police* (Berkeley and Los Angeles: University of California Press, 1988); and Sedgwick, *Epistemology*, p. 3 and passim.

19. John Dagion, ed., *Sex Stop* (San Francisco: Leyland, 1987), pp. 13, 15.

20. Foucault, *History I*, p. 98. Continuing, Foucault denies that there is "a certain sphere of sexuality that would be the legitimate concern of a free and disinterested scientific inquiry were it not the object of mechanisms of prohibition brought to bear by the economic or ideological requirements of power." For a call to abandon all pretensions to the possibility of objective knowledge, see also his *Discipline and Punish*, pp. 27-28.

21. Stein, "Essentials of Constructionism," p. 350.

22. See Karl Popper, *The Poverty of Historicism* (1957; London: Routledge & Kegan Paul, 1986), pp. 94-98. By "science" I mean a structure of beliefs that entail hypotheses that can be tested for falsehood by appeal to the senses or inferences made from the senses.

To be fair, it is worth noting that not all social constructionists are committed to skepticism about empirical science. Carole Vance is a notable exception: "Social construction does not predict a particular answer: whether something we call 'gay identity' existed in the 17th or 19th century, in London or in Polynesia, or whether 19th-century female romantic friendship or crossing-women are properly called 'lesbian', is *a matter for empirical examination*" ("Social Construction Theory," p. 15; emphasis added). Vance even goes so far as to claim at a couple of points that what social construction theory is is a purely *methodological* commitment, one that simply holds questions of sexual identity open to scientific inquiry rather than presuming that such questions are settled in advance by received opinions (pp. 15, 17, 23).

Similarly, David Halperin holds that, as providing "a guide to future research" into sexual matters, social constructionist theory has a "heuristic value," even if the sciences eventually "prove to have been wrong" the substantive claims of social construction "about the cultural determination of sexual object-choice." Halperin's objection to science is not that it is cognitively bogus but that it is morally objectionable: "The search for a 'scientific' aetiology of sexual orientation is itself a homophobic project" (*One Hundred Years*, pp. 42, 49; for accord, see Sedgwick, *Epistemology*, pp. 43-44).

23. Hacking, "Making Up People," pp. 222-36, esp. 230-31. Ian Hacking and Arnold Davidson (discussed below) are the two analytic philosophers who have tried to make Foucault's views about sexuality respectable within mainline philosophical circles.

24. Foucault—without arguments—tries conceptually to distance sexual desire from the drives to eat and drink (interview, reprinted from *The Advocate*

[Los Angeles], #400, August 7, 1984, 26–30, 58, in Mark Thompson, *Gay Spirit: Myth and Meaning* [New York: St. Martins, 1987], pp. 25–35).

25. Robert Padgug, "Sexual Matters: Rethinking Sexuality in History," in *Forms of Desire*, p. 50, reprinted from *Radical History Review*, #20 (Spring/Summer 1979): 3–23.

26. For insightful discussions of the slippage between language and concept, see Boswell, "Concepts, Experience, and Sexuality," pp. 69–70. For a particularly naive identification of language and concepts, see Katz, *Gay/Lesbian Almanac*, pp. 1–2, 14.

27. Koertge, "Constructing Sexual Concepts," p. 2; some emphasis omitted.

28. Steve Barron, director, screenplay by Todd W. Langan and Bobby Herbeck, *Teenage Mutant Ninja Turtles* (1990).

29. The sense in which social constructionists use "discourse" is close only to the *Oxford English Dictionary*'s sense 3a, where "discourse" is a mass noun, in contrast to senses 3c (*a* talk) and 5 (*a* dissertation), where "discourse" is a count noun. All other senses are obsolete.

30. Halperin, *One Hundred Years*, p. 15. Later, Halperin speaks as though he is qualifying this position, but it is unclear what the qualification is (p. 17). The following quotes are from pp. 7 and 29.

31. "For attestations to the strength of individual preferences (even to the point of exclusivity) on the part of Greek males for a sexual partner of one sex rather than another, see, e.g., . . . [followed by twenty-four citations]" (ibid., p. 163, n. 53). And see generally Winkler, *Constraints of Desire*, chaps. 1 and 2.

32. For "homoerotic adult preference" and behavior among the Sambia, see Gilbert Herdt, *The Sambia: Ritual and Gender in New Guinea* (New York: Rinehart & Winston, 1987), pp. 166–67. Greenberg writes: "Herdt has informed me that a minority of the Sambian youth never learn to like homosexuality; they participate because they must, but give it up as soon as it is permissible to do so" (*Social Construction of Homosexuality*, p. 39, n. 70). See also Gilbert Herdt and Robert J. Stoller, *Intimate Communication: Erotics and the Study of Culture* (New York: Columbia University Press, 1990), pp. 279–322, esp. p. 279: "I finally became aware that Kalutwo not only feared women but still preferred erotic contacts with boys. Unlike other Sambia, therefore, Kalutwo comes closest to being like a homosexual in the old sense of that western label."

33. *Greek Anthology*, trans. W. R. Paton (New York: Putnam, 1916), vol. 1, bk. 5, epigram 65. For a discussion, see John Boswell, "Jews, Bicycle Riders, and Gay People: The Determination of Social Consensus and Its Impact on Minorities," *Yale Journal of Law and the Humanities* 1 (1989): 211,

"Revolutions, Universals, Sexual Categories," p. 99, and "Concepts, Experience, and Sexuality," p. 79.

34. Boswell concludes his essay "Concepts, Experience, and Sexuality" thus: "Constructions and context shape the articulation of sexuality, but do not efface recognition of erotic preference as a potential category. . . . Primary ancient and medieval sexual constructs were unrelated to the modern differentiation between homosexual and heterosexual 'orientation,' 'identity,' or 'preference.' This does not mean that there was no awareness of specifically homosexual or heterosexual 'orientation' in earlier societies. Much evidence indicates that these were common and familiar concepts, which received little attention in the records of these cultures not because few people recognized them, but because they had little social or ethical impact" (pp. 81 and 86, n. 50).

35. See the "Addendum" to Halperin's *One Hundred Years*, p. 225, referring to the unpublished work by Keith DeVries, "Homosexuality and the Athenian Democracy."

36. James N. Adams, *The Latin Sexual Vocabulary* (Baltimore: Johns Hopkins University Press, 1982), pp. 125-30.

37. *Jocks* (Los Angeles), September 1987, p. 31.

38. Plato, *Gorgias* 494e4.

39. *New York Times*, August 2, 1990, p. A8; October 10, 1990, p. B1.

40. The photograph, *Richard* (1978), can be found in Richard Marshall, *Robert Mapplethorpe* (Boston: Little, Brown, 1988), p. 69.

41. Carole Vance writes: "At minimum, all social construction approaches adopt the view that physically identical sexual acts may have varying social significance and subjective meaning depending upon how they are defined and understood in different cultures and historical periods" ("Social Construction Theory," p. 18). Depending only on what is meant by "subjective meaning," even *this* chapter could be counted as social constructionist by Vance's standard. If "subjective meaning" means "what I think society thinks sexual categories are," then that will, of course, assuming that I am thinking correctly, vary from society to society simply as classificatory schemes vary between societies. If, however, the claim about "subjective meaning" here entails that I view my sexual behavior in whatever way society happens to view my sexual behavior, then this claim is, with the collapse of labeling and causal theories, simply false.

42. For a catalog of such claims of an absence of same-sex erotic behavior, see Greenberg, *Construction*, p. 74. There are great difficulties in determining whether homosexual behavior occurs in any given society: "At first, Herdt's Sambian informants unanimously denied homosexual practices; only after

293

six months' time did they trust him enough to confess that ritualized sodomy was part of their initiation rituals" (ibid., pp. 78–79).

43. "While blacks may be prone toward skin pigmentation disorders and umbilical cord hernias, . . . they are far less likely than whites to suffer with cystic fibrosis, skin cancer or PKU syndrome" (*New York Times*, September 25, 1990, p. B5).

44. In their antiessentialist mode, constructionists are what might be viewed generically as crypto-Idealists or neo-sub-post-Hegelians, relativizing Hegelians who, like Hegel, believe that what is is webs of concepts, that there is no "reality" over and against the world of concepts, yet who believe that the webs' elements are only loosely connected, are neither necessarily nor causally related to each other—Hegelians, that is, who have abandoned, both as a formal and as a temporal possibility, a belief in the structure of a unidirectional waltz of thesis, antithesis, and synthesis, and who indeed have abandoned any belief that concepts form a complete unified structure either formally or temporally.

In the first volume of the *History*, Foucault advances an idealism that "sublates" the real into the conceptual, i.e., that takes up the real into the conceptual, leaving the real without an independent status. Such idealist commitment is evident in such sentences as: "We must not place sex [i.e., what people desire] on the side of reality, and sexuality [i.e., various scientific 'discourses'] on that of confused ideas and illusions; sexuality is a very real historical formation; it is what gave rise to the notion of sex, as a speculative element necessary to its operation"; sex is "an imaginary point," "the most internal element in a deployment of sexuality" (pp. 155, 157). So it is chitchat that is real; desires are chitchat's dreams.

An even more extreme sexual idealism can be found in Butler's *Gender Trouble*, where even the body and the material conditions of the world are emanations of a social mind (pp. 130–34). Just as the supreme Idealist Bishop Berkeley held that the only things that can exist are God and His ideas, so too Butler holds that the only things that can exist are Social Discourse and Its Ideas.

Beyond the sublation of the real into the conceptual, there are at least two other idealist strands in Foucault and in constructionists more generally. I can only just mention them here. One idealist strand is a belief that all relations are internal relations, i.e., relations in which what the relation's terms are depends on what the relation is, rather than vice versa. That I am a lover, e.g., depends on the relation "loving someone"; love in this way is an internal relation. But "is the same height as" appears to be an external relation: if I am the same height as you, this is so, not because of the relation between us, but because of the height each of us has (say five feet, ten inches) independently of the other. In this case, the relation is what it is because the terms are what they are. Foucault is committed to internal relations most clearly in the synopsis that he gives of his views on power in *History I*, pp. 92–100.

The other idealist strand in Foucault is that truth is a matter of coherence rather than correspondence. Once all relations are internal, and once what is is concepts, then, not surprisingly, not only can there not be any stepping outside the realm of concepts to see if there is any correct correspondence between them and a separate "world," but also there cannot be a separate world "out there" to begin with. However, since there are webs or "matrices" (p. 99) of concepts but no *one* system of concepts either formally or temporally, there is no *one* coherent conceptual story, as there is, say, in Hegel's *The Encyclopedia of the Philosophical Sciences*; and so further for Foucault, there is no one truth, only many incommensurable truths.

This is odd: despite Foucault's commitments to internal relations, to truth as coherence, and to the conflation of concept and reality, he does not bite the final Hegelian bullet and hold that the distinction between concept and instance is an illusion. In consequence, there remains, I think, a tension between his causal account of homosexuality (sec. II above) and his conceptual account (discussed here and below).

45. Jonathan Katz, *Gay American History* (New York: Crowell, 1976), p. 7; emphasis added. Katz's definition is taken by the *Harvard Law Review* as its understanding of the social construction of homosexuality (the Editors of the *Harvard Law Review, Sexual Orientation and the Law* [Cambridge, Mass.: Harvard University Press, 1990], p. 7). The *Review* more or less treats the distinction between constructionists and realists (or what it calls "neutral difference" theorists) as the distinction between those who believe that having a sexual orientation is a matter of choice and those who believe that it is not. Against this too rapid conflation, see Stein's excellent discussion in "Essentials of Constructionism," pp. 326–30.

46. Padgug, "Sexual Matters," p. 58; emphasis added and omitted.

47. For example, D'Emilio and Freedman, *Intimate Matters*, p. 226; Halperin, *One Hundred Years*, p. 162, n. 52; Lynch, "Here Is Adhesiveness,'" p. 68; Janet E. Halley, "The Politics of the Closet: Towards Equal Protection for Gay, Lesbian, and Bisexual Identity," *UCLA Law Review* 36 (1989): 936.

48. Foucault, *History I*, p. 43.

49. Worries over whether the person in fact has those properties or not leads straight back to assumptions about the validity of labeling or causal theories. These worries are irrelevant here.

50. Arnold I. Davidson, "Sex and the Emergence of Sexuality," *Critical Inquiry* 14 (August 1987): 18.

51. Bullet biter Ian Hacking is willing to admit that claims about when homosexuals have existed are necessary truths: "It is not possible [even] for God to make George Washington a pervert" ("Making Up People," p. 230; cf. Davidson, "Sex," p. 22, on conceptual impossibility).

52. Davidson, "Sex," p. 24.

53. Ibid., p. 25. For example, in ordinary English, one says that one is *in* pain, but one (usually) does not say that one is *in* pleasure, suggesting (so it goes) that, in English, we do not consider pain and pleasure to be polar opposites operating in the same logic.

54. *New York Times*, September 13, 1987, sec. 2, p. 22.

55. Halperin, *One Hundred Years*, p. 8. Subsequent references are to pp. 24, 26, 29, 31, 36, 36n.

56. Plato, *Republic* 4.436a to the end, and esp. 9.571a–574a, 586a–b, 588b–590d; on the psychic origins of one's politics, see *Republic* 8; see generally the image of the charioteer from the *Phaedrus* 253c–254e.

57. Plato, *Timaeus* 70d–e with 90e–91d. Indeed, to make good his various claims about the Greeks, Foucault pretty well has to drum Plato, especially the *Republic*, out of the Greek corpus (*Use of Pleasure*, p. 30).

58. Many self-described social constructionists give no account of what they mean by "social construction." Even after wandering around for six hundred pages, David Greenberg fails to state anywhere the theory named in the title of his book (*The Construction of Homosexuality*). His index directs the reader to consult pp. 484–92 for an account of "social construction," but the desired conceptual apparatus is not there.

Many others who do offer an account of what is meant by the social constructionists' thesis are self-defeatingly unclear in their formulations. For example, social historian Martin Duberman formulates the central claim of social constructionism thus: "In other words, the 'modern homosexual,' defined primarily by his or her exclusive sexual orientation and basing a whole way of life on that sexual preference may well be a unique creation of contemporary Western societies" ("Reclaiming the Past," *European Gay Review*, #5 [1989]: p. 75). This formulation can be read at least three ways. (1) If the term "homosexual" here is defined in a culturally neutral way, then, without the bells and whistles given in the participial clauses, Duberman is claiming nothing more than the tautology that the modern homosexual is the modern homosexual. (2) Alternatively, if, on the one hand, by "a whole way of life" Duberman means the specific life that gay men developed in post-Stonewall American gay urban ghettos, with poppers, gloryhole arcades, gay men's choruses, AIDS support groups, and the like, then he has formulated the concept "homosexuality" in a way that simply could not apply to any other cultures and so for this reason too is question-beggingly applied only to our place and era. (3) Or again, if, on the other hand, he defines "a way of life" in a culturally neutral way, then the position just seems to be false. For it looks like the *hijras* of India have a way of life that wholly revolves around their sexuality. The *hijras* are same-sex inclined but ideally ascetic, voluntarily castrated transvestites who live together in caste-less houses, loosely structured around relations of guru and student. Severally and through the houses, they are also part of a loose national network, through which members migrate and which conducts annual festivals and intermittent leadership conventions. Members earn their living by providing entertainments and blessings at marriage and baptism ceremonies (see Serena Nanda, *Neither Man nor Woman: The Hijras of India* [Belmont, Calif.: Wadsworth, 1990]).

Some theorists think that they can remain neutral in the debate between social construction and essentialism, indeed, transcend the debate, by avoiding substantive arguments for each position and treating the positions simply as discursive strategies (see Sedgwick, *Epistemology*, p. 27; Fuss, *Essentially Speaking*, pp. 108–12). But such assumed neutrality is bogus. To believe that language, undeniably a component of the social, is at heart strategic—effects things, accomplishes things, makes up things, rather than describing things, expressing things, or offering insight into things that exist independently of it—is simply to side with the social constructionists' thesis that society makes up categories, either causally or definitionally.

59. In an act of damage control, Hacking tries to limit the scope of such relativity to the social ("Making Up People," p. 229).

60. The Foucault of the later volumes of the *History* is here the chief offender.

61. David Halperin tries to avoid this charge of intellectual hypocrisy by eschewing for himself a claim to epistemological neutrality. He admits to being thoroughly embedded in his time. But this strategy has a high price of another sort. If society thoroughly constructs his concepts of himself (as he admits), then he cannot believe that he is so constructed (since the construction is that sexuality is thoroughly natural): "So I freely admit that, in a sense, I don't, and couldn't possibly, *believe* in what I've been saying . . ." (*One Hundred Years*, p. 53). Still (now mysteriously), he claims that he can have "a solid intellectual conviction" that sexuality is different in different times and places, forgetting (it appears) that convictions are beliefs.

CHAPTER 8. GAY STUDIES AS MORAL VISION

This chapter is an address that was originally written for and delivered to the inaugural conference of Yale University's Lesbian and Gay Studies Center, October 30, 1987. This conference launched an ongoing series of annual national lesbian and gay studies conferences. An earlier version of the chapter appeared in *Educational Theory* 39, no. 2 (1989): 121–32.

1. Some of the sexual signs discussed in this chapter can be found in James Woodward's *Signs of Sexual Behavior: An Introduction to Some Sex-related Vocabulary in American Sign Language* (Silver Springs, Md.: T.J., 1979); others I learned from people associated with Gallaudet University in 1986. Some of the pejorative signs have been reappropriated by gay men to carry a positive connotation—to mean "gay" rather than "queer"—just as in spoken American English gay men and lesbians, even before Queer Nation came along, have reappropriated derogatory terms for positive ends, as in the names of the tabloids *Fag Rag* (Boston) and *Big Apple Dyke News*.

2. See Woodward, *Signs*, pp. 26–43.

3. Martin L. A. Sternberg, *American Sign Language Dictionary* (New York: Harper & Row, 1987), s.vv.

4. Erving Goffman, *Stigma: Notes on the Management of Spoiled Identity* (Englewood Cliffs, N.J.: Prentice-Hall, 1963), p. 4; emphasis added.

5. *Guardian of Freedom* (New York: American Civil Liberties Union, 1986), n.p.

6. See *Doctrinal Congregation's Letter to Bishops: The Pastoral Care of Homosexual Persons* (Rome, October 1, 1986), esp. secs. 3, 12. The Vatican's English-language translation is published in full in *Origins: NC Documentary Service* 16 (November 13, 1986): 377–82.

7. Randy Shilts, *And the Band Played On* (New York: St. Martin's, 1987), p. 554.

8. See, e.g., *New York Times*, August 2, 1987, p. 14.

9. See, e.g., *Jobs For Philosophers* (American Philosophical Association), #89, October 1988, p. 2, item 12.

10. See *New York Times*, March 5, 1988, p. 1.

11. The later part of 1991 saw the publication of two studies that, if correct, suggest that, at least for males, being homosexual is not a matter of personal choice (Simon LeVay, "A Difference in the Hypothalamic Structure between Heterosexual and Homosexual Men," *Science*, #253, August, 3, 1991, pp. 1034–37; J. Michael Bailey and Richard C. Pillard, "A Genetic Study of Male Sexual Orientation," *Archives of General Psychiatry* 48, no. 12 [1991]: 1089–96). Earlier studies pointing in the same direction include Richard C. Pillard and James D. Weinrich, "Evidence of Familial Nature of Male Homosexuality," *Archives of General Psychiatry* 43, no. 8 (1986): 808–12; and the Kinsey Institute study by Alan P. Bell, Martin S. Weinberg, and Susan K. Hammersmith, *Sexual Preference: Its Development in Men and Women* (Bloomington: Indiana University Press, 1981).

12. See *City of New Orleans v. Dukes*, 427 U.S. 297 (1976), which upheld

grandfather provisions against equal protection challenge and reversed an earlier case that had barred them, *Morey v. Dowd*, 354 U.S. 457 (1957), the only case of the modern era to strike down an economic regulation on equal protection grounds.

13. *Dred Scott v. Sandford*, 60 U.S. (19 Howard) 393, 407 (1857).

14. See Blanche Knott, *Truly Tasteless Jokes* (New York: Ballantine, 1982), p. 114.

15. For the locus classicus of this view, see Michel Foucault, *The History of Sexuality*, vol. 1, *An Introduction*, trans. Robert Hurley (1976; New York: Random House, 1978), p. 43. For a discussion of this passage, see the preceding chapter.

16. For examples, see John Boswell, *Christianity, Social Tolerance, and Homosexuality: Gay People in Western Europe from the Beginning of the Christian Era to the Fourteenth Century* (Chicago: University of Chicago Press, 1980); Gilbert Herdt, *Guardians of the Flute: Idioms of Masculinity* (New York: McGraw-Hill, 1981); and Walter L. Williams, *The Spirit and the Flesh: Sexual Diversity in American Indian Culture* (Boston: Beacon, 1986).

17. Joe Gay Studies, assistant professor of English at Withit State University, writes a book titled *Cite und Site* on "the historicity of the problematizations of the intertextuality of the totalizations of the valorizations of the inscriptions, rescriptions, and postscriptions of contingent oppositional discursive gaps in the domains, fields, and streams of the diffusive epistemic registers of the productivitinesses of the positivities and stylizations in the modes of subjectivization to the normalization of the always already performative valences and hypostatized valances of the solidifications in the tropicality of the cultural specificities of the transformative poststructurality of the hegemonic technologies for the *askesis*, *savoirs*, and *jeux de verité* of citationability and sitationability"—and wins a prize from the Modern Language Association.

18. For a discussion of the rationales for *representational* democracy and their relation to gay rights, see Richard Mohr, *Gays/Justice—A Study of Ethics, Society, and Law* (New York: Columbia University Press, 1988), pp. 181–86.

19. Elsewhere, I have offered arguments for a couple of specific gay affirmative action programs based on compensatory justice (ibid., pp. 235–38, 246). For the general architecture for this type of argument, see Marilyn A. Friedman and Larry May, "Harming Women as a Group," *Social Theory and Practice* 11, no. 2 (1985): 207–34.

20. An empirical study has found that, without being aware of it, straight people literally distance themselves from people whom they suppose are gay: in conversation, they stand on average three times the usual "personal" distance from a person labeled "gay." Can such people—who may well

think that they are not prejudiced against gays—be counted on to be fair to gays, say, in hiring decisions for positions entailing collegiality with the employer? Surely not. (See Paul Siegel, "Androgyny, Sex-Role Rigidity, and Homophobia," in *Gayspeak: Gay Male and Lesbian Communication*, ed. James W. Chesebro [New York: Pilgrim, 1981], p. 145). For the general architecture of arguments for "current fairness" affirmative action programs, see Mary Anne Warren, "Secondary Sexism and Quota Hiring," *Philosophy and Public Affairs* 6 (1977): 240–61.

21. For the general architecture for this type of argument, see Justice Brennan's opinion in *University of California Regents v. Bakke*, 438 U.S. 265, 324 (1978).

22. For gender, see chap. 6, sec. IV, above; and Mohr, *Gays/Justice*, pp. 255–56.

23. Eve Kosofsky Sedgwick, *The Epistemology of the Closet* (Berkeley and Los Angeles: University of California Press, 1990), pp. 1, 11.

24. *New York Times*, December 7, 1991, p. 8.

25. *New York Times*, August 31, 1991, p. 9; *The Advocate*, #587, October 8, 1991, p. 48.

INDEX

Abjection, 30

Abortion, 25, 64, 65

ACT UP, 5, 17; demonstrations by, 52, 99n; graphics of, 192; on The NAMES Project, 126; slogan of, 49

Adam, Barry, 222n

Adhesiveness, 201, 226n

Adoption, 28, 79

Affirmative action: arguments for, 257; Court cases on, 72–74; and gays, 257; reversals of, 72n, 74, 99; types of, 257

Agency, moral, 14, 32, 88, 245–47

Agency, sexual, 179–81, 203–5

AIDS, 3, 6, 16, 106; and animal rights, 100–101; art, 206; funding, 49–50, 93–94, 99, 124; and outing, 17–18; and politics, 43–44, 246–47; and state coercion, 90–91, 97; and terrorism, 259; testing, 90–91. *See also* The NAMES Project

Alcoholics Anonymous, 27

Allen, Jeffner, 129

American Civil Liberties Union, 80, 245

American Sign Language, 243–45

Americans with Disabilities Act, 93

Analingus, 88

Animal rights, 5, 7, 100–101, 164

Animals, 31, 118, 162, 171, 229

Anti-semitism, 40, 244

Anus, 203–5

Arendt, Hannah, 40

Aristotle, 117, 122–23, 200

Autobiography, 110–11

Awe, 6, 117

Bailey, J. Michael, 248n

Bakker, Jim, and Tammy Faye, 24–25

Baldwin, James, 92n, 172

Bathhouses, 29, 165, 200, 203

Bellows, George, 175; *fig.*, 176

Benjamin, Walter, 2

Bentley, Eric, 12

Berg, Alban, 135–36

Bérubé, Allan, 222n

Betrayal, 28, 30, 46, 99, 101

Bias. *See* Prejudice

Bieber, Irving, 213

Biology, 228–29, 234, 248, 250. *See also* Science; Sex

Bisexuality, 232–33

Black and White Men Together, 113

Blackmun, Harry A., 63–64, 67